Paul: A Man of Two Worlds

Paul:

A Man of Two Worlds

C. J. den Heyer

SCM PRESS

Translated by John Bowden from the Dutch *Paulus. Man van twee werelden*, published 1998 by Uitgeverij Meinema, Zoetermeer, The Netherlands.

0 334 02756 X

This edition first published 2000 by
SCM Press
9–17 St Albans Place London N1 0NX

SCM Press is a division of
SCM-Canterbury Press Ltd

Printed in Great Britain by
Biddles Ltd, Guildford and King's Lynn

Contents

Introduction

A risky venture

In the first century of our era in the region of the Mediterranean Sea there lived a man who has left an indelible stamp on Christian tradition, the Jew Paul. He came from Tarsus in Asia Minor. He was an erudite man, fond of travelling, creative and many-sided; an expert in scripture and tradition but at the same time by no means a stranger in the cultural world of his day. He was a passionate preacher of the gospel of Jesus Christ, he founded an unknown number of Christian communities and wrote letters which have gained a canonical status by being included in the New Testament. It goes without saying that over the course of the centuries a tremendous amount has been written about this man.[1] He is one of the great influential spirits of human history.[2] Those who steep themselves in his writings will meet a complicated and controversial person, a pioneer in the sphere of Christian theology. There is no avoiding the fact that such a many-sided thinker evokes conflicting feelings, as he always has done. For some he is an inexhaustible source of inspiration, while for others he seems to be a source of offence. He has been admired and celebrated, but also reviled and vilified.[3]

Writing a book about this man is a risky venture. Scholarly objectivity proves an unattainable ideal. Paul himself was anything but 'objective'. Despite a gulf of centuries he also challenges modern readers. No one can avoid being partisan about him. For or against Paul? Do we find him sympathetic or antipathetic? His views and insights are often so original and unexpected that they not only compel admiration but also provoke rejection.

Already during his lifetime Paul provoked resistance and was regularly the focal point of conflicts. It is evident from the opening of his letters that he saw himself as an apostle who was called by Jesus Christ himself (Rom. 1.1; I Cor. 1.1; II Cor. 1.1; Gal. 1.1). This assured conviction came up against opposition within the early Christian community. That was not surprising. No admirer of Paul will fail to understand this opposition. He claimed that he was 'called to be an apostle', but by what right did he give himself this honorific title? There is no indication that he belonged to the very first group of disciples. After Jesus' death on the cross, to begin with Paul was not even part of the early Christian community. On the contrary, he found himself in the opposition camp. Afterwards he was not ashamed of this. With a certain pride he declared that he had been among the fiercest opponents of this new messianic movement within the Judaism of those days (Gal. 1.13, 23).

Paul was a controversial man and he has remained one to the present day. After he had become a follower of Jesus Christ himself, he also provoked opposition within the Christian community. His apostleship remained a point of discussion (I Cor. 9.1–2). He made no secret of the fact that he wanted to be independent of the leading figures in the early Christian community in Jerusalem (Gal. 1.15–24). He came into conflict with his first travelling companion, Barnabas (Acts 14.35–16.3), and did not hesitate to rebuke even Peter sharply (Gal. 2.11–14). He was certain that he had been chosen by God to make known the gospel of Jesus Christ in the pagan world (Gal. 1.16). He took account of the consequences. His daring vision of the relative importance of the Torah for Gentile Christians brought him into conflict with those members of the Christian community who thought that no distinction might be made: everyone, whether Jewish or non-Jewish, had to observe the whole Torah. Paul would not yield here: 'If anyone preaches another gospel than the one which you received (from me, Paul), let him be accursed' (Gal. 1.9).

Paul was not an easy man. He antagonized some people with his sharp, complicated arguments (II Cor. 7.8–16). However, it is also evident from his letters that he could win people's loyalty and make lasting friendships. Timothy, Titus, Silvanus and others accompanied him on his journeys. He calls a certain Phoebe 'our sister', and relates that she also gave him personal support (Rom. 16.1–2). In Corinth he met a Jewish couple from Rome, Aquila and Priscilla (or Prisca), tentmakers like himself (Acts 18.2). He held them in high esteem, as is evident from the following passage: 'Greet Prisca and Aquila, my fellow labourers in Christ, who have risked their necks for my life' (Rom. 16.3–4).

The *man* Paul died in the 60s of the first century. His letters have made him unforgettable. They are among the most read and studied writings in world literature. They have been highly praised for their profundity and fiercely criticized for the perplexing complexity of Paul's arguments.[4] Those who have criticisms find themselves in 'canonical' company. The critic can refer to the New Testament itself. 'So also our beloved brother Paul wrote to you according to the wisdom given him, speaking of this as he does in all his letters. There are some things in them hard to understand, which the ignorant and unstable twist to their own destruction, as they do the other scriptures' (II Peter 3.16).

So after his death Paul entered history. Without being able to defend himself he fell into the hands of his readers. Did they do him justice? Did they let him say what he had wanted to say? Or did they make him a ventriloquist's dummy? Anyone who has left complicated, controversial writings to posterity runs that risk. An exciting study could be written about the fate of Paul's letters in the course of church history.[5] Sometimes they were not very popular. At other moments they played a prominent role. In this connection, by way of illustration I might mention the names of Augustine in the fourth century, Luther in the sixteenth century and Karl Barth in the twentieth century.

The approach

Paul wrote letters. These three words need to be heavily underlined; in what follows they cannot be repeated often enough.
The apostle sent *real* letters to *specific* communities. He was
not a desk-bound scholar but a practical man. In his writings
he was reacting to questions which were alive in the early
Christian communities. Paul emerges from this correspondence
as a creative man with a keen eye for reality. Here it must be
remembered that he was treading on virtually unexplored
ground. He knew that he had been called by God to preach the
gospel to the Gentiles. Hitherto unprecedented questions arose
in this exciting confrontation with other cultures and thought-
worlds. As a result Paul's letters cover a rich variety of themes:
from circumcision to eating meat dedicated to idols, from
marriage and sexuality to speaking in tongues at meetings of
the community.

In the course of church history the writings of Paul became
above all the domain of systematic theology. The specific
character of the questions discussed in them fell into the background or was even forgotten, and they were transformed into
a theological discussion which went beyond the limits of any
time-conditioned character and claimed to be topical for all
times and all places and people. That the 'practical' Paul,
perhaps to his own amazement, became a normative voice in
the dogmatic reflection of the Christian church is abundantly
clear from the three names in the last sentence of the previous
paragraph: Augustine, Luther and Barth. At a decisive moment
in their lives they were surprised – sometimes even 'converted'
– by the content of the letters of the apostle Paul.

On mentioning the above great names from the history of the
church and theology I also want to indicate a danger which
constantly threatens from the interpretation of Paul's letters.
Men like Augustine, Luther and Barth enjoyed so much
authority and influence that their interpretation of Paul's
insights has taken on almost 'canonical' character. It is the task
of the exegete to go back behind this dogmatic reflection, to the

texts. Of course it is interesting to know what Luther had to say about Paul's letters and the same thing applies to the views of Augustine, Barth and all those others who have grappled intensively with Paul's thought in the course of centuries, but they do not have the last word in exegetical discussion.

The plan of this book shows clearly that as far as possible I have taken seriously the consequences of what I have just said. I have not found my approach to the life and thought of Paul through dogmatic reflection in the present and the past. I did not begin my investigation in the hope that I would rediscover the picture of a 'Lutheran' or a 'Reformed' Paul in the New Testament. Nor have I been guided by those pictures of Paul which have been drawn in New Testament scholarship since the last century: an eschatological Paul, an apocalyptic Paul, a mystical Paul, a Gnostic Paul, a Hellenistic Paul or a Jewish Paul.[6]

I would say that the way in which I have tried to approach the life and thought of the apostle to the Gentiles is primarily *historical* and *biographical*. That means that I start with an investigation of those facts in the New Testament which make it possible to sketch a profile of the apostle. Who was the man who achieved so much? His letters leave no doubt that his thought developed gradually. This observation makes it necessarily to analyse his writings *chronologically*. Here each letter needs to be treated separately: in what *historical context* was Paul writing? What was his aim, and what did he want to achieve? Because the apostle wrote *letters* and not theological treatises, the question of 'the historical context' is of key significance. Paul was a many-sided and creative man. Every letter is different and cannot easily be compared with any other of his other letters which have been preserved in the New Testament. So it is a challenge to the exegete, on the basis of an analysis of the individual writings, to look for *constants* in Paul's thought. It is an even greater challenge to enter into discussion with dogmatic theology on the basis of exegesis, but that debate falls outside the scope of this study.

Literature

As I have already remarked, a tremendous amount has been written about Paul over the course of the centuries. It is impossible to attempt to refer to it all, nor would that make sense. My book would become unreadable and 'drown' in a sea of footnotes.[7] At the same time I need to explain myself. I am indebted to many New Testament colleagues. Sometimes perhaps I am not even aware of what I owe them. Their books and articles have been my companions for many years and have inspired me in finding my own way into Paul's life and thought. I trust that they themselves will discover how much they have been a source of inspiration to me and how much I have learned from all that they have brought to birth. I have not completely banished footnotes from my book. However, I make sparse use of them. In the footnotes I mention literature which can help readers further when, as I hope, their interest has been aroused by my view on a particular topic. In my choice of literature I have remembered that books must be accessible. Preference has therefore been given to recent studies (above all after 1970), and I mention more books than scholarly articles.

A number of books need separate mention. I have listed them below. Without these works my book would have remained unwritten. The authors have enriched me with their insights. I mention them out of gratitude. I do not agree with all that they have written. That is not necessary, nor is it possible. It might be said that birds of very different plumage have set me thinking. I mention their studies in chronological order.

Albert Schweitzer, *The Mysticism of Paul the Apostle*, London 1931

R. Bultmann, *Theology of the New Testament*, London and New York 1952, 1955

H. J. Schoeps, *Paul. The Theology of the Apostle in the Light of Jewish Religious History*, London 1961

H. N. Ridderbos, *Paulus. Ontwerp van zijn Theologie*, Kampen 1966

G. Bornkamm, *Paul,* London and New York 1971

G. Eichholz, *Die Theologie des Paulus im Umriss*, Neukirchen-Vluyn 1972

E. P. Sanders, *Paul and Palestinian Judaism. A Comparison of Patterns of Religion,* London 1977

J. C. Beker, *Paul the Apostle. The Triumph of God in Life and Thought,* Edinburgh 1980

J. Becker, *Paulus. Der Apostle der Völker*, Tübingen 1989

A. F. Segal, *Paul the Convert. The Apostolate and Apostasy of Saul the Pharisee,* New Haven and London 1990

H. Maccoby, *Paul and Hellenism*, London and Philadelphia 1991

K. Berger, *Theologiegeschichte des Urchristentums,* Tübingen and Basel 1994

J. Gnilka, *Paulus von Tarsus. Zeuge und Apostle,* Herders theologischer Kommentar zum Neuen Testament. Supplementband 6, Freiburg 1996

H. Hübner and D. Flusser, 'Paulus I and II', *Theologische Realenzyklopädie* 26, Berlin and New York 1996, 133–60

E. Lohse, *Paulus. Eine Biographie*, Munich 1996

J. Murphy O'Connor, *Paul: A Critical Life,* Oxford 1996

M. Hengel and A. M. Schwemer, *Paul Between Damascus and Antioch,* London 1997

J. D. G. Dunn, *The Theology of Paul the Apostle*, Edinburgh 1998.

Finally, I am writing about Paul but I also allow Paul himself to say a great deal. His writings are well worth quoting.

I

The 'historical' Paul

The historical Jesus

The question arises how far it makes sense to begin a chapter on the 'historical' Paul with a section devoted to the historical Jesus. Since the beginning of the last century this question has stood high on the agenda of New Testament scholarship.[1] Since then a flood of literature has appeared; countless books and articles have been published. Experience has shown that a consensus will remain an unattainable ideal. In the end of the day every scholar creates his or her own picture of Jesus. Of course objectivity needs to be striven for, but it will never be possible to exclude subjective feelings and emotions completely. That applies not only to the discussion of the historical Jesus but in fact to any historical and biographical undertaking. All facts and data which may be relevant take on significance only when they have been collected, put in order and interpreted by an exegete or historian. Anyone who is interested in the life and thought of Paul must adopt the same approach. We know that the result of all investigations has a subjective character. In the following pages I shall present *my* view. It is *my portrait* of the apostle to the Gentiles.

There are both agreements and differences between the debate on the historical Jesus and the investigation of the 'historical' Paul. I shall begin with the agreements. The apostle lived in the first century of our era. He was a younger contemporary of Jesus. Both figures played a role in human history. Therefore historical investigations can be made into their words and actions. That investigation has not been without its problems. It has experienced the inevitable difficulties and obstacles. The time in which Jesus and Paul lived lies almost two thousand years behind us. It is impossible for us to question eye-witnesses. They are long since dead, and to an important degree have taken their stories with them into their graves. Fortunately not everything has disappeared for good. Their recollections have been preserved in the writings of the New Testament. The investigation needs to be based on these sources. That applies both to the quest of the historical Jesus and to attempts to get a picture of the life and thought of Paul.[2]

But how *reliable* are the sources at our disposal? At this point we come up against a complicated problem. Opinions are very divided on the question of the 'reliability' – in the *historical* sense! – of the New Testament writings. Four evangelists relate the life and death of Jesus. However, anyone who carefully compares their writings will have to recognize that they contain different pictures of Jesus.[3] The evangelists were not modern historians. They did not strive for scientific objectivity. Their writings are not biographies of Jesus Christ. They look at the past through the spectacles of their belief that God had raised the crucified Jesus from the dead.

The words and actions of Paul were not put down in writing by four evangelists. He was not accorded this honour. He himself wrote, and a number of his letters proved to be worth including in the canon of the New Testament. In addition, his fortunes receive much attention in the book of Acts. The result is that the investigation of the 'historical' Paul is similarly confronted with something like a 'synoptic problem'. The picture of the apostle sketched in Acts only partly corresponds to the content of his letters. Events which Paul mentions are absent from Acts or are put in a different light there, and often the opposite is the case. In the letters a good deal of attention is paid to theological themes and ethical conflicts, whereas the author of Acts seems to concentrate above all on the long journeys which Paul undertook. Sometimes the personal reports which the apostle gives in his letters fit easily into the account in Acts, but it also happens that they contradict one another.

As I have said, there are both agreements and differences in respect of the historical investigation of both Jesus and Paul. They were contemporaries, but they played different roles in the history of the origin of Christianity. The imminent coming of the kingdom of God was central to the preaching of Jesus (Mark 1.14–15).[4] In Paul's preaching the accent shifted radically: Jesus himself becomes the one who is *preached*; the one who preaches the coming kingdom becomes the content of the preaching. The discovery of the shift in accent indicated here is one of the consequences of investigation into the life of Jesus. Since then a distinction has been drawn in scholarly literature between 'the historical Jesus' and the 'Christ of preaching'.[5] There is no consensus about precisely how great that difference is, but it is certain that this historical investigation soon brings the exegete into conflict with traditional insights and presuppositions in church and theology. Paul appeared as a preacher of the gospel of Jesus Christ. He himself never becomes the central content of the preaching. In that respect the consequences of the investigation of the 'historical' Paul are considerably less radical and far-reaching.

Sources

Paul plays a prominent role in the New Testament. There are no less than thirteen letters in his name – in the 'canonical' order: the letter to the Romans, two letters to the Corinthians, letters to the Galatians, Ephesians, Philippians and Colossians, a couple of letters to the Thessalonians, another two to Timothy and finally a letter to Titus and one to Philemon. Moreover more than half of Acts is largely devoted to his fortunes (Acts 9.1–28.31). We follow him on his journeys through Asia Minor and Greece. He visited cities which in his time were renowned for their economic, cultural and religious significance: Jerusalem, Ephesus, Athens, Corinth and even Rome, the nerve centre of the immense Roman empire.

On the basis of all this, is it right to suppose that we are well informed about the 'historical' Paul, perhaps even better than about the 'historical' Jesus? Little is known with certainty about the first decades of the history of the early Christian community. Much is hidden in the darkness of the past. The apostle Paul seems to be a favourable exception to this rule. Despite a gulf of many centuries, he encounters us in his letters. We can note his view of a large number of subjects which occupied people's minds in his time. The author of Acts thought it worth while to pay considerable attention to the activities of Paul. His life is not a closed book to us. We know the efforts he made to spread the gospel of Jesus Christ outside the limits of Jewish territory. He is more than a vague shadow from antiquity.

But all that does not alter the fact that caution is called for. Paul was a much-travelled man. According to the descriptions in Acts he caused a stir in communities in various cities of Asia Minor and Greece. He was arrested several times (Acts 16.19– 40) and had to account for himself before city rulers (Acts 17.1–14) and even before the Roman governor of Achaea – the southern part of present-day Greece (Acts 18.12–17). However, Paul has left no trace in contemporary literature. Roman historians do not mention him. His speech on the Areopagus in Athens found no response in the works of Greek philosophers of this time (Acts 17.15–34). Even in early Jewish writings from the first and second centuries of our era we look in vain for reactions to the difficulties that his appearance caused in Jewish communities inside and outside the land of Israel (I Thess. 2.14–16). Anyone who reads the New Testament will never be able to overlook Paul. He caused a great stir by his words and actions. He founded communities and thus laid the foundation for the spread of the Christian faith in the Roman empire. He did important work but – at least as far as we know – it was not noted in extra-biblical sources.

Therefore for a description of Paul's life and thought we have no other sources than the writings in the New Testament: his letters and the book of Acts. This observation provokes the question of the historical reliability of the sources mentioned. Were all the letters attributed to Paul really written by him? Then we need to be clear about the relationship between the content of the letters and the descriptions in Acts. As I have already remarked, sometimes the two sources supplement each other, but they also prove to contradict each other on essential points. One example is that nowhere in Acts is it mentioned that Paul wrote letters to communities which he had founded or still wanted to visit. Why was the author of Acts silent about Paul's correspondence? How reliable is his description of the past?

The authenticity of the letters: Hebrews

Discussion of the authenticity of the letters of Paul began in the nineteenth century.[6] Before this time people had few if any hesitations. Letters bearing the name of Paul had been written by him and by no one else. In this connection one book of the Bible played a notable role for centuries: the letter to the Hebrews. The name of Paul does not occur anywhere in the work. But already at a relatively early state of church history it was presupposed that he was the author of this work. This thought is encouraged by a sentence at the end of the letter: 'You should understand that our brother Timothy has been released, with whom I shall see you if he comes soon' (Heb. 13.23). Paul could have written these words. However, it is very questionable whether he really did.

In the first centuries of church history there was a fierce discussion over the value of the letter to the Hebrews. A harsh statement about the impossibility of a second repentance did not contribute to the popularity of the work: 'For it is impossible to restore again to repentance those who have once been enlightened, who have tasted the heavenly gift, and have become partakers of the Holy Spirit, and have tasted the powers of the age to come, if they then commit apostasy, since they crucify the son of God on their own account and hold him up to contempt' (Heb. 6.4–6). Did this letter deserve to gain a place in the list of 'canonical' books? For a long time views were divided. Finally Hebrews was accepted into the canon. What arguments proved decisive? In the process that led to the formation of the New Testament, among other things value was attached to a criterion which can be described by the term 'apostolicity'. The 'canonical' authority of a work increased depending on the degree to which it could be connected with an apostle – if the author himself or the source on which an author who was not himself an apostle drew was apostolic.[7] The passage quoted earlier about 'our brother Timothy' made it possible to connect the letter with Paul and to give the work an authoritative status.

Thus the letter to the Hebrews got its place in the canon of the New Testament; as the fourteenth letter of Paul it follows directly after the series of thirteen letters which are explicitly attributed to the apostle. Already in the first centuries of church history there was disagreement over the Pauline authorship, and in the course of the centuries doubt increased.[8] In our time the dominant view in exegetical circles is that the letter to the Hebrews cannot have been written by Paul. The text in which Timothy is mentioned is no longer accepted as proof. Many scholars regard these words as a later addition which was necessary in order to be able to attribute the letter to Paul.

Of course a comparison of content is decisive for a definitive verdict. On reading this letter, anyone who has no knowledge about the church tradition about the authorship of Hebrews will not quickly come to the conclusion that it could have been written by Paul. The differences from the letters which do stand in the name of the apostle are in fact too great. Traditionally Hebrews is indeed called a letter, but the writing has few if any characteristics of this form of literature. Nothing is said in the opening about the author or those to whom it is addressed (Heb. 1.1–4). References to concrete situations, very usual in the letters of Paul, are strikingly absent. According to present-day insights indeed it has become unusual to classify Hebrews as a letter in the strict sense of the word. Some exegetes refer to the conclusion of the writing, which speaks of 'this word of admonition' (Heb. 13.22). Is that in fact meant to indicate a 'sermon'? In any case we have an extended, profound and original theological treatise.[9]

Central to the christology of Hebrews is the notion of Jesus Christ as the high priest who 'has offered up himself once for all' (Heb. 7.25–28). In the letters of Paul we look in vain for such a reflection on the meaning of the suffering and dying of Christ. The author of Hebrews was familiar with scripture and tradition. Moreover he was not afraid to adopt unusual approaches. He emphatically associated the high priesthood of Jesus Christ not with Aaron but with the mysterious figure of Melchizedek (Heb. 7.1–17). Paul too often referred to the scriptures; however, there is no allusion in his letters to this enigmatic priest-king from the Old Testament (Gen. 14.17–20; Ps. 110.4).[10]

The consequence has to be that Hebrews will be left out of account in the investigation into Paul's life and thought. In the chapter in which I consider the influence of the apostle on following generations, we need to examine how far trains of thought from his letters influenced the thought of the author of Hebrews.

Thirteen or seven letters?

The question remains what judgment must be passed on the thirteen letters which do bear the name of Paul. Is it absolutely certain that they were written by the apostle? This is not the place to discuss this question in detail and at length. I shall limit myself to a brief survey of the most important insights which are the result of research into the New Testament that already began in the nineteenth century.[11]

The vast majority of exegetes think that the three Pastoral Epistles (I Timothy, II Timothy and Titus) cannot come from Paul himself. They were written some decades later by an anonymous author, who in all probability came from the circle of his disciples. In language and style these writings differ so much from the other letters which are attributed to the apostle that it is difficult to imagine how they all came from one and the same pen. There are also differences in content. These relate above all to two important areas of theological reflection, christology and ecclesiology. The authentic letters of Paul are central to an extended discussion of both. That is particularly true of the cross and resurrection. Secondly, the community in the Pastoral Epistles, unlike that in the time of Paul, proves to be tightly ordered and structured. The church has become an institution. There are different ministries, and those who exercise these ministries give leadership to the community. There is mention of 'overseers (= elders) and deacons', men with an impeccable lifestyle (I Tim. 3.1–13; Titus 1.5–16). It is difficult to say with any certainty precisely when the Pastoral Epistles were written. Generally speaking, it is assumed that they were written some decades after Paul's letters, which means around the end of the first century or shortly afterwards.[12]

So we do not have thirteen letters of Paul, but only ten. Or is even that number too high? In New Testament scholarship there is little difference of opinion over the authorship of the second letter to the community of Thessalonica. Already at the beginning of the nineteenth century the Pauline authorship was doubted, and since then this doubt has become almost a certainty.[13] In terms of content there is hardly any connection between the two letters to the Thessalonians. Whereas in the first letter it is emphasized that the day of the Lord will come suddenly and unexpectedly 'as a thief in the night' (I Thess. 5.1–3), the second letter speaks about a series of visible 'signs' which will precede the end (II Thess. 2.3–8). This striking contrast could be said to be the explanation of the origin of II Thessalonians. From the first letter to the community of Thessalonica it proves that Paul lived in a tense expectation of the *parousia*, the coming of Jesus Christ (I Thess. 4.13–18; 5.1–11). Time goes on, but the day of the Lord still has not come. This problem, usually described as 'the delay of the *parousia*',[14] also underlies some other New Testament writings, like the Gospels of Luke and John. Had Paul made a mistake? An anonymous author, presumably between the years 80 and 120, thought that he had to give a positive answer to this crucial question. The day of the Lord will come, but less quickly than Paul supposed. For pastoral reasons – see the advice in II Thessalonians 3 – the unknown author thought it wise to replace Paul's letter to the community of Thessalonica with a fictitious letter from the apostle. In his view the content of this new writing fitted better the situation in which the early-Christian community had meanwhile found itself as a result of the 'delay of the parousia'.[15] In retrospect it has to be said that the anonymous critic of Paul was only partially successful: his letter gained a place in the canon of the New Testament, but Paul's letter did not disappear from the scene.

The number ten has become nine. Two letters still need to be discussed, the letter to the Ephesians and the letter to the Colossians. Both letters show striking agreements with each other. They form a separate category. They are less remote from the authentic letters of Paul than the Pastoral Epistles, but at the same time there is sufficient reason to doubt their authenticity. The first question which needs to be answered is: in what way are the two letters dependent on each other? I follow a view widespread in scholarly literature that Ephesians must be dependent on Colossians and not vice versa; the latter position is defended only by one scholar. The language and style of the letter to the Ephesians differ in many respects from the other letters which are attributed to Paul. Here we come upon a surprising phenomenon. Among many scholars the apostle has gained the reputation of being fond of constructing long, incomprehensible sentences. He owes this reputation above all to the letter which he is said to have written to the community in Ephesus. In scholarly literature the same long and complicated sentences in the letter to the Ephesians are an important argument for questioning the authenticity of this work.

The anonymous author of the letter to the Ephesians thought it important that his writing should be recognized as 'Pauline'. He deliberately wrote 'in the spirit' of the apostle. He attached so much importance to this that his writing changed character. It is not a real letter. Concrete situations are never explicitly mentioned. It has become a theological treatise in letter form which was intended to function as a circular letter.[16] In the letter to the Ephesians it is no longer Paul himself who is speaking; he is being spoken about. His appearance belongs to the past. Posthumously he has become a man of great authority: 'For this reason I, *Paul,* a prisoner for Christ Jesus on behalf of you Gentiles . . . You have heard of the stewardship of God's grace that was given to me for you, how the mystery was made known to me through revelation' (Eph. 3.1–3). Once again it can be said that time has moved on. New questions and problems mean that old conflicts in the past have been forgotten. In this rapidly changing situation there was need for an authoritative word. The author of the letter to the Ephesians hoped to be able to write that, and for that reason he deliberately 'hid' behind the figure of Paul. The consequence was that a confusing situation arose, of which readers need to be thoroughly aware. The apostle is giving his view of developments which had not yet taken place in his time; he is making statements about a universal church which has become a remote ideal for him, and he is focussing with great force on the union of Judaism and Christianity, while he himself was still opposing a parting of the ways.[17]

The letter to the Ephesians is dependent on the letter to the Colossians. The anonymous author of Ephesians is unmistakably indebted to the latter. He himself will have been convinced that he had an *authentic* letter of Paul in his hands. At the moment New Testament scholars are no longer convinced of this. The letter to the community of Colossae stands as it were between the authentic letters and Ephesians. The content is not predominantly un-Pauline. One can find unmistakable Pauline notions in it, but there are also differences. In New Testament scholarship the striking combination of Pauline and non-Pauline arguments has led to the presupposition that the letter to the Colossians was written by one of the apostle's closest fellow-workers. The name of Timothy is mentioned in this connection (Col. 1.1).[18] It is indeed an attractive thought. Timothy belonged to the small circle of faithful followers of the apostle. Without any doubt he was familiar with his theological insights and he will have warmly subscribed to an important part of them. At the same time he was a different person and therefore will have handed on the Pauline insights in his own way.

Seven letters in the New Testament are attributed to Paul by the majority of exegetes: the letter to the Romans, the two letters to the community of Corinth, the letters to the Galatians and the Philippians, the first letter to the Thessalonians and the short letter to Philemon. Consequently only these letters will be used as a basis for investigating the life and thought of Paul. Attention will be paid to the six writings which bear his name but were not written by him in the chapter which tries to sketch out the influence and effect of his thought.

The letters and Acts

Two different sources are at our disposal: on the one hand the seven letters which were written by Paul himself, and on the other the book of Acts, in which an extended account can be found of his fortunes. Initially he emerged as a fanatical persecutor of the Christian community; on the way to Damascus he had a vision which made him change his mind; then as a preacher of the gospel of Christ he crossed wide areas of Asia Minor, Macedonia and Greece. Finally he arrived in Rome, the administrative centre of the Roman empire. The author of Acts gives the impression of having been a trustworthy chronicler. Some passages even suggest that from time to time he was among Paul's travelling companions. At these moments he writes in the first person plural and no longer speaks about 'them' but about 'us' (Acts 16.9–18; 20.4–16; 21.1–18; 27.1–28.16).

Earlier I wrote that the investigation into the 'historical' Paul is similarly confronted with something like a 'Synoptic problem'. We have two sources which at first sight seem historically trustworthy. We can put them side by side (= the synopsis) and compare them with each other, as we are accustomed to do with the three Synoptic Gospels. Sometimes the personal reports which Paul has included in his letters can be matched without much difficulty to the account in Acts. But that is by no means always the case. Paul and the author of Acts often contradict one another. Another, milder description of this difference of view is difficult to give. As an example here is an evocative illustration.

Acts pays a good deal of attention to the 'conversion'[19] of Paul on the way to Damascus: the event itself is related in detail (Acts 9.1–31). After that we hear the story twice more from the mouth of Paul, both times as an explanation and defence of his controversial way of acting (Acts 22.3–16; 26.9–18). However, in his letter to the Galatians the apostle gives an account which differs on important points from the descriptions in Acts. He emphatically writes that after the decisive event he did not travel to Jerusalem, 'but I went away into Arabia; and again I returned to Damascus' (Gal. 1.17). Acts tells another story. Paul fist stayed several days in Damascus. In the synagogue he preached the gospel 'that Jesus is the son of God' (Acts 9.23–25). From Damascus he travelled directly to Jerusalem and there, with Barnabas as an intermediary, met the other apostles (Acts 9.26–27). He also spoke bluntly in Jerusalem and again got into difficulties. Because there was even a threat to his life, the 'brothers' escorted him to Caesarea (from Jerusalem) and from there he travelled – presumably by sea – to Tarsus (Acts 9.29–30).

According to the letter to the Galatians the apostle undertook the journey to Jerusalem only three years later. Paul relates little about that first stay. It lasted fifteen days and he met only Peter and James, 'the brother of the Lord' (Gal. 1.18–19). It is striking that the apostle links this summary report with a formula which suggests that he is engaged in something like swearing an oath: 'In what I am writing to you, before God, I do not lie' (Gal. 1.20). Why these heavy assertions? Did Paul know or guess that other readings of the event were possible? In any case it is clear that the narrative in Acts is difficult to reconcile with Paul's own account in his letter to the Galatians. In the same passage the apostle emphatically declared: 'Then I went into the regions of Syria and Cilicia. And I was still not known by sight to the churches of Christ in Judaea' (Gal. 1.21–22).

Who gives the right view of the event: Paul or the author of Acts? Which description is historically reliable? It is obvious that Paul must be given the benefit of the doubt. As the one directly involved he will have known best precisely what happened. Obvious as this may seem, caution is called for. It was not Paul's custom to sprinkle his letters with auto-biographical notes. He was sparing with these and inserted them only when he thought it necessary. His apostolate was controversial (see especially II Cor. 10–12). His opponents pestered him incessantly. He stated his conviction briefly, but powerfully, at the beginning of his letter to the Galatians: 'Paul, an apostle – not from men nor through man, but through Jesus Christ and God the Father . . .' (Gal. 1.1). His apostleship proves to be of 'a higher order'. God himself has called him (Gal. 1.15). The consequence was that he felt independent of the leading figures in the early church and even from the first disciples, the apostles in Jerusalem: the 'pillars' of the early Christian community (Gal. 2.9). This striking self-confidence also colours the other personal notes in the letter to the Galatians. Paul forthrightly declares that he did not travel to Jerusalem immediately. However, he did go three years later. His stay was of short duration and his encounters with other apostles remained limited to Peter and James. After fifteen days he returned and spent some time far from Jewish territory. Only fourteen years later did he undertake a journey to Jerusalem for the second time. Again Paul emphasizes his independence: 'I went up by revelation' (Gal. 2.2). It is certainly no coincidence that he uses the same word in his account of the decisive event on the way to Damascus (Gal. 1.12,16). He did not go to Jerusalem because he had been invited by his fellow apostles. They had nothing to say about him. He arrived in Jerusalem because God had shown him the way.

In his letter to the Galatians Paul was writing with a special perspective on the past. He wanted to offer a historical proof of his special, independent position as an apostle. His view of what happened in the past is doubtless coloured by personal interests. The consequence is that the historian, in search of the truth, is confronted with a difficult dilemma. Did Paul deliberately keep silent about a previous visit to the members of the early-Christian community in Jerusalem (cf. Acts 9)? Or must the attractive accounts in the Acts of the Apostles be assigned to the realm of fable? There is no doubt that the author of this book of the Bible, too, had 'theological interests'. He wanted to show that the early Christian community could delight in a high degree of unanimity. Of course he was realistic enough not to keep completely silent about existing tensions (Acts 6.1; 15.35–16.3), but he emphasized above all that the Christian community which had received the Spirit of the Lord at Pentecost lived in an exceptionally close fellowship (Acts 2.41–47; 4.32–37). In this framework we need not be surprised that the author of Acts was primarily concerned to show that even the controversial apostle Paul did not destroy the unity. Eventually he was lovingly received by the original community in Jerusalem – though as the 'thirteenth apostle', since he would never belong to the circle of the Twelve.[20]

Again we face the question of the reliability of the sources. The letters contain some of the apostle's personal recollections, but not many. Paul referred to the past in order to prove or to support his own view. His reminiscences are coloured, and that is not surprising, since sometimes there are from ten to twenty years between past and present. The discussion would be considerably easier if one could put an objective, reliable historical work alongside the subjective recollections of Paul. However, that is not possible. Acts certainly presents itself as such a work, but nevertheless there is every reason to doubt this.

The Acts of the Apostles evokes trust. The author makes a connection with the Gospel of Luke: 'In the first book, O Theophilus, I have dealt with all that Jesus began to do and teach, until the day when he was taken up into heaven' (Acts 1.1–2). In the first verses of the Gospel the author showed himself to be a man who attached great importance to accuracy (Luke 1.1–4). We would seem justified in concluding that the Third Gospel and the Acts of the Apostles were written by one and the same author.[21] But who was he? The church tradition has called him Luke. The letter to the community of Colossae speaks about 'my friend Luke, the physician' (Col. 4.14). At the end of his letter to Philemon Paul mentions three 'fellow-workers': Aristarchus, Demas and Luke (Philemon 24). The 'we-passages' in Acts (16.9–18; 20.4–16; 21.1–18; 27.1–28.16) seem to confirm what has been said above: Luke was a fellow-worker of Paul and he accompanied the apostle on his missionary journeys on some occasions.

The traditional view does not make the problem easier, but considerably more complicated. If the author of Acts really was a contemporary and sometimes even a travelling companion of Paul, how are we to explain the fact that his account of events corresponds so little with the personal recollections in the apostle's letter? Was he really an eye-witness? Did he know Paul? The author of Acts was also the author of the Third Gospel. According to current views in New Testament scholarship that writing was only completed in the 80s or 90s of the first century.[22] Given the introduction quoted earlier, Acts took its definitive form after that. The unknown author – 'doctor' Luke will meanwhile have died – also made use of sources in writing Acts, including Peter's speeches and the 'we passages', which related above all to Paul's voyages by sea.[23]

To sum up. Anyone interested in the life and thought of Paul has to use two kinds of sources: seven letters and the Acts of the Apostles. His letters contain personal reminiscences, which are unmistakably coloured by the context. The Acts of the Apostles was not written by an eye-witness. It was composed only around the 80s or 90s of the first century. This is long after the time when Paul lived: thirty to forty years. However, that does not mean that the historical reliability of the stories in Acts must be belittled all along the line. The author made use of sources. At the same time his view of the past was also coloured by the time and circumstances in which he lived. All this means that it is impossible to lay down a general guideline about the relationship between the letters and Acts. Time and again the accounts need to be assessed for their historical reliability.

2

The life of Paul.
Biographical information

A cosmopolitan

Paul was a man with a complex background. He lived and worked in different worlds and cultures. He boasted of his Jewish origins (Phil. 3.5–6) but also made grateful use of the prominent position which Roman citizenship offered him (Acts 16.37–39). Paul was a Diaspora Jew. He grew up in Tarsus, a Greek-Hellenistic city in the eastern part of Asia Minor. As a young man he went to Jerusalem, there to be instructed in scripture and tradition by Gamaliel, an influential leader of the Pharisaic movement (Acts 22.3).

Thanks to his cosmopolitan background, Paul spoke various languages. In his youth, which he spent in the Hellenistic culture of Tarsus, he became familiar with Greek (Acts 21.37). He wrote his letters in *koine* Greek. In the period around the beginning of our era many non-Greeks spoke this simplified form of classical Greek. Like English in our time, in antiquity *koine* Greek made it possible to communicate with people from other cultures and peoples. Paul was a Roman citizen. We do not know for certain, but it seems probable that he spoke Latin. To the amazement of furious Jews in Jerusalem he also spoke their language – Hebrew or Aramaic (Acts 21.40; 22.2). Paul's knowledge of languages put him in a position to travel across the Roman empire and make himself understood almost everywhere. He paid visits to important urban centres like Antioch in Syria, Ephesus in Asia Minor, Philippi, Corinth and Athens in

Greece, and finally – as the crown of his work – to Rome in Italy.

Hundreds of years have gone by since Paul's travels. Some of the cities which he visited are now in ruins. They are interesting to archaeologists and to modern pilgrims who 'in the footsteps of Paul' try to form a picture of the world in which the apostle moved. In Rome and Athens there is the hubbub of modern life in all its force and energy, of a kind that can also be found in places like New York, which cannot boast of a particularly venerable past. Paul would not believe his eyes if he were to visit Rome and Athens again today. History has not stood still after the first century. Everything is changed. Even the Roman empire – great, powerful and vast: the world seemed to stop at its frontiers – disappeared from the earth long ago. Ruins tell an age-old, always fascinating story of rise and fall: of emerging, of flourishing and decay.

Paul had no great expectations for the future of this world (Rom. 8.18–30). Together with many of his contemporaries he lived in the conviction that the end was near: 'the time is short' (I Cor. 7.29). The (second) coming of the Lord would take place soon: 'maranatha' (I Cor. 16.22). For this reason, it seems doubtful whether Paul ever dreamed that a follower of Jesus Christ would take his place on the imperial throne in Rome. But that did happen in the fourth century. Martyrs became authorities. This had its consequences. Accents shifted in theological reflection and focal points were moved. In these circumstances the disappointment at the failure of the kingdom of God to materialize gave place to joy at the fact that the powerful Roman empire had become a Christian empire. However, this joy was short-lived. Christian faith proved no guarantee of success. The Roman empire fell into decay and disappeared from the map. It was not forgotten. In numerous places, from the coasts of Western Europe to the Middle East, there are still the remains of impressive buildings once put up by the Romans. These are only ruins. But they still cause wonderment, even among people at the beginning of the twenty-first century, who are well accustomed to the sight of imposing buildings.

After all these centuries it has become impossible for us to get an idea of the fascinating classical world in which Paul lived and which he came to know thoroughly during his long trips. Even if we were able to follow in his tracks as accurately as possible, that cannot be, since the travel account in Acts is not precise enough, while the geographical indications in his letters have an extremely summary character – moreover other images strike our retinas from those which the apostle once looked on. Can a gulf of centuries ever be bridged?

Honesty compels us to recognize that we cannot give a positive answer to this question. We are not contemporaries of the apostle. We never will be, however often we read his writings. I think it theological arrogance to pretend that it is possible not only to make a complete reconstruction of the apostle's 'thought' but also to fathom it with the help of less than ten letters and a number of travel accounts in Acts.

Anyone who makes a careful attempt to analyse Paul's theological insights needs to be well aware of the gulf which I have just indicated. To begin with, it would be a great misunderstanding to underestimate this classical world. Paul was shaped by a conglomerate of cultures which cannot in the least be described as primitive. Western European civilization would have lost important values and strengths had it not been fed by the thought of 'classical' figures with famous names: Homer, Socrates, Plato, Aristotle, Julius Caesar, Tacitus, Livy and many other philosophers, thinkers and writers of plays, romances and historical works. They have left traces on history which have proved worth investigating down to our day.

The dimensions of the Roman empire were unimaginably great. Under the command of skilled and creative commanders with notorious reputations – like Pompey and again Julius Caesar – Roman legions conquered one people after another. As a result, the empire increasingly took on the character of a real melting pot of languages, cultures and religions. The Romans were usually very tolerant of those with different opinions. Their admiration for Greek culture – religion, philosophy and plays – came from the period before the empire.

And even when they had reached the height of their power, the Roman authorities were usually wise and understanding enough not to provoke the conquered peoples to rebellion by challenging and abolishing their religions. These peoples were not forced to bow to the gods of their conquerors. With one exception, Roman tolerance went so far as to accept the gods of the conquered people and give them a full place alongside their own religious ideas.[1]

But despite this conglomeration of religions and cultures, which seems as confusing as it is chaotic, we can say that there was a degree of cultural unity with in the Roman empire. This 'spiritual' unity found its basis in the philosophical and religious notions of the thinkers and authors whom I mentioned earlier. Their writings were read and studied everywhere. Their ideas were part and parcel of the culture of all those who had had an education. It is not irresponsible to assume that this also applied to Paul. He grew up in a Hellenistic Greek city which was prominent in both the cultural and the philosophical sphere. On his many journeys he crossed a lively, colourful world. Those who want to grasp his letters and understand his thoughts must steep themselves in the culture of this world.[2]

'I am a Jew'

According to the author of Acts Paul twice in close succession emphatically declared that he was a Jew. He did that during his last stay in Jerusalem, after other Jews had recognized him and threatened him over his activities as a preacher of the Christian faith (Acts 21.39; 22.3). There is no difference of opinion between Acts and the letters on this point. Paul was a Jew and he saw no reason to be ashamed of his Jewishness: 'Of the people of Israel, of the tribe of Benjamin' (Phil. 3.6); 'I myself am an Israelite, a descendant of Abraham, a member of the tribe of Benjamin' (Rom. 11.1). On one occasion he made use of a rhetoric which speaks for itself: 'Are they Hebrews? So am I. Are they Israelites? So am I. Are they children of Abraham? So am I' (II Cor. 11.22).

His Jewish origin stamped his life. He grew up as the Jew Saul (Acts 7.58). The age-old faith of the fathers meant a great deal to him (Gal. 1.14), but he became a convinced follower of Jesus Christ. Saul became Paul. His life changed radically, but he never denied his Jewishness. Paul always also remained Saul.[3] He died as a Christian and as a Jew. By virtue of his birth he was taken up soul and body into a community of faith with an old, venerable tradition.

In the first century of our era Judaism had spread widely in the Roman empire.[4] Jews were living in a number of cities – usually they were small in number, but sometimes there were quite a lot of them and they were influential. That was the case in Antioch in Syria and above all in Alexandria in Egypt. Throughout the Roman empire archaeologists have found the remains of buildings which served as synagogues. There is no convincing evidence – Matt. 23.15 is a notable exception – that Jews engaged intensively in disseminating their belief among Gentiles.[5] But at this time Jewish belief exercised a marked power of attraction on non-Jews. The reason must be sought in the unambiguous monotheism which may be said to be characteristic of the Jewish tradition. The uniqueness of the God of Israel was of a quite different, higher order than the stories which went the rounds about the Greek supreme god Zeus and his fellow gods. Anyone who was not attracted by the scandalous actions of Zeus found an inspiring counter-balance in the Old Testament-Jewish stories about the unique and exalted God of Israel. Moreover the behaviour of Jews made an impression and their modest way of life earned them the respect of their non-Jewish fellow-citizens. Those who prized a lofty morality sought and found their salvation in the local synagogue.

'Born in Tarsus in Cilicia'

The author of Acts leaves no doubt about Paul's sense of a close tie with the city of Tarsus in Cilicia. He was born there (Acts 22.3) and he is said to have settled there again when after his flight from Damascus Jerusalem threatened to become too hot for him and he was even in danger of his life (Acts 9.30; 11.25). There is no doubt about his identity in Acts: he was widely known as Saul/Paul from Tarsus (Acts 9.11; 21.39). Remarkably, not a single reference to Tarsus can be found in his own letters. In his autobiographical notes in the first chapter of the letters to Galatians Paul certainly says that after his first visit to Jerusalem he went 'to the region of Syria and Cilicia' (Gal. 1.21), but he does not say a word about the city of Tarsus. Does his silence contradict the reports in Acts?

In all probability it does not. Paul's silence could be explained from the fact that in his letters he needed to prove and defend above all his Jewish identity. In the discussion about the significance of the commandments of the Torah for Gentile Christians he chose a position which made some Jewish Christians suspect that he no longer wanted to take the Torah as a whole seriously. In such a discussion several times he referred with great emphasis to his Jewish origin and upbringing (Gal. 1.11–24; Phil. 3.5–9). He would have played into the hands of his opponents if, for the sake of completeness, in the autobiographical passages he had mentioned that he had seen the light of day outside the frontiers of Jewish territory. A Diaspora Jew was at any rate open to the suspicion of not taking faithfulness to the Torah as seriously.

It seems legitimate to conclude that Paul's origin lay in the Jewish Diaspora. In his time he was not the only Jew whose cradle had not been in the age-old land of Israel. In the first century of our era the Jewish Diaspora was already an ancient and widespread phenomenon.[6] Influential Jewish families had been living in the old cultural area of Mesopotamia from the time of the Babylonian exile. Their forebears had not listened to the summons to return to the land of Judah. For various reasons they had preferred to stay in Persia. Some proved successful in trade and business. In these circumstances the study of scripture and tradition also flourished. In the period after the destruction of the temple in AD 70 the scribes in Persia played an important rule in the development of the Jewish tradition. Moreover it is no coincidence that the Babylonian Talmud was in general thought more highly of than the Palestinian Talmud.

The great Egyptian city of Alexandria was also an important centre of Diaspora Judaism.[7] Little can be said with any certainty about the origin of this Jewish community, but we cannot rule out the possibility that here too the Babylonian exile played a decisive role. Thus the book of the prophet Jeremiah tells of inhabitants of Judah who after the destruction of the temple in 586 BC fled to Egypt for fear of reprisals from the Babylonians (Jer. 41.16–18). Alexandria – founded by Alexander the Great, as the name suggests, in the fourth century – grew rapidly into an important, cosmopolitan city with a distinguished and influential Jewish minority. Because it had a good harbour, Alexandria was a focal point of trade and business, but in addition it was also a cultural centre and a melting pot for religious convictions and philosophical currents.[8] Because Alexandrian Judaism had opted not to live in spiritual isolation, it saw itself compelled to reflect on the relationship between its own convictions and insights which derived from old Egyptian traditions and from Hellenism.

Alexandrian Judaism was also important for early Christianity. At any rate, well before the beginning of our era it tried to become a bridge between Judaism and Hellenism. In the second century BC, under the tolerant government of the Ptolemies,[9] a beginning was made in Alexandria on a Greek translation of the scriptures of the Hebrew Bible. In reaction to pagan notions a form of wisdom theology developed within the Jewish community of Alexandria which had a surprisingly speculative character, and was less exclusively focussed on the Torah.[10] The influential Hellenistic Jewish thinker Philo lived in Alexandria in the first century of our era. It is significant that to the present day, Orthodox Jewish circles are critical about the value and significance of Philo's insights. He was indeed a Jew, but a Diaspora Jew, and his thought was said to be strongly influenced by Hellenism.

The Diaspora was vast. Around the beginning of our era

its extent steadily increased. Ancient centres like Persia, Alexandria and cities in Asia Minor might rejoice in the influx of new emigrants from the home country. Jesus' well-known parable about the 'prodigal son' (Luke 15.11–32) is not a time-less story but seems to have been taken from life. That is how things often were at that time. The oldest son inherited the business and the younger sons went away. Jewish territory was relatively small, and fertile only in parts. The numerous building activities of Herod the Great – palaces and fortresses, but above all the temple in Jerusalem – had provided many opportunities for employment, but after his death this activity declined sharply. Therefore enterprising young men looked for possibilities of making a future outside the frontiers of the land of the Jews.

Once Paul's ancestors also took this step – it is not impossible that we should have to go back further in his genealogy and put the responsibility for Paul's birth as a Diaspora Jew on his grandparents or great-grandparents. Why did they go to live in Tarsus? It is almost impossible to give a meaningful answer to this question. But I have a suggestion. It is speculative and there is no proof, but it is not completely plucked out of thin air. Both the letters and the book of Acts make no secret of the fact that the apostle was financially independent. His many missionary activities did not prevent him from providing for himself. He mentions this with pride (Acts 20.34; II Cor. 11.9; I Thess. 2.9). He was a tent-maker by profession (Acts 18.3). It is natural to suppose that he learned this trade from his father. That's how things were in those days. And once his father or grandfather had settled in Tarsus. Why? Tarsus was the capital of the Roman province of Cilicia. So the city was a government centre, and consequently also had a garrison. Even in our day armies need tents. It is not inconceivable that Paul's father earned his living as a tent-maker for the garrison of Tarsus. That could explain how at the end of his short spell in prison in Philippi Paul appealed to his Roman citizenship (Acts 16.37–39; 22.23–29).[11]

Tarsus lay in Cilicia. It was an ancient city which is already mentioned on an inscription from the time of the Babylonian king Shalmaneser III (around 830 BC). The history of the city bears the traces of the political and military developments in the Middle East; the Babylonian empire was conquered by the Persians, with the result that Tarsus fell into Persian hands; after the campaign of Alexander the Great the city was for a long time part of the kingdom of Syria; in 66 BC it was incorporated into the Roman empire. Tarsus was widely known and had a high reputation. The city had a mixed population and was regarded as an influential centre of Hellenistic culture. Philosophers and poets adopted it as their home. According to some, Tarsus even challenged renowned cultural centres like Athens and Alexandria for the crown.[12]

If we go on to try to form a picture of Paul's life and to analyse his thought, it is important not to forget all this. The apostle was no stranger to the world of his days, dominated as it was by Hellenism. He spoke Greek and was a Roman citizen. Thanks to his youth in Tarsus he need not feel uncomfortable in a big city. The daily hustle and bustle did not bewilder him. Far less was he surprised by the morals and customs in Hellenistic cities. He had grown up in such a sphere in Tarsus. From his youth on he knew that the world of the Roman empire was particularly rich in gods and goddesses.[13] There were also various temples in Tarsus. Paul will have known to whom they were dedicated. He certainly also knew the place where the gymnasium stood, the sports school which enjoyed great popularity. Throughout the Roman empire, much attention was devoted to sport and games and the development of the body had become a real cult. Paul will have been familiar with all these expressions of Hellenistic Greek and Roman culture, but in all probability he did not take part in them. As a Jew in the Diaspora he lived in a world dominated by pagan ideas and notions. It seems almost impossible that he was not influenced by them in one way or another. At the same time, even as a Diaspora Jew he remained thoroughly aware of his Jewish identity.

'Circumcised on the eighth day'

In the letter to the community of Philippi, Paul himself relates that he was 'circumcised on the eighth day' (Phil. 3.5). In Acts there is no reference to Paul's circumcision. In the auto-biographical passage in Philippians the clause is functional. In the face of criticism of his position that Gentile Christians need not be circumcised (Phil. 3.2–4; for a more extended discussion of this problem see the letter to the Galatians), Paul clearly wanted to leave no room for doubt about his Jewishness. Completely in keeping with the regulations of the Torah he was circumcised on the eighth day (Lev. 12.3; cf. Luke 2.21, where it is said that Jesus was similarly circumcised on that day).

The report on Paul's circumcision also sheds some light on the religion of his parents. They lived in the Diaspora, but they observed the commandments of the Torah. How consistently they did that is impossible to say, because we do not have sufficient information. With some caution one could infer from certain remarks which Paul made and decisions which he took that he grew up in a milieu conscious of its Jewish identity. Paul knew his origins, and he will have received this knowledge from his parents: an Israelite, a descendant of Abraham and belonging to the tribe of Benjamin (Phil. 3.5; Rom. 11.1). His decision to travel to Jerusalem in order to steep himself in scripture and tradition there under experienced guidance also says something about his parents. Given the relationship between parent and child at this time it seems reasonable to suppose that they encouraged him to take this course. In orthodox Jewish families it was (still is) thought important to have many descendants. We do not know whether Paul grew up in a large family. According to Acts, at any rate he had one sister (Acts 23.16).

Like many Diaspora Jews, from his youth Paul was someone who lived in different worlds. He grew up in a typically Hellenistic city, but he did so as a Jew, as someone who had been circumcised on the eighth day. In the Graeco-Roman world, circumcision was regarded as a barbarian custom, an irreversible mutilation of the body. As a consequence of his circumcision Paul was 'marked' for life and could be recognized as a Jew.

We can only guess at the year of his birth. The author of Acts reports his presence at the stoning of Stephen and calls him a 'young man' (Acts 7.58). This report does not leave us any the wiser. For up to what age was someone at this time still 'a young man', and when did the stoning of Stephen take place?

Both questions can only be answered with many 'ifs and buts'. Stephen did not meet his tragic end (Acts 6.7) immediately after the outpouring of the Spirit at the feast of Pentecost (Acts 2). Some time elapsed between the two events. How many days, months or perhaps years it is difficult to indicate precisely. The name of Stephen is mentioned in Acts in the first instance in connection with disputes which had broken out within the original community (Acts 6.1–6). Partisan disputes posed a real threat to the unity of the community and led to some widows going short. Clearly this situation stood in sharp contrast to the fortunes of the original community in the period immediately after Pentecost (Acts 2.41–47; 4.32–37). When did this insidious split become manifest? After a year or only after a number of years? How long can an ideal situation last? Or is the picture that Acts sketches of the original community in fact the ideal that is desirable,[14] but never existed in this form?

It is not absolutely certain in what year Jesus was crucified. 7 April 30 is the date which is usually mentioned in this connection.[15] In that year the early Christian community in Jerusalem came into being. It is not inconceivable that the disputes described in Acts developed relatively quickly. Tensions between different groups of Jews – e.g. between those who spoke Aramaic by preference and others who preferred Greek because they came from the Diaspora and had been influenced by Hellenism – already existed long before the beginning of our era. It was inevitable that Jews who became followers of Jesus Christ took their different backgrounds and tendencies into the new community of faith. The result was that the tensions indicated could also spread easily and quickly there.

The stoning of Stephen could thus have taken place around two years after the death of Jesus – in the year 32.[16] Paul witnessed the execution, and according to the author of Acts, at that moment he was 'a young man' (Acts 7.38). It is well known that people at this time were regarded as adults sooner than they are today. They married young – girls around the age of thirteen or fourteen and boys also some years later, but at all events before they were twenty. It also seems likely that at this time the age of twelve was regarded as the moment when someone of the male gender was declared adult in a religious sense (cf. the story of the twelve-year-old Jesus in the temple, Luke 2.40–52). A short time later the young Paul will have gone off to Jerusalem. Since nowhere in his letters does he mention encounters with Jesus in Jerusalem, he probably arrived in the city only after the crucifixion, between 30 and 32. All this means that the one who was later to become an apostle must have seen the light of day in Tarsus around the year 15.

'Brought up at the feet of Gamaliel'

We look for the name Gamaliel in vain in the letters of Paul. We owe the information that the apostle was a pupil of this influential scribe to the author of Acts (22.3). The name Gamaliel has already appeared in that work. He is then introduced as follows: 'but a Pharisee in the council named Gamaliel, a teacher of the law, held in honour by all the people, stood up' (Acts 5.34). He speaks at a session of the Sanhedrin at which Peter and the other apostles are being questioned. Some members of the supreme Jewish legal body seem to be of the opinion that the followers of Jesus deserved the death penalty, but Gamaliel forcefully opposes this. On this occasion he gives his colleagues wise advice: 'Keep away from these men and let them alone; for if this plan or this undertaking is of men, it will fail; but if it is of God, you will not be able to overthrow them. You might even be found opposing God!' (Acts 5.38–39).

At first sight it is surprising that the name of Gamaliel does not occur in Paul's letters. Can this silence on the part of the apostle be cited as proof that the author of Acts had given an incorrect picture of events? At all events Gamaliel was not a fictitious figure. His name is mentioned with honour in Jewish literature. He formed a link in a dynasty of influential scribes. He himself was a grandson of Hillel, the founder of one of the most important schools within Pharisaism. At the end of the first century one of his grandsons belonged to the generation of the first rabbis who devoted themselves to the ongoing existence of the Jewish tradition after the catastrophe of the year 70. This rabbi too bore the name Gamaliel. To distinguish between grandfather and grandson, the contemporary of Jesus is usually called Gamaliel I and his grandson Gamaliel II.[17]

It is understandable that in the book of Acts there is no reticence about the relationship between the wise Gamaliel and the young Paul. Anyone who was brought up at the feet of this venerable and authoritative teacher might be regarded as an expert in scripture and tradition. No one would have found it strange if the apostle had mentioned the name of his teacher with pride. However, he did not do this. He will have had his reasons for that silence. Paul knows himself to be called by God (Gal. 1.1, 15). Without reserve he emphasized his independent position. People had not influenced him and made him think otherwise (Gal. 1.11–12), not even the first apostles, the leaders of the primitive community in Jerusalem (Gal. 1.16). So it is not so strange that he also kept quiet about having been taught by Gamaliel. Moreover it is possible that Paul had a second reason for not mentioning the influential leader of the Pharisaic movement. Certainly the suggestion is made in Acts that Gamaliel was Paul's most important teacher, but it is not inconceivable that the man who was later to become an apostle had already been inspired and influenced by other scribes during his studies in Jerusalem.

'As to the law a Pharisee'

Paul's parents observed the commandments of the Torah. As a young man he travelled to Jerusalem, there to qualify in the exegesis of scripture and tradition under the direction of Gamaliel, who was mentioned above. As a scribe Gamaliel belonged to the Pharisaic current within the Judaism of his days (Acts 5.34). When Paul writes in the autobiographical passage in his letter to the Philippians that he was 'as to the law a Pharisee', this characterization fits the profile that I have been able to draw of him so far. In following his parents and teacher he belonged to the party of the Pharisees and subscribed to their aims and ideals.

For a good understanding of the background of Paul's thought it is important to pay attention to the motives of the Pharisees. Various texts in the four canonical Gospels have contributed towards giving their name negative connotations in the Christian tradition: Pharisees are hypocrites (Matt. 6.1–18; 23.1–39; Luke 18.9–14). They have been depicted as those who constantly discussed with Jesus his supposed transgressions of the Torah (Mark 12.13–17; Luke 14.1–6; John 9.40–41). Thanks to a better insight into the religious situation within Judaism at the time of Jesus we now know that the evangelists paint a distorted picture of the Pharisees. The Pharisees are said to have been the opponents of Jesus. In reality they were certainly not. They had no reason to have him put to death (Luke 13.31–35).[18]

When Jesus arrives in Jerusalem the Pharisees disappear into the background. They play no role in his trial and their name is not mentioned again. It seems probable that the evangelists' view of the attitude of the Pharisees has been influenced by the time in which they themselves lived, with the result that consciously or unconsciously they projected this situation back into the time of Jesus. After the destruction of the temple in 70 the influence of the Pharisees quickly increased and they became the spiritual leaders of Judaism. At the same time the tensions between Jews and Christians became so great that a schism proved unavoidable. In the debate Christians found themselves confronted with predominantly Pharisaic scribes, men who knew scripture and who were not easily convinced by their opponents. Who will blame the evangelists for projecting their own polemic against Jewish leaders back into the time of Jesus? What they were going through now, without doubt he had already gone through earlier. He too was constantly threatened by fanatical Pharisees. They will have even tried to put him to death (Mark 3.6)![19]

What has been said above leads to the following conclusion: those who want to know more about the aims and ideals of the Pharisees in the time of Jesus will need to reckon with the fact that the texts about them in the New Testament are not historically reliable.[20] Of course there will also have been hypocrites in Pharisaic circles – as in every religious grouping – but it is certainly wrong to brand them collectively as hypocrites. The Pharisees took their lives very seriously. They knew the scriptures and were deeply convinced that God would not let himself be mocked by them. For this reason the Torah played a central role in their lives.

The roots of Pharisaism as it manifested itself in different schools and tendencies in the first century of our era go far back into the Old Testament-Jewish tradition. The terrible reality of the Babylonian exile had once more raised the question of the hand of God in history. Why did God let this happen? Was even God powerless against the violence of the Assyrian and Babylonian authorities? Or was it his will that the people of Israel should be led into captivity? In the book of the prophet Jeremiah we find the following bewildering sentence: 'Now I (= God) have given all these lands into the hand of Nebuchadnezzar, the king of Babylon, my servant' (Jer. 27.6). However, according to the prophet all this did not happen behind God's back. The dramatic defeat, the conquest of Jerusalem, the destruction of the temple, the end of the dynasty of David, the deportation of part of the population – the prophet Jeremiah concluded that all this was indeed the will of God. But why did God will this? The readers of the prophetic work are not left in ignorance for long about the answer to this question: 'How can you complain against me (= God)? You have all been unfaithful to me – says the Lord. In vain have I smitten your sons, they have learned nothing from it' (Jer. 2.29–30). Destruction and captivity are seen as God's punishment, because the people of God has proved disobedient and has constantly failed to walk in the ways of the Lord.

The tone which is set here is of essential importance for the history of the Jewish people to the present day.[21] Pharisaism also fits into that perspective.[22] The movement arose in the period shortly after the successful revolt of the Maccabees in 167–164 BCE. The 'pious' (= Hasidim), who had refused to obey the demand of their Syrian overlord that they should modernize and Hellenize the Jewish faith despite threats and torture, came closer together after the conquest and formed a movement of like-minded people. They regarded themselves primarily as a penitential movement, inspired by prophets like Jeremiah, Ezra and Nehemiah. To their sorrow they discovered that the warnings from the distant past were still relevant and that the majority of the Jewish people had apparently learned little or nothing from the past. Was history to repeat itself? In this critical situation the Pharisees thought that they had been called on to oppose with all their power the danger which threatened. Therefore they concentrated on the commandments of the Torah in the hope that others would follow their example. However, they met with bitter opposition. In their 'zeal' for the Torah they came into conflict with all the Jews who did not disapprove of Hellenistic influence on their own tradition of faith. This group also included the descendants of the Maccabees, who as the dynasty of the Hasmonaeans ruled as kings over the Jewish people up to the coming of the Romans in 63 BCE. Around the year 100 BC the conflict came to a climax which was as tragic as it was dramatic, and a number of Pharisees were killed on the orders of the Hasmonaean ruler.[23]

The Pharisees never had a tremendous following, but they were quite influential. That was also the case at the time of Jesus. Their serious way of life commanded respect. Sobriety characterized their actions. They thought it of the utmost importance that theory and practice, convictions and daily life should be combined as closely as possible. Pharisees were regarded as experts in scripture and tradition, but they combined the permanent study of the Torah with the practice of a profession. Many had learned a trade: they were saddle-makers or tanners; they earned their living as tent-makers (like Paul and his family) or as carpenters (like Joseph and Jesus – cf. Matt. 13.55). In the later rabbinic literature carpenters are even praised for their learning; they in particular are said to be particularly skilled in the close study of the commandments of the Torah.

The Pharisees combined their strict, devout piety with a striking sense of reality. They had to, since they deliberately stood at the centre of ordinary life. Marriage and family were highly esteemed in Pharisaic circles. The father or the house had the duty of providing for his wife and children (often many). That was the consequence of the choice which the Pharisees thought they had to make in accord with scripture and tradition. They did not retreat from the everyday world like the Essenes – who were in fact kindred – seeking the solitude of the wilderness in the region of the Dead Sea in order to be able to observe the commandments of the Torah as strictly as possible there. Because the Pharisees stood firmly in the society of those days and had to earn their living, they felt compelled to teach the commandments of the Torah in such a way that they did not make life an intolerable burden. In Pharisaic circles there was much difference of opinion over the exposition of the Torah. And that is understandable. Creativity was necessary for dealing with the Torah like this, and among some members this came up against misunderstanding and even opposition. In the writings of the Qumran community, the Essenes pass a harsh judgment on the attitude of the Pharisees; they are called half-hearted and even hypocritical.[24] Of course it was easy for those who had withdrawn from society and refused to dirty their hands in everyday work to talk like that.

A passionate zealot

Paul's profile is slowly taking shape. However, it is not yet complete. We noted that his background was complex. As a cosmopolitan he spoke several languages and was no stranger to the Hellenistic world of the Roman empire. Divergent cultures came together in Paul, the Diaspora Jew. His letters show that he was a literate man who apparently without difficulty could speak and argue in a way which corresponded to the rules which had long been regarded as authoritative in Greek and Roman rhetoric.[25]

Paul was a man of two worlds. He grew up in a city which was dominated by Hellenistic Greek culture. At the same time, from his youth up his Jewish identity played no less important a role in his life. In the Diaspora his parents observed the commandments of the Torah, and they will have made efforts also to bring up their son in this atmosphere. Paul's stay in Jerusalem will have stimulated him all the more to establish himself as a dedicated, enthusiastic adherent of Pharisaism. Even in the letters which he afterwards wrote as a follower of Jesus Christ, he did not keep quiet about his Jewish identity, far less did he see reasons for concealing his Pharisaic background. Paul was not ashamed of his past. Perhaps it can even be stated that he looked back with some pride on the period in which he appeared as a convinced Pharisee. In the recollections which he put down in writing, several times he used a term which makes one think and which is worth further discussion.

Paul preferred to describe himself as a 'zealot': 'I excelled many of my own age among my people *in my boundless zeal* for the traditions of my forefathers' (Gal. 1.14). This terminology also occurs in other letters: 'as to zeal a persecutor of the community' (Phil. 3.6). Here it is striking that Paul did not reserve his 'zeal' for the past. Just as once he had been a passionate zealot for the Old Testament Jewish tradition, so now he was zealous with the same passion for the Christian community: 'I am zealous for you with the zeal of God' (II Cor. 11.2). Paul also called himself a 'zealot before God' in the biographical passage in Acts which I have already quoted. He was proud of his 'zeal', but evidently he did not feel superior to his Jewish fellow-believers. Without reservations he praised their 'zeal' (Acts 22.3). The apostle sometimes expresses himself less modestly in his letters. By his own account he surpassed most of his contemporaries in his zeal (Gal. 1.14). He was a passionate man. He drew the motivation for his action from scripture.

Paul was not the first 'zealot' – nor the last! – in the history of the Jewish people. He had predecessors. They inspired him to his 'zeal'. In the centuries after Paul their example stimulated others to be 'zealous' for God and the Torah with no less dedication and sacrifice. God asks them to choose. He is 'a zealous God' (Deut. 5.9). The consequence is that it is sometimes necessary for short shift to be made of anyone who thinks he has to rebel against God and his commandments. At these moments in history 'zealots' appear. The series opens in the Old Testament with Phinehas, a priest, grandson of Aaron (Num. 25.11); after him in succession come the prophet Elijah (I Kings 19.10–14) and king Jehu (II Kings 10.16, 30–31).[26]

The story of the appearance of Phinehas in Num. 25 gives a good picture of the intention of the 'zealot'. On the verge of entering the promised land the people of Israel commits idolatry on a large scale. Given the covenant that God made with Israel, syncretism is one of the every worst sins. It is a form of unfaithfulness which can be compared with prostitution (Hos. 2.1–22). The narrative in Num. 25 begins like this: 'When Israel was staying in Shittim, the people began to engage in prostitution with Moabite women. The women invited the people to the sacrifices of their gods. The people took part and bowed down to their gods' (Num. 25.1–2). One thing leads to another. It goes from bad to worse. In the course of the centuries the story was repeated several times: foreign women bring foreign gods and goddesses with them. Thus even the wise king Solomon succumbed in his old age (I Kings 11.1–13). There was a terrible outbreak of idolatry in the time when king Ahab married a princess of pagan origin, Jezebel, the daughter of the king of the Sidonians (I Kings 16.29–34).

In such a situation the wrath of God flares up and the consequences are disastrous: there is talk of a 'plague' and the death of no less than twenty-four thousand people (Num. 25.9). How can God's anger be stilled? That is evidently possible only if one or more pious men become 'zealous'. In Num. 25 that is the role of Phinehas. The way in which he is introduced is characteristic (Num. 25.7). Phinehas, the zealot *par excellence,* is a grandson of Aaron, the priest *par excellence.*

Thanks to the zeal of Phinehas, 'the plague' ended and death and destruction lost their grip on the people of Israel. In public Phinehas, driven by his zeal for God, openly killed with his own hands an Israelite and a Midianite woman who had been practising fornication. After this God spoke the following words to Moses: 'Phinehas, the son of Eleazar, son of Aaron the priest, has turned back my wrath from the people of Israel, in that he was zealous with my zeal among them, so that I did not consume the people of Israel in my zeal. Therefore say, "Behold, I give to him my covenant of peace, and it shall be to him, and to his descendants after him, the covenant of a perpetual priesthood, because he was zealous for his God and made atonement for the Israelites"' (Num. 25.11–13).

The powerful intervention of Phinehas, his zeal for God, result in God's anger being turned away and thus the plague comes to an end; a new covenant is made, and the destroyed relationship between God is restored. It can be concluded that the zeal of Phinehas has brought about 'reconciliation'. However, that is not the end of the story in the book of Numbers. Clearly a new orgy of violence is unavoidable. At God's command, the people of Israel takes vengeance on the Midianites: 'And Moses sent them to the war, a thousand from each tribe, together with Phinehas the son of Eleazar the priest, with the vessels of the sanctuary and the trumpets of the alarm in his hand. They warred against the Midianites, as the Lord had commanded Moses, and killed all the males' (Num. 31.6–7).

The same motifs return in the stories about the two other zealots in the Old Testament: the prophet Elijah and king Jehu. Again we hear of idolatry, and the honour and holiness of God are at stake. Again the zealot can decide the dispute in his favour and much blood flows: 'And Elijah gave the command: Seize the prophets of Baal, let not one of them escape. And they seized them, and Elijah brought them down to the brook

Kishon, and killed them there' (I Kings 18.40). We know from an earlier account that there were four hundred and fifty priests (I Kings 18.22). Thus Elijah was zealous (I Kings 19.10,14), and so too was Jehu when he killed Jezebel, exterminated the whole house of Ahab and knew no mercy for all those who continued to persist in the service of the god Baal (II Kings 10.16).

It says much that the name of Phinehas is to be found in the list of the ancestors of Ezra, 'a scribe skilled in the law of Moses' (Ezra 7.1–6), who was leader of the Jewish people at the end of the Babylonian exile. One of the abuses that he tried to combat was syncretism, which was still prevalent. Soon after his arrival he was told: 'The people of Israel, the priests and the Levites, have not separated themselves from the peoples of their lands with their abominations, from the Canaanites, the Hittites, the Perizzites, the Jebusites, the Ammonites, the Moabites, the Egyptians and the Amorites. For they have taken some of their daughters to be wives for themselves and their sons; so that the holy race has mixed itself with the peoples of the lands. And in this faithlessness the hand of the officials and chief men has been foremost' (Ezra 9.1–2). Afterwards, on his advice a decision was taken which sounds harsh in our ears today, but which was in line with expectations on the basis of what has been said above: 'And Ezra the priest stood up and said to them (= the people): You have trespassed and married foreign women, and so increased the guilt of Israel. Now then make your confession to the Lord the God of your fathers and do his will; separate yourselves from the peoples of the land and from the foreign wives' (Ezra 10.10–11).

From the conclusion of the book of the Bible which bears the name of Nehemiah – he was like-minded with Ezra and was also a leader of the returned exiles – it can be seen that this line of thought was continued. The commandments of the Torah determined human life from the cradle to the grave.[27] Nehemiah put great emphasis among other things on hallowing the sabbath, and he too stipulated that marriages with non-Jews needed to be ended (Neh. 13). The ideal is summed up briefly at the end of the book: 'I cleansed them of all that is alien to us' (Neh. 13.30).

Some centuries later, at the time of the Maccabaean revolt,[28] the old traditions inspired the pious – the Hasidim – successfully to oppose the persecution of the faith. That is evident from the deutero-canonical writing called I Maccabees, which in all probability was written some decades after the revolt. This book contains the address which Mattathias is said to have delivered to his sons when his hour of death was approaching (I Macc. 2.49–70). Here are some passages from the speech which are important for this theme: 'Now, my children, show zeal for the law, and give your lives for the covenant of our fathers' (vv. 50–51). Then the names of Abraham and Joseph are mentioned, and afterwards also that of Phinehas, the zealot of the book of Numbers: 'Phinehas, our father, because he was deeply zealous, received the covenant of everlasting priesthood' (54); then Joshua, Caleb and David follow: 'Elijah because of great zeal for the law was taken up into heaven' (v. 58). These 'heroes' from the past, zealots for God and the Torah, are presented by Mattathias to his sons as examples, so that despite the superiority of the Syrians they do not fear the battle: 'Do not fear the words of a sinner, for his splendour will turn into dung and worms. Today he will be exalted, but tomorrow he will not be found, because he has returned to the dust, and his plans will perish. My children, be courageous and grow strong in the law, for by it you will gain honour' (I Macc. 2.62–64).

The zeal of Phinehas is also mentioned with honour in the book of the wisdom teacher Jesus Sirach: 'Phinehas the son of Eleazar is the third (i.e. after Moses and Aaron) in glory, for he was zealous in the fear of the Lord, and stood fast, when the people turned away, in the ready goodness of his soul, and made atonement for Israel. Therefore a covenant of peace was established with him, that he should be leader of the sanctuary and of his people, that he and his descendants should have the dignity of the priesthood for ever' (Sir. 45.23–24).

In the first century of our era, the time when Jesus and Paul lived, the age-old 'zeal for God and the temple' took on a strong political as well as religious colouring with the Zealots.[29] The forced departure of Archelaus as tetrarch of Judaea in AD 6 and the change in the form of government introduced by the Romans made a census necessary. There was much opposition to this census not only in Judaea but also in Galilee. A man with charismatic gifts and leadership qualities known as Judas the Galilean (cf. Acts 5.37) succeeded in concentrating the opposition. This was the beginning of the Zealot movement. Despite the failure of the revolt, they did not disappear, but above all in Galilee continued forms of opposition which constantly caused unrest. Because of the difficult economic position, many tenant farmers in the north had been driven from their land, so the Zealots had no problems over recruitment. In the 40s and 50s their influence steadily increased. In 66 there was finally a widespread revolt against Roman domination. Initially this revolt seemed successful – and thus aroused memories of the course of the Maccabean revolt – but finally it ended in a tragic catastrophe. This time the 'zeal' was not rewarded by God.

In the tradition of those of like mind from the past the Zealots strove for a clean and holy land which would no longer be polluted by pagan authorities and their troops. They lived in expectation of the speedy coming of the kingdom of God, but thought that here they could not remain passive. Their activity would be an important condition. If the kingdom of God was to come, they must prepare the way for it by cleansing the land and driving out the godless enemy. Then what prophets had proclaimed long ago would become a reality: 'the Lord will be king over the whole earth; on that day the Lord shall be the only Lord and his name the only name' (Zech. 14.9).

For the Zealots, as for the Maccabees, the zeal of Phinehas was the great example. His independent intervention gave them the theological legitimation and justification for their violent opposition. The action of Phinehas brought about reconciliation between God and the people. The Zealots were convinced that they had been called to the same action. The godless called the tune in the land of the Jews; numerous Jews were collaborating with the enemy; alien gods were being worshipped and mixed marriages entered into. God's wrath would again flare up. Therefore the action of Phinehas had to be repeated. Then as priest he led the Israelites in their 'holy war' against the Midianities – a battle of revenge and therefore a battle that knew no compromises.

Jesus preached the speedy coming of the kingdom of God. However, he was no zealot in the spirit of the Zealot movement. That does not mean that his words and actions did not exercise a certain power of attraction on (former?) adherents of Zealotism. The circle of his followers included Simon the Zealot (Mark 3.18). Other disciples had suggestive nicknames: John and James, the sons of Zebedee, were called Boanerges, 'sons of thunder' (Mark 3.17). Peter is given the name Bar Jonah (Matt. 16.17); according to some exegetes the name is connected with an old word which means something like 'terrorist'; finally, the name Iscariot was attached to Judas (Mark 3.19) – possibly a reference to an extreme trend among the Zealots, the Sicarii.

Did Jesus' behaviour perhaps prompt Zealot-like dreams? He called Herod a 'fox' (Luke 13.32) and also on other occasions spoke out fiercely against the authorities and those in power (Mark 10.42–45; Luke 22.25–27). His entry into Jerusalem and his aggressive and challenging appearance in the temple could have aroused expectations among the Zealots. Pilate's view in this connection is also eloquent: he condemned Jesus as a ridiculous and failed pretender to the throne and had a board fixed to the cross with the shameful title 'king of the Jews' (Mark 15.18,26).

And Paul? He proudly called himself a 'zealot', but in all probability he never belonged to the Zealot movement. According to the author of Acts, Gamaliel was his teacher (Acts 22.3). In an earlier episode in the same book of the Bible Gamaliel appeared as a moderate man (Acts 5.34–39). He was a grandson of Hillel, a Pharisaic scribe who had a school and was regarded as 'liberal' over the exposition of the commandments of the Torah.[30] Did Paul therefore belong to 'the school of Hillel'? It seems to me that this question cannot immediately be answered in the affirmative.[31] Paul was certainly not moderate; rather he was a fanatic, consciously a zealot in the spirit of the Old Testament-Jewish tradition. His zeal was directed wholly in particular against the adherents of a new movement within the Judaism of those days: men and women who called themselves followers of Jesus of Nazareth. Gamaliel made a plea to maintain an attitude of waiting. Paul did not accept this advice and opted for confrontation. Now a second answer can be given to the question raised earlier why the apostle never mentions the name of Gamaliel anywhere in his letters: in the course of time perhaps Paul ceased to regard Gamaliel as his teacher. In the long run his moderate standpoint did not attract Paul.

'A *thorn in the flesh*'

The picture that the New Testament sketches of Paul is complex. He radiates power, appears self-confident, has boundless energy and can cover great distances. It seems legitimate to conclude that in body and spirit he must have been an extraordinarily healthy man. However, a fascinating passage in the letter to the Galatians shows another side of Paul: 'You know it was because of a bodily ailment that I preached the gospel to you first; and though my condition was a trial to you, you did not scorn or despise me, but received me as an angel of God, as Christ Jesus. What has become of the satisfaction your felt? For I bear witness that, if possible, you would have plucked out your eyes and given them to me' (Gal. 4.13–15). Paul arrived a sick man. What ailment did he suffer from? On the basis of the last sentence of this quotation people have supposed that he could have suffered from a serious eye disease. Intrinsically that was not impossible. Blindness and other eye ailments were by no means unknown in the classical world. However, Paul's words can also be interpreted in a figurative sense. In that case he means that the Galatians were even ready to give him the most important thing that they had – the light in their eyes.

In II Corinthians the apostle gives a report which is worth

quoting in this connection: 'Though if I wish to boast, I shall not be a fool, for I shall be speaking the truth. But I refrain from it, so that no one may think more of me than he sees in me or hears from me. And to keep me from being too elated by the abundance of revelations, a thorn was given me in the flesh, a messenger of Satan, to harass me. Three times I besought the Lord about this, that it should leave me; but he said to me, "My grace is sufficient for you, for my power is made perfect in weakness"' (II Cor. 12.6–9). The history of the exegesis of this passage has shown that it is impossible to make a reliable diagnosis of Paul's ailment. Often a form of epilepsy is thought of, but that too is not certain. Moreover we cannot rule out the possibility that in this part the apostle was not writing primarily about bodily ailments, but was drawing attention to the spiritual pressure under which he threatened to give way at certain moments in his life.[32] Sometimes life pressed heavily on him and he knew from his own experience what it was to have to suffer. In these circumstances it was a support if he could associate his own difficulties and cares with the suffering of Christ: 'always carrying in the body the death of Jesus, so that the life of Jesus may also be manifested in our bodies. For while we live we are always being given up to death for Jesus' sake, so that the life of Jesus may be manifested in our mortal flesh. So death is at work in us' (II Cor. 4.10–12). Paul was no intrepid hero. While he went his way boldly, he knew his shortcomings. He knew from his own experience that human beings are vulnerable in body and spirit. This knowledge did not make him timid or inactive. He had the capacity to draw strength in particular from his weaknesses, in order to perform the task that God had laid on him according to his sure conviction at his calling.[33]

Curriculum vitae[34]

Around 15	born in Tarsus
30	crucifixion of Jesus
32	stoning of Stephen
34	Paul's vision near Damascus
34–37	Paul in Arabia and Damascus
37	first visit to the apostles in Jerusalem
37–42	Paul in Tarsus
42–44	Paul in Antioch
45–48	first missionary journey with Barnabas
48/49	meeting of the apostles in Jerusalem
49–52	second missionary journey – eighteen months' stay in Corinth
	first letter to the Thessalonians
52–54	third missionary journey: two and a half years in Ephesus
	correspondence with the communities in Corinth and Philippi
	letter to Philemon
winter 54/55	continuation of third missionary journey – Macedonia
	conclusion of the correspondence with Corinth and Philippi
	three months in Corinth
	letter to the Galatians
	letter to the Romans
55–56	journey to Jerusalem
56–58	imprisonment in Caesarea
winter 58/59	journey to Rome
59–61	imprisonment in Rome
?	died – presumably as a martyr in Rome.

3

From persecutor to preacher

A 'conversion'

Paul is a model for all those who have experienced a radical change in their lives. Suddenly, like a thunderbolt from a clear sky, they became another person. That is also said to have happened to Paul. By his own account he started as an impassioned persecutor of the early Christian community (Gal. 1.13). The author of Acts emphasizes that Paul carried out the task that was assigned to him with all his might. After reporting that Saul/Paul showed endorsed the condemnation of Stephen (Acts 8.1), he tells of persecutions which resulted in the Jerusalem community being dispersed over the regions of Judaea and Samaria: 'Saul wanted to destroy the church; he entered house after house, dragged off men and women and committed them to prison' (Acts 8.3).

In his 'zeal', Paul knew no rest. He wanted more action and sought to enlarge his territory: 'But Saul, still breathing threats and murder against the disciples of the Lord, went to the high priest and asked him for letters to the synagogues at Damascus, so that if he found any belonging to the Way,[1] men or women, he might bring them bound to Jerusalem' (Acts 9.1–2). On the way, on the approach to Damascus, the event took place which radically changed the career of Saul/Paul. The one who was feared everywhere as a fanatical persecutor of the early Christian community soon proved to be no less a passionate proclaimer of the Christian faith.

The section in Acts in which the story is told is often referred to as *the conversion of Paul*. This interpretation is centuries old:

Saul becomes Paul; the Jewish zealot for the Torah is converted and becomes a follower of Jesus Christ. However, the world 'convert' does not occur in Acts 9. And that also applies to both passages in the same book of the Bible in which Paul looks back on what happened to him near Damascus.

Nor does the apostle use the term 'conversion' in his letters. After he has explicitly gone into his past as a persecutor of the Christian community in the first part of the letter to the Galatians, he describes the radical change which happened to him as follows: 'For I did not receive it (= the gospel) from man, nor was I taught it, but it came through a revelation of Jesus Christ' (Gal. 1.12). Some verses later he says the same thing in other words: 'But when God, who had set me apart before I was born, and had called me through his grace, was pleased *to reveal his Son in me* in order that I might preach him among the Gentiles . . .' (Gal. 1.15–16).

The vocabulary of both Paul and the author of Acts is surprising. Why do they not speak of 'conversion'? How is what happened on the way to Damascus to be interpreted, then? Paul himself made use of a terminology which obscures matters rather than clarifying them. For precisely what is a 'revelation'?

The early Christian community

Judaism at the beginning of our era was a variegated community. The New Testament gives us some insight into the divergent groups and parties that there were at this time: Pharisees, Sadducees and Zealots. Extra-biblical sources confirm this image, but also add nuances to it. Thus it proves, among other things, that the movement of the Pharisees did not form a close unity, but consisted of several schools, which differed from one another on essential points. Moreover the above-mentioned extra-biblical sources speak of groups and parties which are not mentioned in the New Testament.[2] That applies in particular to the Essenes. The discovery of the Qumran writings has in all probability brought us into direct contact with the thought of this remarkable – sectarian! – group of pious Jews.

The Jews lived in occupied territory. The Romans exercised power. However, they could not do so without Jewish agents. So it was attractive to collaborate with the enemy. The toll collectors did this and were hated because they were able to enrich themselves through the unjust Roman system of taxation. There was also opposition to Roman domination, sometimes even armed opposition, above all from the Zealots. They saw it as their task to cleanse the Jewish land of pagans in preparation for the coming of the kingdom of God. Many who hoped for change lived between these extremes, but did not dare to take the law into their own hands. They looked longingly to the definitive intervention of God. These pious included the Pharisees and the Essenes – the essential difference between them being that the second group had withdrawn into the wilderness, while the Pharisees wanted to take their place in the midst of society.

The variegated nature of Judaism in the first century is reflected in the composition of the circle of disciples around Jesus. Some were fishermen, but even within this professional group there was rank and status: the brothers Peter and Andrew cast the net while they were standing in the water and clearly had no ship; John and James worked in a ship, presumably owned by their father Zebedee, who moreover employed day labourers (Mark 1.16–20). Jesus' disciples even included men who because of their background should have hated and abhorred one another with all their hearts: Simon the Zealot (Mark 3.13–19) and Levi the publican (Mark 2.13–14).

Although Jesus appeared as a teacher,[3] he did not formulate any 'teaching' or doctrine. He called on his contemporaries to *repent*, because the kingdom of God would come soon (Mark 1.14–15). However, he did not leave things at that, for he saw it as his task to go in search of all those who risked being lost (Luke 15.1–32). Jesus told stories. The Synoptic Gospels have preserved the memory that he tried to unveil the mysteries of the kingdom of God to his disciples with the help of 'parables' (Mark 4.1–34; Matt. 13.1–52). Precisely when would the kingdom come? According to the evangelists Jesus said that it was so near that it was already 'at the door' (Mark 13.29). Unfortunately things were not much clearer than that.

After this memorable Easter morning a totally new phase in their existence dawned for the circle of disciples. They had no 'doctrine', but they did have their memories. They told one another stories about Jesus and lived in the firm conviction that he would return soon (Mark 13.24–27). The followers of Jesus initially formed a messianic sect within the Judaism of those days. They differed from other messianic sects because they not only directed their attention to the near future, but could also look back. The Messiah whom they expected was none other than the Jesus whom they had known, who had died on the cross and who would be raised by God 'on the third day' (I Cor. 15.4).

The descriptions of the quarrels in the first community in Jerusalem in the book of Acts make it clear that the community lived within the limits of Judaism and was perhaps particularly inspired by ideals of the Essenes: 'All who believed were together and had all things in common; and they sold their possessions and goods and distributed them to all, as any had need. And day by day, attending the temple together and breaking bread in their homes, they partook of food with glad and generous hearts, praising God and having favour with all the people' (Acts 2.44–46).[4]

It seems legitimate to ask whether this almost idyllic situation is not too good to be true. The book of Acts also contains narratives about apostles who were executed in prison and had to defend themselves before the Sanhedrin (Acts 4.1–31; 5.17–42; 12.1–19). So there was not just the sympathy of many among the people but also the mistrust of others. In all this we shall have to take account of all the differences within the Judaism of those days which were indicated earlier. What one person admired, another abhorred. There was no unanimity about the attitude to be adopted towards this new messianic movement even in the Sanhedrin, the highest legal body on religious matters. As an illustration I can refer to the advice of Paul's teacher Gamaliel mentioned earlier: 'Keep away from these men and let them alone; for if this plan or this undertaking is of men, it will fail; but if it is of God, you will not be able to overthrow them. You might even be found to be opposing God' (Acts 5.38–39).

The way in which action was taken against Stephen some time later stands in sharp contrast to Gamaliel's sound judgment. The author of the books of Acts describes how he was killed by stoning (Acts 7.54–60). Stephen is the first martyr of the Christian church.[5] His death was an event which seemed to put a definitive end to the more or less peaceful co-existence of church and synagogue which had prevailed hitherto. Was the church at that moment already put out of the synagogue for good? This is a question which arises all the more urgently because in Acts there is then mention of persecutions of the Christian community. Saul/Paul is said to have played a central role in these actions (Acts 8.1–3).

Here again we come upon questions which cannot easily be given a satisfactory answer. In Acts 8.1 we read: 'And on that day a great persecution arose against the church in Jerusalem, and they were all scattered throughout the region of Judaea and Samaria, *except the apostles*.' The clause printed in italics calls for our special attention in this connection. Why is an exception made for 'the apostles'? The New Testament contains more indications from which it can be inferred that in the first decades of church history there was permanently a Christian community in Jerusalem which was led by apostles. At the end of the 40s an important meeting of apostles took place in Jerusalem (Acts 15). Paul travelled to Jerusalem several times to meet apostolic colleagues there (Gal. 1.18; 2.1).

It is conceivable that the persecution did not affect the whole of the Christian community in Jerusalem, but only one particular group. The author of Acts does not disguise the fact that relations within the 'ideal' original community quickly became disturbed. Old oppositions which had already divided the Jewish people earlier also meant that there were difficulties and tensions in the Christian community: 'In those days, when the disciples were increasing in number, the Hellenists (= Greek-speaking Jewish Christians) murmured against the Hebrews (= Aramaic-speaking Christians) because their widows were neglected in the daily distribution' (Acts 6.1).

Seven men were given the task of putting things in order and preventing the formation of groups. Stephen was one of these seven. According to the book of Acts there was vigorous opposition to him in certain Jewish circles, with the result that he was brought before the Sanhedrin. The accusation against him ran: 'This man never ceases to speak words against this holy place and the law; for we have heard him say that this Jesus of Nazareth will destroy this place, and will change the customs which Moses delivered to us' (Acts 6.13–14).

Stephen was presumably opposed to a particular interpretation of the Torah of Moses – which, it is difficult to say – and in so doing at least in the view of some put himself outside the limits of Judaism. Is his attitude typical of the whole Christian community in Jerusalem at that time? It can be inferred from a number of the New Testament writings that this was one of the most difficult problems with which the early Christian community rapidly found itself confronted. What significance does the Torah of Moses have for this messianic movement – and especially for those Christians who were not Jewish by origin? The marked increase in the number of Christians from the Gentiles – also thanks to the successful missionary journeys of the later apostle Paul – made this question particularly pressing in the early Christian churches.

In his letter to the community of the Galatians Paul gives us some insight into how views were divided, and the book of Acts also brings clarification. At any rate it is clear that there was an influential group in the Jerusalem community led by James, 'the brother of the Lord' (Gal. 1.19), which argued that the whole Torah should continue to be valid without diminution even for Christians who came from paganism. In the year 62 the execution of James led to fierce protests from the Pharisees. He was executed on the orders of the then high priest, who not only belonged to the movement of the Sadducees but came from the same family as his predecessors in office, Annas and Caiaphas,

who played an important role at the time of the execution of
Jesus. Despite the fact that James had already been leader of the
early Christian community in Jerusalem for some time, the
Pharisees were said to have called him 'a righteous man'. The
Jewish historian Flavius Josephus tells us this, and we have no
reason to doubt the historical value of his account. That would
mean that at the beginning of the 60s James had yet to become
an outsider or a heretic for Jews inclining towards Pharisaism
who put great emphasis on observing the commandments of the
Torah.[6]

What has been said above leads to the following conclusion:
in all probability the persecution spoken of in the book of Acts
in which the young Paul is said to have played a leading role
was limited in scope. In other words, this persecution only
affected the group within the Christian community which
under the leadership of Stephen opposed an interpretation of
the Torah of Moses accepted as authoritative above all in wide
circles of the Pharisees. For this reason Paul was 'zealous'
against that specific group within early Christianity. Evidently
James and the original apostles were left in peace. They could
continue their stay in Jerusalem without difficulty.

'I persecuted the community of God beyond measure'

Nowhere in the New Testament are attempts made either by
the apostle himself in his letters or by the author of the book
of Acts to keep quiet about Paul's activities as a persecutor of
the early Christian community or at least to some degree to
trivialize them. Rather, the opposite seems to be the case. In a
passage from his letter to the Galatians which has already been
mentioned several times Paul openly writes: 'You have heard of
my former life in Judaism, how I persecuted the church of God
violently and tried to destroy it' (Gal. 1.13). In all honesty it
needs to be recognized that Paul had little to hide. The story of
his past was widely known, as is witnessed by the following
passage from the same letter: 'Then I went into the regions of
Syria and Cilicia. And I was still not known by sight to the

churches of Christ in Judaea; they only heard it said, "He who once persecuted us is now preaching the faith he once tried to destroy"' (Gal. 1.21–23). The book of Acts is no less restrained in describing what in Christian eyes were the dubious ways that the apostle had taken. As an illustration I can repeat an earlier quotation: 'Saul wanted to destroy the community: he entered house after house, dragged off men and women and committed them to prison' (Acts 8.3).

After what has been said above about the complicated relationship between the variegated early Christian community and the no less variegated Judaism of the first century of our era, one is inclined to ask whether this persecution by Paul can really have been so 'devastating'. What, for example, are we to imagine by the following sentence: 'Saul was still breathing threats and murder against the disciples of the Lord' (Acts 9.1)? If we take the words literally, then they imply that Paul had the death of one or even more adherents of early Christianity on his conscience. In the previous chapter we saw that it may be said to be typical of all those who are 'zealous for the Lord' that they do not shrink from the consequences of their convictions. Words and actions are very closely connected, and these actions can result in the death of enemies.

Could Paul have killed people – members of the early Christian community – in his 'zeal' as Phinehas and Elijah once did? Not without pride, he reminded his readers of his 'boundless zeal for the traditions of my fathers' (Gal. 1.14). Here the exegete with a historical interest comes up against questions which are difficult to answer. The writings of the New Testament contain insufficient facts to give us a clear picture of the 'persecution' of the early Christian community. The information is so summary that we cannot say anything with certainty about the duration and extent of Paul's dispute with the early Christian community.

At the time of the stoning of Stephen, according to the author of Acts Paul was still 'a young man' (Acts 7.58). The first persecutions of the Christian community must already have begun shortly after that. Does it seem likely that a young man, who moreover had come from the Diaspora, would have played a leading role in the action against the early Christian community? It seems to me that the answer to this question must be no; that leads to the conclusion that the later apostle had a less dominant role in the event.[7] Once we have drawn this obvious conclusion, a new question arises: why did both Paul himself and the author of Acts have the need to attach more importance to the influence of the later apostle? This question is all the more pressing, because we already noted earlier that the 'persecution' affected only part of the early-Christian community.

One satisfactory solution to the problem is that for different reasons Paul and the author of Acts thought it necessary to put the past in another perspective. It may be regarded as certain that some members of the early Christian community caused difficulties because of their view of the significance to the Torah. On the basis of the narrative in Acts about tensions within the Christian community and the appearance of Stephen and his followers, it seems probable that it affected the Jewish Christians, who were so influenced by Hellenism that they were known to be Greek speakers (Acts 6.1–15). At that moment there was still no question of a schism between Judaism and Christianity, with the result that the tensions within the early Christian community of Jerusalem could not possibly remain internal. Influential leaders of one of the radical orthodox wings within the Pharisaic movement thought it necessarily to deal harshly with Stephen's circle. Thus a legal case was undertaken against him, which led to his execution and the persecution of those of a like mind. In both the execution and the persecution, a young man who still bore the name of Saul showed himself to be a dedicated 'zealot' (Acts 7.58; 8.1).

Around fifteen years later, Paul was writing his letter to the Galatians, in which he gave a short survey of his past. Here it is striking that he did not anxiously keep quiet about his appearance as a persecutor of the early Christian community but was open and honest and even made his role more important than it had really been. What drove the apostle to write like this?

In the autobiographical passage in the letter to the Galatians Paul was particularly concerned to emphasize two aspects of his life. In the first place his whole career must be judged from the perspective that he constantly takes decisions independently of others. From his birth his career had been determined by nothing and no one other than God: 'but when God, who had chosen me when I was still in my mother's womb, and who had called me through his grace, resolved to reveal his son in me . . .' (Gal. 1.15–16). Paul also wanted to leave no doubt that he knew what he was talking about when later in the letter the Torah was discussed: '. . . and I advanced in Judaism beyond many of my own age among my people, so zealous was I . . .' (Gal. 1.14). Perhaps his opponents had expressed their suspicions about him in the community and suggested that as a Jew from the Diaspora he was not sufficiently interested in the commandments of the Torah. The apostle countered these assertions with both passion and indignation. That in the fire of his argument he may have made some blunt remarks and given more weight to his own role in the persecution is understandable, and can be forgiven him.

Some decades later the author of Acts put Paul's role in the persecution even more strongly in the foreground. He too had a reason to approve of it – in the context of the time. A good deal had happened in the meantime. The gulf between Judaism and Christianity had become so broad and deep that one could already speak of a real schism. Like the Gospel of Luke, the book of Acts is dedicated to a certain Theophilus (Luke 1.1–4; Acts 1.1). He is spoken of with respect:: 'most excellent'. Theophilus must have been an important man in the Roman empire, a non-Jew interested in religious questions. Perhaps he had come into contact with the Christian preaching through the local synagogue. In theory he could have met no less a person than Paul there. According to the book of Acts, when the apostle had arrived in a city during his missionary journeys, he usually went to the local synagogue (Acts 17.1–4; 18.4, 19; 19.8). That was his base, and from it he developed his activities as a preacher of the gospel of Jesus Christ. Of course in a large number of cities that led to difficulties, and Paul was accused by the Jewish leaders and even dragged before the court (Acts 17–18). The dedicated reader of the book of Acts here comes upon a fascinating motif in the story: one day the persecutor became preacher, and as a preacher he too was persecuted. One can imagine that the author of Acts did not want to trivialize this motif, but tried to give it more emphasis.

An apocalyptist

Paul belonged to the Pharisaic current. He was a pious man and zealous for God and the Torah. In the autobiographical passages in his letters he writes little or nothing about his future expectation in the first phase of his life. From the fact that he is silent about this we may conjecture that on this point he did not differ fundamentally from his fellow-believers. Noting this, however, does not get us very much further, for the question of the future expectation of the Pharisees is not easy to answer. We already noted that the Pharisaic movement was divided into different tendencies or schools.

The spiritual ancestors of the Pharisees of the time of Jesus and Paul include the Hasidim (= pious), who under the leadership of the Maccabees fought tooth and nail against the persecution of the faith by the Syrian king Antiochus IV Epiphanes in the years 167 to 164 BC. In their perilous situation, inspired by their faith in God's faithfulness, they created a vision of the future of human beings and the world which contained surprising new facets by comparison with the prophetic expectation.[8] It is customary in scholarly literature to speak about 'apocalyptic' in this context. The last word has yet to be spoken about the origin of this thought. According to some scholars the roots of the 'apocalyptic' view of human beings and the world go back into the history not only of Israel but also of the surrounding peoples.[9] In fact it is said to be a universal phenomenon. Others emphasize the special character of this thought and call it more typically Old Testament and Jewish. Be this as it may, in some prophetic writings in the Old

Testament which were written after the Babylonian exile – was that chance? or is it an indication that an exchange of religious ideas and notions did take place – we already find thoughts which could be defined as 'apocalyptic'.[10] In general the book that bears the name of the prophet Zechariah can be mentioned as an example in which prophecy increasingly begins to take on apocalyptic features.[11] The book of Daniel in its last redaction, composed when the Maccabean revolt was still raging vigorously and the outcome was uncertain, can be seen as the earliest writing known to us which is unmistakably stamped by an apocalyptic view of present and future.[12]

Prophets and apocalyptists – at first sight their thought-patterns show some affinity, but in substance they differ fundamentally from one another on a number of essential points. Prophets were more interested in the present than in the future. They were fiercely critical of kings and other authorities who were not interested in the well-being of the powerless and those with little opportunities in society. Their ideals were directed towards the victory of right and justice. So they looked hopefully to the future: there will be *shalom* on earth; one day a shoot from the family of David will sit on the throne in Jerusalem who will tread in the footsteps of his illustrious father and follow the will of God with heart and soul (Isa. 11.1–10). Apocalyptists would presumably have liked to have had such a 'simple' faith, but they could no longer do so. Time had not stood still, and too much had happened: the terrors of the Babylonian exile; the surprising, glorious return which was not, however, followed by a period of peace; the little Jewish temple state had once more become a powerless toy in the midst of the great powers which surrounded it.

Where was God – the redeemer (Isa. 44.24)? Had he withdrawn from the world? Apocalyptists realized that the world had changed and that traditional perspectives were threatening to lose their evocative power. Experience had taught them that the powers of evil had a force which could not be under-estimated. They no longer believed in the ongoing existence of this world. Prophets had still set their hope on change, on conversion. The apocalyptists thought that they knew better and drew a far-reaching conclusion: this world had to perish. They looked expectantly for this cosmic catastrophe (Mark 13.24–27). The terrors would be great and fearful. Indeed they had already begun. The 'signs of the times' spoke a clear language. Wars, natural disasters, persecutions and oppressions – the apocalyptists interpreted these events as the 'messianic woes' which had to precede the birth of the new world – the new Jerusalem (Rev. 21–22).

Apocalyptists waited – impatiently, but also full of confidence – for the definitive intervention of God. He would not forsake his 'elect' (Mark 13.20). The perspective of prophets and apocalytists was not the same. Their view of life differed considerably. Prophets were interested in the present and called on their contemporaries to walk in the ways of the Lord. Apocalyptists looked expectantly to the future and to heaven. Prophets called for activity and strove to change people on *this* earth, whereas apocalyptists interpreted the terrors of the present as a necessary 'evil'. The pious, the elect, stood powerless. There was nothing for them to do but to wait for God's intervention. But it is also the case that the boundary between prophecy and apocalyptic cannot be drawn too precisely. Discussions in the Jewish tradition teach us that terms like 'active' (= prophecy) and 'passive' (= apocalyptic) are inadequate.[13] The Hasidim in the time of the persecution of the faith by the Syrian ruler Antiochus Epiphanes were influenced by apocalyptic thought, but that did not prevent them from engaging in armed assistance under the leadership of the Maccabees.

History teaches us that the ideas which people have of the future are strongly dependent on the times and circumstances in which they live. In the period round about the beginning of our era, in all probability apocalyptic thought played an important role within the early Jewish tradition. From the writings from this period which have been preserved it can also be inferred that it is impossible to speak of a firmly defined 'apocalyptic dogma'.[14] Independently of the situation, people could also be inspired by prophetic ideals. That is evident among other things from a writing known as the Psalms of Solomon.[15] The author is unknown. His work breathes a spirit which suggests that he belonged to the circle of the Pharisees. He wrote shortly after the downfall of the Jewish royal house of the Hasmonaeans. They were the descendants of the Maccabees, but had forgotten the ideals of their forefathers. In 63 BC the Roman general Pompey put an end to this government. In this comfortless situation an anonymous writer drew courage from age-old prophetic texts which said that the kingship of the house of David would last for ever (II Sam. 7.14): 'See, Lord, and raise up for them their king, the son of David, to rule over your servant Israel in the time known to you, O God. Undergird him with the strength to destroy the unrighteous rulers, to purge Jerusalem from Gentiles who trample her to destruction; in wisdom and in righteousness, to drive out the sinners from the inheritance; to smash the arrogance of sinners like a potter's jar; to shatter all their substance with an iron rod; to destroy the unlawful nations with the word of his mouth. At his warning the nations will flee from his presence; and he will condemn sinners by the thoughts of their hearts. He will gather a holy people, whom he will lead in righteousness; and he will judge the tribes of the people that have been made holy by the Lord their God. He will not tolerate unrighteousness even to pause among them, and any person who knows wickedness shall not live with them. For he shall know them, that they are all children of their God. He will distribute them upon the land according to their tribes; the alien and the foreigner will no longer live near them. He will judge peoples and nations in the wisdom of his righteousness' (Ps. Sol. 17.21–29).

Around a century earlier the apocalyptist who completed the book of Daniel did not look back to the past. He directed his gaze hopefully above, to heaven: 'I saw in the night visions and behold, with the clouds of heaven there came one like a son of man' (Dan. 7.13). He too will reign as a king, but his kingship has no dynastic basis. He will receive it from the hand of God: 'his dominion is an everlasting dominion which shall not pass away, and his kingdom one that shall not be destroyed' (Dan. 7.14). This remarkable vision of the future has left traces not only in the early Jewish tradition – in some passages in the apocalypse of Enoch – but also in the New Testament. Each of the four evangelists tells in his own way how Jesus was very restrained towards disciples and others who called him the Messiah from the house of David (Mark 8.27–30), while he himself preferred to identify himself with the enigmatic figure of the Son of Man (e.g. Mark 8.31; 13.26; 14.62).[16]

An earthly Messiah or a heavenly son of man – at first sight the two notions are mutually exclusive. That is the case, but it does not mean that they could not be combined in one way or another: a limited period in which the Messiah will rule as king on earth followed by the coming of the everlasting kingdom of God. Such a future expectation can be found in an early-Jewish writing known under the name IV Ezra, which was written shortly after the destruction of the temple of Jerusalem in 70. It can be said of the anonymous author that he too belonged to the Pharisaic movement.[17] The future is divided into two periods: 'He answered me and said: Listen to me, then I will teach you and again instruct you. Precisely for that reason the Most High has created not one time but two' (IV Ezra 7.49–50). Kindred thoughts can be found not only in the early Jewish tradition but also in the last book of the New Testament, which was given its definitive form around 96. 'And I saw thrones, and seated on them were those to whom judgment was committed. Also I saw the souls of those who had been beheaded for their testimony to Jesus and the word of God, and who had not worshipped the beast or its image and had not received its mark on their foreheads or their hands. They came to life, and reigned with Christ *a thousand years*. The rest of the dead did not come to life until the thousand years were ended. This is the first resurrection. Blessed and holy is he who shares in the first resurrection. Over such the second death has no power, but they shall be priests of God and of Christ, and they shall reign with him *a thousand years*' (Rev. 20.4–6).

The Christian apocalyptist who hoped to encourage his

fellow believers and comrades in oppression (Rev. 1.9) had a complicated picture of the future. The coming kingdom in which the Messiah will rule with his followers is of limited duration: a thousand years. IV Ezra speaks of four hundred years, while yet other figures are given in the later rabbinic literature: two thousand, seven thousand.[18] At the end of the messianic kingdom comes the apocalyptic downfall of all that exists; there will be a judgment on all the living and the dead, on all people and nations; the new heaven and the new earth will appear, and after that the eternal kingdom of God will dawn.

An apocalyptic vision[19]

To go back to Paul. He was a Pharisee. Was he influenced by apocalyptic ideas, like many of his like-minded colleagues? There is no consensus on this in exegetical literature.[20] The apostle himself knew no hesitations. He was not secretive in his description of the event which had made him think in a radically different way: 'For I did not receive it from man, nor was I taught it, but it came through a revelation of Jesus Christ' (Gal. 1.12). Some verses later he said that God has resolved 'to reveal his son in me' (Gal. 1.16).

In both texts Paul uses Greek terms which are usually translated as 'revelation' and 'reveal'. The last book of the Bible begins with the same word: 'The revelation of Jesus Christ, which God gave him to show his servants what must soon take place' (Rev. 1.1). Was Paul an apocalyptist in the spirit of the author of the last book of the Bible? The question requires a careful answer. Paul wrote letters and – as far as we know – not apocalypses. In this sense of the word he was no apocalyptist. However, there are passages in his letters which can be described as apocalyptic (e.g. Rom. 8.18–25; I Thess. 4.15–18). There was often a dispute about his apostolate within the early Christian community. Paul had to defend himself more than once. In the letter to the Galatians, written around ten years later, he did that confidently with a reference to the 'revelation' that he had received on the way to Damascus. At that moment it became clear that he had been chosen by God. The apocalyptic vision formed the firm basis of his apostolate. There is no doubt about it: Paul was an apocalyptist[21] before he received the vision on the way to Damascus, and after that he remained an apocalyptist. Obviously the vision changed his thinking at particular points, but it remained the foundation of his belief in Jesus Christ.

Paul was a many-sided man: a skilful biblical scholar, a passionate zealot and a creative apocalyptist. His zeal for the Torah stimulated him to persecute the early Christian community. Close study of the scripture and tradition did not make him think otherwise. An apocalyptic vision was the cause of a feared persecutor becoming a convinced disciple. The question still remains: is it correct to speak of Paul's *conversion* in this connection? In answering this question it is important to know precisely what we must understand by conversion. In the Synoptic Gospels a link is made between 'conversion' and the speedy coming of the kingdom of God (Mark 1.14–15). 'Conversion' literally means change, change on the way that one takes. The religious meaning picks this up: conversion is turning away from sin and turning to God; making an effort from then on to walk in God's ways. It is significant that Paul did not describe the event near Damascus in terms of 'conversion'. He did not regard himself as a sinner. He was a passionate zealot for the Torah, and not a man who refused to obey the commandments of God. The apocalyptic vision did not lead him to think that he needed to convert in the sense of the word described above. But his life did change, deeply and radically.[22]

What was revealed to Paul? Anyone who looks for an answer to the question of the nature and content of a 'revelation' in the texts of the New Testament will come to realize that this is a complex phenomenon. It is certain that a 'revelation' cannot be the result of a human activity. It was all-important for Paul to emphasize his independence of human beings (Gal. 1.12). The first words of the last book of the Bible emphasize this: 'revelation of Jesus Christ which God has given him' (Rev. 1.1). A 'revelation' is a gift of God. Paul would firmly have endorsed that (Gal. 1.16).

But that does not yet say what the *content* of this revelation was. The question can be answered relatively simply in the case of the last book of the Bible: the seer of Patmos 'was in the Spirit on the Lord's day' (Rev. 1.10) and was ordered to write letters to seven communities in Asia Minor (Rev. 2–3).Then followed a new 'exaltation of the spirit' in which he was told: 'Come up here, then I will show you what must happen next' (Rev. 4.1). During this second rapture he could not only look into heaven but it was also made possible for him to see the future. His 'vision' forms the content of the last book of the Bible from the fourth chapter to the end, the decisive intervention by God and the coming of a new heaven and a new earth (Rev. 21–22).

The last book of the Bible does not stand alone. Related ideas and notions can be found in apocalyptic writings of Jewish origin. There too there is often talk of exaltation in the spirit and the seers have visions which make it possible for them to acquire knowledge of the future. This world of ideas was also known to Paul. This is attested by a marvellous passage in one of his letters: 'I must boast: there is nothing to be gained by it, but I will go on to visions and revelations of the Lord. I know a man in Christ who fourteen years ago was caught up to the third heaven – whether in the body or out of the body I do not know, God knows. And I know that this man was caught up into Paradise – whether in the body or out of the body I do not know, God knows – and he heard things that cannot be told, which man may not utter. On behalf of this man I will boast, but on my own behalf I will not boast, except of my weaknesses' (II Cor. 12.1–5).

Of course this fascinating text raises new questions: who is this 'Christian' about whom Paul wants to boast? From the last verse it could be inferred that he is someone other than Paul. But it seems legitimate to approach these words of Paul with some suspicion. The whole closing part of the second letter to the community of Corinth is characterized by a way of speaking and arguing which runs between irony and sarcasm.[23] Paul is tormented by all those who think that they must doubt his integrity and his apostolate (II Cor. 10–12). Who is this man who fourteen years ago was taken to the third heaven and heard inexpressible words? It happened fourteen years ago (II Cor. 12.2). Paul gives the same figure in a passage in his letter to the Galatians: 'Then after fourteen years I went up again to Jerusalem with Barnabas, taking Titus along with me. I went up by revelation' (Gal. 2.1–2). Again the tone in this part of the letter is striking: the apostle claimed to be able to be independent of others. His life is guided by 'revelations'. That already happened fourteen years ago, and has happened again now. At those moments he is as it were taken above the ordinary human level. He is temporarily transformed into another Paul. Against this background and despite the fierce tone of the passage we can explain why the apostle suggested that another person was involved. Presumably the attentive readers in Corinth knew better. They knew Paul and were familiar with his emotional outbursts.

All this makes us all the more curious about the question of *what* Paul saw. From the fact that he deliberately speaks of an '*apocalypse*' I think that it can be inferred that he was granted a glimpse of heaven and that he could see the future. That is what happened to the apocalyptic visionaries, and it will also have happened to Paul. By comparison with the extensive visions in both Jewish and Christian apocalyptic literature his account is notably sober. For him in fact only one aspect was of essential importance. Everything that he saw in heaven was overshadowed in his memory by one figure, Jesus. Therefore in the letter to the Galatians Paul writes this wonderful sentence: 'God resolved to reveal his son in me' (Gal. 1.15–16). How important this was for him emerges from a text in his first letter to the community of Corinth. In defence of his controversial apostolate he put the following emotional questions: 'Am I not an apostle? Have I not *seen* Jesus our Lord' (I Cor. 9.1).

Paul's emotion is understandable if we realize that on the basis of the 'apocalyptic vision' he came to realize that Jesus was alive. The implications of this discovery must have been as bewildering to the apostle as they were enriching. As a passionate zealot for the traditions of his forefathers he had collaborated in the persecution of followers of Jesus who allowed freedoms in respect of the commands of the Torah which as a convicted adherent of Pharisaism he abhorred. He stood on his rights, but the 'apocalypse' made it necessary for him to revise his thoughts. It must have been offensive for him that the members of the early Christian community spoke of Jesus as the Messiah. As a Pharisee Paul did not find the expectation of the coming of the Messiah strange, but it was impossible for him to imagine that someone who had died on the cross could be the Messiah. In scripture and tradition there were no indications which pointed in such a direction. The only text that Paul could think of in this connection expressed a totally different standpoint: 'If a man has committed a crime punishable by death and he is put to death, and you hang him on a tree, his body shall not remain all night upon the tree, but you shall bury him the same day; for a hanged man is accursed by God; you shall not defile your land which the Lord your God gives you for an inheritance' (Deut. 21.22–23). Of course this passage did not refer explicitly to someone who was crucified, but that will have made little or no difference to Paul's feelings. Moreover also as a Roman citizen he must have found it difficult to think positively of someone who had been crucified. What salvation could be expected from a failed rebel or a runaway slave?

In his 'apocalypse' Paul was granted a glimpse of heaven, and there he saw Jesus 'sitting at the right hand of God' (Col. 3.1; cf. Eph. 1.20). For the apocalyptist who was later the apostle, that could only mean that the crucified man had been raised from the dead by God. The consequences which Paul drew from this discovery will occupy us at length in the following chapters. Here we need only note that the apostle can speak in different ways about his apocalyptic experience: in one of his letters he writes simply that he has seen Jesus (I Cor. 9.1), but in another letter he expresses himself in a much more complicated way and claims that God had resolved to reveal his son in him (Gal.

1.15). The vision that Paul saw was clearly of such a kind that it could be interpreted in different ways. In what follows I shall bring out the implications of these notions at greater length.

4

Between Damascus and Antioch

The 'unknown' years

The man who was actively involved in the persecution of particular groups within early Christianity became an inspired preacher of the Christian faith. The man who was passionately zealous for his ancestral traditions proved to be a passionate champion of the spread of the Christian faith in the non-Jewish world.

The apocalyptic experience which led Paul to the radical change in his thought about the crucified Jesus was central to the previous chapter. Subsequently we shall be discussing his letters in chronological order so as to trace the development of his theologizing. In this chapter we are as it were on the bridge which links his past – that of the passionate zealot – to his future – the passionate preacher of the Christian faith.

On the way to Damascus a light dawned on Paul. What did this 'enlightenment' mean for him personally? His life changed radically. Friends became enemies and those who had learned to fear him as their opponent saw themselves compelled to accept him into their circle as a colleague. It is regrettable that the Bible only gives us summary information about the period which preceded the time when Paul wrote the letters that have found a place in the New Testament. The apostle himself also seems to be silent about his experiences. He will not have led a quiet life. It was not in his nature to let things take their course. He had a great deal to do. The consequences of his apocalyptic experiences will have gradually become clearer to him, with the result that his thought gained momentum. He saw himself confronted with a complex problem: was it possible to be an enthusiastic follower of Jesus without doing violence to the Old Testament-Jewish tradition? Could he integrate the new insights which he had acquired into his views from the past?

Paul was a Jew and he remained a Jew all his life. He was never ashamed of his origins. In some autobiographical passages he even praises them (Gal. 1.11–13; II Cor. 11.21–22). That does not alter the fact that he can also write that a break has come about between his past and his present life: 'But whatever gain I had, I counted as loss for the sake of Christ. Indeed I count everything as loss because of the surpassing worth of knowing Jesus Christ my Lord. For his sake I have suffered the loss of all things, and count them as refuse, in order that I may gain Christ and be with him' (Phil. 3.7–8).

The task of the historian/biographer is difficult because of a lack of information. The New Testament provides little information about the first years of Paul's apostolate.[1] In the scanty autobiographical passages in his letters Paul gave a different reading of the course of events after his Damascus vision from that of the author of Acts. Which of the two is closest to reality is impossible to say for sure. In Acts much importance is attached to the *unity* of the early Christian community. In that perspective it is understandable that Paul travelled from Damascus directly to Jerusalem (Acts 9.23–29). His stay there was of short duration. His appearance aroused the displeasure of Jews who had not been followers of Christ. Thereupon he left Jerusalem and went to Tarsus, the city in Asia Minor where he had been born and grew up (Acts 9.30). Then Paul disappears from the scene for a while. Acts is initially silent about his fortunes. His name only crops up again when it is related that Barnabas travelled from Antioch to Tarsus to seek Paul: 'and when he had found him he brought him to Antioch' (Acts 11.25).

Paul the apocalyptist put much emphasis on his independence from others. On the way to Damascus he received a vision, a divine 'revelation'. His life changed radically. He became a convinced follower of Jesus Christ, but for him that evidently did not mean that he too now had to fall in with the views of the authoritative leaders of the original community in Jerualem. Paul went his own way. He did not travel immediately from Damascus to Jerusalem. He went to Arabia and then went back to Damascus again (Gal. 1.15–17). Only 'three years later' did he arrive in the city where he had been trained by Gamaliel in the Pharisaic interpretation of scripture and tradition. Much had happened in a relatively short time. Accoridng to Paul's reading of events he stayed with Peter for fifteen days and also had a meeting with James the 'brother of the Lord' (Gal. 1.18–19). After that he moved on, by his own account, to the regions of Syria and Cilicia (Gal. 1.21). Tarsus lay in Cilicia. On that point Paul and the author of Acts seem to agree. The differences in their accounts can be explained by 'interests' which did not run parallel: unity or independence? Who is right? I am inclined to give Paul the benefit of the doubt. He had his 'interests', but he was closer to the past than the author of Acts.

Dependent on the tradition

Paul certainly emphasized his independence, but that does not mean that he found himself in a spiritual vacuum. In his letter to the Galatians he himself made no secret of the fact that he had had contact with apostles in Jerusalem (Gal. 1.18–19). On Paul's authority there seems no reason to doubt the reliability of his reports, 'In what I am writing to you, before God I do not lie' (Gal. 1.20).

The curiosity of the readers of the text has been aroused. What will Paul have discussed with Peter during his visit to Jerusalem? Much may have been said in a period of fifteen days. There was plenty of opportunity for intensive meetings and deep conversations. Paul is silent about the content of his contacts, and we have no other sources at our disposal. Therefore we cannot do much more than guess. It is not difficult to guess at a number of the subjects of conversation. Without any doubt Peter and Paul talked together about Jesus, about his life and death, about his words and actions. The same subjects will also have been on the agenda in the meeting between Paul and James, the brother of the Lord.

That makes it all the more amazing that in his letters Paul almost never refers to the earthly life of Jesus. In a much-discussed text he himself seems to assert that the past has become unimportant for him: 'So from now on we know no one after the flesh. If we once knew Christ after the flesh, we no longer do now' (II Cor. 5.16). There is no unanimity in the exegetical literature over the interpretation of these words.[2] In what way should the clause *'knew Christ after the flesh'* be interpreted? Do the words *'after the flesh'* say something about our 'knowing' or do they need to be related to 'Christ'? In the latter case the apostle would be speaking negatively of our 'knowing Christ *after the flesh'*. With this strange expression he could have been referring to Jesus' life on earth – in the theo-logical jargon of our time the historical Jesus – but that is not at all certain. Finally, it can be concluded that the exegetical debate about the above-mentioned text is certainly interesting but does not in fact prove to be of decisive significance for the problems indicated. At any rate, wherever we look, virtually nothing is said in the letters of Paul about the words and actions of Jesus during his life on earth.[3]

Why was the apostle silent? Was he really uninterested in recollections of the 'historical' Jesus? In giving an answer to these questions it is important to realize that we run the risk of confronting Paul with a problem that he did not know. The investigation into the historical Jesus, the 'authentic' Jesus, began in the nineteenth century. Paul simply did not know that problem.[4] Moreover he was not writing gospels but letters. His apocalyptic sense of life inspired him to direct his gaze to the imminent future. His personal reminiscences do not play a major part in his letters. He alluded to them only when he thought that they could be 'functional' and could clarify his view (II Cor. 10–12; Gal. 1–2; Phil. 3.5–8). According to Paul the time was 'too short' (I Cor. 7.29) for him to be able to occupy himself at length with the past. For Paul, Jesus Christ was a living reality, not because he had gone round with Jesus through Galilee and Judaea nor because he could tell fascinating and moving stories about him but because on the way to Damascus he had encountered him as the crucified one whom God had raised from the dead.

Paul emphasized his independence from the apostles, but at the same time he knew that he was dependent on the early Christian tradition. It is highly significant that the relevant passages in his letters concentrate on the event of cross and resurrection. That seems to have been of central significance for him. In his first letter to the community of Corinth he twice refers emphatically to the early Christian tradition and in so doing begins by making use of a characteristic formula: 'For I received from the Lord what I also delivered to you, that the Lord Jesus Christ on the night that he was betrayed took bread . . .' (I Cor. 11.23). So Paul saw himself as a link in the tradition. He handed on a tradition which he himself had first received. In the first formula the apostle suggests that he 'received' this 'tradition from the Lord' (I Cor. 11.23). Is it again Paul's purpose to show his independence from other people? That seems hard to imagine in this case. It will have been known in the early Christian community that these words were not introduced by Paul. He was dependent on the tradition and he knew it. His reference to 'the Lord' gives the tradition an almost unassailable authority.

In the previous chapters we have come to know Paul as a complicated person. In a number of respects he was a man of two worlds. In the letter to the Galatians he vigorously defended his independence from others. In the first letter to the community of Corinth he lets another voice be heard. Measured by present-day standards Paul was a 'contextual' theologian. He had principles, but he was also a realist, with his eyes open to reality. The community of Corinth was torn apart by conflicts (I Cor. 1.10–17). In this situation, Paul saw it as his task to further unity. He did so, among other things, by emphasizing that he knew that he was independent from the tradition which was handed down in the early Christian community.

The scandal of the cross

In his letters Paul makes only sparse use of the possibility of referring to the early Christian traditions. His statements might perhaps have gained in authority and influence had he done so often, but presumably he was not very interested in the question of success. Paul was never afraid of adopting a minority stand-point, and when he thought that he had right on his side he was not afraid of isolation. In such a situation he was even ready to stand up against an angel from heaven (Gal. 1.8).

Paul attached importance to the early Christian tradition, but it was not so sacred to him that he did not dare to deviate from it. Nor did his respect for the very first apostles prevent him from going his own way (Gal. 2.11–14). It emerges from his letters that his dependence on the tradition was limited to references to the suffering and death of Jesus. That makes it all the more striking that Paul developed a personal view of this event. The four Gospels, written some decades after the letters of Paul, pay a great deal of attention to the account of Jesus' passion. Readers are put in a position to follow the dramatic event more or less at close quarters. It seems justified to suppose that the nucleus of that passion narrative had already been laid down in writing within the circle of the primitive community at a relatively early stage – at the end of the thirties of our era.[5] Paul could have come to know it during his visit to Jerusalem. However, from his letters it does not seem that the passion narrative as such had any decisive influence on him. It is not the *suffering* Christ but the *crucified* Christ who is central to his thought. The offensiveness of the account of the suffering and death of Jesus lies in the fact that he died on the *cross*.

Paul was an original thinker. He was not afraid of treading paths which others perhaps thought impassable. No one with-in the early Christian community made the 'scandal' of the cross an important theological theme. In the Gospel of John the crucifixion is even connected with words like 'lifting up' and 'glorification' (John 12.20–36). We do not know for certain how Paul would have reacted to such images, but I suppose that he would have opposed them with all his might. For him the cross was the absolute nadir in Christ's 'humiliation' (Phil. 2.8); it was a curse (Gal. 3.13), a folly and a 'scandal' (I Cor. 1.23; Gal. 6.14). For Paul, moreover, the cross was more than just a theological concept. He was an emotional man, and from a single text it can be inferred that he felt Jesus' death on the cross personally in his own body: 'I bear in my body the marks of Jesus' (Gal. 6.17).[6]

Paul's 'independence' finds a satisfactory explanation in this special relationship to Jesus Christ. His apostolate has a unique basis and therefore cannot be compared with that of his fellow apostles. There is no doubt that this was the source of many conflicts within the early Christian community. For Peter and his followers the paradox will sometimes have been difficult to understand. The one who had not been a follower of Jesus and had persecuted the community found himself suddenly bound up emotionally and existentially with the crucified and risen Christ. The vision on the way to Damascus radically changed his life and thought. However, he did not banish the past from his memory. Years later he remembered all too well that to begin with he had thought quite differently about it. He would never be able to forget that he had challenged followers of the crucified Jesus because he saw the cross as a 'curse' (Gal. 3.13) and as an 'offensive' symbol (= a scandal, I Cor. 1.23). The apocalyptic vision had opened his eyes to a new reality, a paradox which he had gradually begun to see as the heart of the Christian faith: the crazy scandal proved to be God's deepest wisdom and the curse of God had changed into a blessing with world-wide consequences.

For want of sufficient information it is almost impossible to get a clear picture of the development of Paul's thought in his 'unknown' years. On the way to Damascus he was surprised by an 'apocalypse', a vision which convinced him that the crucified Jesus was not dead but alive. It does not seem plausible that the apostle's thought changed completely from one day to the next. However overwhelming that apocalyptic experience was, the event near Damascus will have been the beginning of a long process of reflection. Paul did not keep diaries – at any rate, they have not been preserved. So we cannot follow the development of his thought closely. However, we do have a reliable picture of the world in which he lived and worked. He was a Diaspora Jew. We know the intellectual and religious baggage which he had brought with him from the start. We know that being a Jew meant a lot to him. He was a 'zealot' and was not ashamed of that, even when he had become a convinced follower of the crucified one whom God had raised from the dead.

In search of continuity

As a consequence of the apocalyptic vision Paul's life changed radically: the persecuter became a disciple. Nevertheless he always remained fully aware of his Jewishness. He never allowed himself to be led to deny his origin. Unlike the evangelists Matthew and John he spoke about 'the Jews' in negative terms only very exceptionally (I Thess. 2.14–16). In contrast to age-old Christian presuppositions, on the basis of the texts of Paul that we do have it cannot be proved conclusively that he deliberately broke his bond with the Jewish tradition – and if we are to understand this bond properly, we need to realize that it did not rest on a free choice, but on birth, covenant and election.[7] Paul never interpreted the death of Jesus as the definitive end of God's concerns with the Jewish people (Rom. 9.11). For him the cross was not of historical, but of exclusively theological, interest. He does not make any statements in his letters about who was responsible for the death of Jesus. He does not mention the name of Pontius Pilate, and he is silent about the share of the Jews in the condemnation of Jesus. One looks in vain in the letters of Paul for sharp condemnations of the Jewish leaders of the kind that appear in the mouth of Peter in the book of Acts: 'and killed the author of life, whom God raised from the dead' (Acts 3.15). Paul was not afraid of fierce debate but was also motivated pastorally, concerned for the welfare of the Christian community and also for that of his Jewish contemporaries who had not (yet) found their way into that community. Perhaps he knew some of them personally, members of the family and good friends. Here, too, he remained a man of two worlds.[8]

In Paul's time the ways of Judaism and Christianity had not grown so far apart that the choice of the Christian faith automatically led to a definitive break with the Jewish past. Paul's Pharisaic background guaranteed that he was familiar with scripture and tradition. During his stay in Jerusalem this knowledge deepened, thanks to the teaching of Gamaliel. After Paul's apocalyptic vision. knowledge of his past obviously did not disappear from one day to the next. It is evident from Paul's letters that even as an apostle he remained an expert in scripture and thus was in a position constantly to anchor his newly acquired insights in scripture and tradition.

We already noted that Paul was an apocalyptist. His view of human beings and the world was determined by the remarkable combination of pessimism and optimism which may be said to have been typical of the apocalyptic expectation of the future. He was pessimistic about this world, for it had to perish. He was optimistic about the fate of the elect. After the destruction of the old world and the judgment in which all evildoers and godless have been condemned to eternal punishment, they will receive their 'reward': they will inhabit *the* new world – they and no one else will be admitted to the new Jerusalem which will descend from heaven to the new earth (Rev. 21–22). In his letters Paul seldom allows himself to be diverted into describing the extensive apocalyptic visions of the future. Concrete problems demand all his attention and are given priority. Paul once gives readers a glimpse of his 'inner world' and describes his view of the imminent future. Here is one example as an illustration: 'I consider that the sufferings of this present time are not worth comparing to the glory that is to be revealed to us' (Rom. 8.18). In these words, too, we find that remarkable combination of pessimism and optimism.

Apocalyptists live in the certain conviction that the end of the world is near. Jesus' announcement of the rapid approach of the kingdom of God has an unmistakable apocalyptic character: 'The time is fulfilled and the kingdom of God is at hand' (Mark 1.15). In the letters of the apostle Paul one looks in vain for the term 'kingdom of God', but that does not mean that Paul attached no importance to the hope of the evil end of this wicked word. Just once, he leaves no doubt about his consciousness that one has to live in the certainty that the limit of history is within reach: 'the time is short' (I Cor. 7.29).

It seems legitimate to conclude that Paul was an apocalyptist and remained one, even after his Damascus experience. With this perspective he by no means found himself in an isolated position in the circle of apostles. Stimulated by the apocalyptic preaching of Jesus, the early Christian community initially lived in the firm conviction that the Lord would return very soon (I Thess. 4.15). When this failed to happen and people grew tired of waiting, the interest shifted from the future to the present and less emphasis was put on the coming of the kingdom of God, which was said already to be present on earth (Luke 17.21; John 3.3,5) and more on 'seeing' and entering' it. Paul wrote his letters at an early stage of church history. The developments in thought about the future mentioned above presumably took place only in the second half of the first century.

The early-Jewish apocalyptic world-view and expectation of the future form the basis of Christian faith.[9] In this sphere Jesus and Paul were of the same mind. The differences between the two were caused by the changed situation. Jesus lived in the expectation of the kingdom of God. After his death and resurrection a process of reflection had begun, as a result of which the proclaimer had become the proclaimed The consequences of that process are abundantly clear in Paul's letters: 'I decided to know nothing among you except Jesus Christ and him crucified' (I Cor. 2.2). At first sight the contours of Paul's view of the future have not fundamentally changed. But a decisive shift has taken place. In his apocalyptic thought since his Damascus experience the figure of the crucified Christ has had a central place. This conclusion immediately raises the

question: how did Paul come to begin to talk about Jesus
Christ?

Messiah/Christ [10]

The evangelists – Mark in particular – have preserved the
memory that Jesus never called himself Messiah, and when
others gave him this title, he usually reacted with a restraint
which suggested repudiation (Mark 8.27; 14.61–62).[11] Why
did Jesus hesitate to identify himself unambiguously and without any reservations with the Messiah? In the course of church
history the notion developed in Christian theology that the
expectation of the Messiah was the core of both the Old Testament and the Jewish tradition in past and present.[12] Since the
rise of historical criticism of the Bible in the nineteenth century
it is impossible to avoid relegating this view of things to the
realm of fable. In the Old Testament the coming of *the* Messiah
– a saving figure who will appear in the near future – does not
at all stand at the centre of interest.[13] Prophets like Isaiah and
Micah set their hopes on a spiritual revival which would be
powerfully stimulated by a new king from the dynasty of
David. He would tread in the footsteps of his illustrious forefather and predecessor (Isa. 7.14–16; 8.23–9.6; 11.1–10;
Micah 5.1–14). The birth of a new offshoot of the family of
David, a new anointed of the Lord, is greeted with joy because
it is experienced as an encouraging sign. The period of the reign
of king Hezekiah corresponded to the heightened expectations
and therefore could be characterized as 'messianic'. Just like his
distant forefather David, Hezekiah was a man after God's
heart: 'he did what was right in the eyes of the Lord, just as his
father David had done' (II Kings 18.3).

Unfortunately, the joy was short-lived. Hezekiah reigned for
twenty-nine years and was followed by his son Manasseh.
Manasseh's reign lasted for twenty-five years and was anything
but messianic. The son did not follow the example of his father.
Manasseh is one of the kings of Judah who is judged critically
in the books of Kings: 'He did what was evil in the eyes of the

Lord, according to the abominations of the peoples whom the Lord had driven out before the Israelites' (II Kings 21.2). Some verses later the criticism becomes devastating: 'He did much evil in the sight of the Lord, provoking him to anger' (II Kings 21.6). In religious terms the dynasty of David reached an absolute nadir with this king. At least that is the view of the book of Kings. In Chronicles the biographical sketch of Manasseh does not end in the minor. 'But when he was in distress he entreated the favour of the Lord his God and humbled himself greatly before the God of his fathers . . . Then Manasseh knew that the Lord was God' (II Chron. 33.12–13).

In the end this unexpected humiliation for the kingdom of Judah proved to be only a stay of execution. Only Josiah forms a favourable exception in the series of the successors of Manasseh, the last kings from the house of David. His 'reform' offered the best hope (II Kings 22–23), but could not prevent things continuing to go rapidly downhill. The kingdom of Judah was hopelessly lost. It could not assert itself successfully against the supremacy of the troops of the Babylonian king Nebuchadnezzar. In 586 BCE Judah disappeared for good from the world map as an independent state. All down the ages this dramatic end has made an indelible impression on the Jewish people. After the destruction of Jerusalem the Babylonian soldiers set fire not only to large parts of the city but also the temple, 'the house of the Lord' (II Kings 25.9). In the midst of this violence the dynasty of David also perished. The last king of Judah shared the fate of the majority of his subjects and died as an exile in Babylon. From that point on the age-old throne of king David proved unattainable for his successors.

The survivors saw themselves faced with a painful dilemma. 1. The terrors of 586 BC showed that belief in the God of Israel had been folly, for this God proved not to exist or was not in a position to protect his people. 2. Those who did not want to give up their faith in the power of the God of Israel were compelled to conclude that the catastrophe of 586 BCE had to be seen as God's punishment for the ongoing unfaithfulness of the people of Israel. From the Old Testament writings it can be inferred that the prophets and chroniclers opted for this last possibility. At the time of the Babylonian exile critical light was shed on that past, with the consequence that the history of the people of Israel is described from the perspective of sin, guilt and punishment.

The Babylonian exile did not last for ever. The pious were convinced that God intervened. The consequence was a new 'exodus'. History repeated itself. Again liberated exiles went through 'the wilderness' to 'the promised land' (Isa. 40.1–11). One of the psalmists expressed their feelings in an impressive way: 'When the Lord made the prisoners of Zion return, we were like those who dream. Then our mouth was filled with laughter and our tongue with rejoicing' (Ps. 126.1–2). A new phase in the history of the people of God had dawned. It had been decimated. Politically it no longer played a significant role. The age-old 'land of the fathers' continued to be occupied territory. Persians, Greek, Egyptians, Syrians and Romans alternated. For centuries there could be no talk of an independent Jewish state. The spiritual centre was no longer the throne of David; it became the temple in Jerusalem. A temple state was created, governed by a high priest with limited authority – religious and hardly, if at all, political.

Prophets and scribes tried to draw the lesson from history. Understandably a great deal of attention was paid to the commandments of the Torah. They offered a hopeful perspective. Those who consistently walked in 'the way of the Lord' might expect that there would be no repetition of the catastrophe of 586 BC. Thus the early Jewish tradition was built on two pillars: temple and Torah. After the return from the Babylonian exile the throne in Jerusalem remained empty. The dynasty of David no longer played a significant role. What was to be made of prophetic statements about an eternal kingship (II Sam. 7.14), about the birth of a new offshoot of the family of David (Isa. 7.14; 11.1), and about the dawn of a time of shalom, a period in which right and justice would have the last word (Isa. 11.1–10; Micah 4.1–5; 5.1–14)? It is not easy to answer this

question. The thought that in the near future 'the Messiah', a
son of David, will appear to fulfil the prophetic promises crops
up only late in early Judaism. Around the year 50 BC an
unknown writer from the circle of the Pharisees wrote the hopeful words that I quoted at length earlier: 'See, Lord, and raise up
for them their king, the son of David, to rule over your servant
Israel in the time known to you, O God' (Psalms of Solomon
17.21).

An anonymous author from the circle of the Pharisees wrote
these words almost a century before Paul arrived in the city of
Jerusalem from Tarsus. Apart from the fact that Paul also
belonged to the movement of the Pharisees, it is not inconceivable that he had this text in view. In any case we may
assume that, sitting at the feet of Gamaliel or in discussions
with fellow students, he came to hear this 'messianic' future
expectation mentioned. Paul's knowledge of this view of the
coming of the Messiah must have been an extra handicap for
him in believing the assertions of followers of Jesus. In the eyes
of some, a crucified man was perhaps a tragic hero, but the
most thoughtful people – Jews and Greeks and Romans –
regarded him as a failure: in the light of scripture and tradition
a crucified Messiah was a contradiction in terms. The expected
Messiah would overcome his enemies and certainly would not
be conquered and crucified by his enemies. For this reason, for
Paul in the first instance the crucified Jeus was a source of
scandal, a godforsaken scandal.

Was Paul the first to name Jesus the Christ? It is certain that
he had a preference for this title. He so often connects the words
Jesus and Christ that the combination Jesus Christ – sometimes
also Christ Jesus – has become virtually a proper name. Jesus
did not regard himself as the Messiah. The early Christian
community began to give him this title. We cannot say precisely
when that happened. In his first letter to the community of
Corinth the apostle made use of an early Christian confessional
formula in which the word 'Christ' already occurred: 'In the
first place I delivered to what I received as tradition, namely
that Christ died for our sins in accordance with the scriptures,

that he was buried, that he was raised on the third day in accordance with the scriptures' (I Cor. 15.3–4). Even if it may be true that Paul was not the first to name Jesus the Messiah, he certainly gave a quite distinct content to the early Jewish title. That also emerges from the fact that he did not hesitate to translate the Hebrew/Aramaic word consistently into Greek: Jesus is the *Christ*.

The Torah

What did Paul think of the Torah in his 'unknown years'? Honesty requires us to recognize that no clear answer can be given to this question. The texts are silent about this period in the apostle's life. That does not alter the fact that it is possible to make some statements which are not purely built on sand.

We came to know Paul as a zealot for the Torah. The apocalyptic view that he had on the way to Damascus led him to discover that the one who had been crucified had been raised by God from the dead. Evidently nothing was communicated about the significance of the Torah. In the apocalyptic literature the Torah is not pushed to one side as being without significance. Paul had no difficulty in combining his zeal for the Torah with his apocalyptic view of human beings and the world. After his vision he will not have taken the commandments any less seriously than he did before this time.

Did Paul perhaps gradually come to think otherwise? There is much discussion in the Gospels about the interpretations which relate to rest on the sabbath (Mark 2.23–3.6; Luke 13.1–17; 14.1–8), but nowhere is there a fundamental criticism of the Torah. On the contrary, Jesus says: 'Do not think that I have come to abolish the law or the prophets. I have not come to abolish but to fulfil' (Matt. 5.17). Jesus' parents had him circumcised on the eighth day in accordance with the commandments (Luke 2.21; Lev. 12.3). In the Gospels the question of the significance of the ritual of circumcision is not raised. Jesus was circumcised, and the same can also be said of his disciples. As long as the preaching was limited to the frontiers of Jewish territory and the Jewish tradition there were no problems over the Torah.

Paul was a Diaspora Jew. He grew up outside Jewish territory. He knew the problems that the commandments of the Torah – circumcision, sabbath, eating clean and unclean food – could pose for Jews and non-Jews who were interested in the Jewish religion in a Greek-Hellenistic city within the Roman empire. In his youth Paul went to Jerusalem to steep himself further in scripture and tradition. How did Saul experience the 'transition' from the Diaspora to Jerusalem? Was he already a passionate zealot for the law or did he only become that in Jerusalem? This last possibility should be considered, all the more so since we have already noted that in the course of time Paul will have distanced himself from his moderate teacher Gamaliel. Thus the later apostle became a fanatical persecutor of those who in his view did not take the Torah seriously enough. The apocalyptic vision brought about a radical change in his life and thought. He more or less turned his back on Jerusalem and became the Diaspora Jew that he had already been from birth. Thus the zealot again became the Hellenistic Pharisee which he had been before his stay in Jerusalem.[14]

5

It began in Antioch

The early Christian community in Antioch

Thanks to Barnabas, an end came to Paul's 'unknown years'. According to the book of Acts the two men had known each other since Paul's first stay in Jerusalem after his rapid departure from Damascus. For understandable reasons the reception from the members of the primitive community was not particularly warm: 'And when he (=Paul) had come to Jerusalem, he attempted to join the disciples; and they were all afraid of him, because they did not believe that he was a disciple. But Barnabas took him, and brought him to the apostles and declared to them how on the road he had seen the Lord, who spoke to him, and how at Damascus he had preached boldly in the name of Jesus' (Acts 9.26–27). It could be inferred from this text that Barnabas already performed a leading role in the community in Jerusalem before the coming of Paul. That is all the more striking, because he is not mentioned in the Gospels as one of the twelve disciples of Jesus. However, his name already appears at an early stage in the book of Acts: 'Thus Joseph who was surnamed by the apostles Barnabas – which means, son of encouragement – a Levite, a native of Cyprus, sold a field which belonged to him and brought the money and laid it at the apostles' feet' (Acts 4.36–37). Like Paul, Barnabas too was clearly a Diaspora Jew. That could explain why initially the two men got on well with each other. They made a number of journeys together (Acts 12.24–15.34) until a personal conflict put an end to their collaboration for good (Acts 15.35–41).[1]

For want of sufficient information we cannot say for certain precisely when 'Paul's hidden years' came to an end. In what year did Barnabas travel from Antioch to Tarsus to look for Paul? We do not know. Around the year 40 – that is the only thing that can be stated without objection. Evidently Barnabas had not yet forgotten the man whom he had introduced in Jerusalem to the circle of the apostles. According to the author of Acts Barnabas's quest had a clear purpose: 'when he had found him, he brought him to Antioch' (Acts 11.26). Why to this city outside Jewish territory and not to Jerusalem? Would it still have been dangerous for Paul to return to the centre of Judaism? Or did other considerations play a role?

If we are to be able to answer these questions we need to form a picture of the situation in which the early Christian community lived in Antioch. Whereas Jesus mainly stayed in smaller towns and in the countryside of Galilee – his pilgrim journeys to Jerusalem were an exception to the rule – after his cross and resurrection, his followers were to be found above all in the larger cities of the Roman empire:[2] initially in Jerualem and later in Antioch in Syria. This city had been founded by Seleucus I around 300 BCE and for a long time functioned as the residence of the Seleucid dynasty (I Macc. 3.37). The occupation of the city by Roman troops in 64 BCE did not turn it into a ruin and therefore did not mean the end of its existence. In the first century of our era Antioch was regarded as the third city of the world after Rome in Italy and Alexandria in Egypt.[3]

From its foundation, many Jews lived in Antioch. The first Jewish inhabitants had settled in the city after following the armies of Alexander the Great as traders on his campaigns of conquest in the East. Like Alexandria in Egypt, Antioch in Syria was relatively close to Jewish territory. Well before the beginning of our era, both cities attracted all those Jews who could find little or no employment in their own land. In the metropolis to the north of Galilee, about ten per cent of the population were Jews. There were various synagogues, and as that was also the case elsewhere in the Diaspora, the Jewish faith continued to be attractive to non-Jews. This is also attested by an interesting passage in the book of Acts in which a kindred spirit to Stephen is described in the following way: 'Nicolaus, a fellow-Jew from Antioch' (Acts 6.5).

The distance between Jerusalem and Antioch did not pose any obstacle; connections were good and beyond doubt there will have been numerous personal contacts – family, friends and business relationships. So it need not surprise us that already at an early stage of church history an important Christian community came into being in Antioch. The author of Acts gives us some insight into this history. After the execution of Stephen, those of a like mind fled from Jerusalem, 'and all were dispersed over the regions of Judaea and Samaria' (Acts 8.1). Things did not stop there. In a later phase, the 'dispersed' sought their salvation further north: 'Now those who were dispersed because of the persecution that arose over Stephen travelled as far as Phoenicia and Cyprus and Antioch' (Acts 11.19b). Thus the readers of Acts become aware that there was as yet no organized and systematic mission among the Gentiles. This is a surprising discovery, because attractive stories have already been told of the baptism of two important Gentiles: first of the chamberlain from Ethiopia by Philip (Acts 8.26–40), and then of Cornelius, the centurion of the so-called Italian cohort, in Caesarea by Peter (Acts 10.1–48). The way to the Gentiles has been opened up: not only have the 'first fruits' been baptized, but at the same time the restrictive regulations about 'clean and unclean' have been annulled: 'When they heard his they were silenced. And they glorified God, saying, "Clearly to the Gentiles also God has granted repentance unto life"' (Acts 11.18). What is there still to wait for? When will the decision be taken for an organized mission among the Gentiles? Who will give the sign?

On their way north, those dispersed from Jerusalem were not yet in a position to do this. However, the time does seem to have been ripe in Antioch.[4] There a beginning was made on the mission among the Gentiles: 'But there were some of them, men of Cyprus and Cyrene, who on coming to Antioch spoke to the Greeks also, preaching the Lord Jesus. And the hand of the

Lord was with them, and a great number that believed turned to the Lord' (Acts 11.20–21). A frontier was crossed in Antioch. The decision to take this way had already been prepared for in the circle of Stephen and his sympathizers in Jerusalem. Unlike Peter and his followers they were influenced by Hellenism. The result was that they had a different view of the relationship between Israel and the Gentiles from their Jewish contemporaries, who anxiously guarded themselves again alien notions and ideas. The Hellenistic Jews in the Diaspora were very important for the spread of Christian faith in the Gentile world.[5]

How did the 'Jewish' primitive community in Jerusalem react to these developments? As has been said, the contacts were good, and reports will very soon have reached the apostles. They took a far-reaching decision. They resolved to send Barnabas to take soundings in the community of Antioch (Acts 11.22). It need not surprise us that he was the person chosen: he was a Diaspora Jew from Cyprus (Acts 4.36). It might be expected that he would be able to assess the surprising developments in Antioch at their true value. His verdict proved to be favourable (Acts 11.23–24). And then he went in search of Paul (Acts 11.25)!

Why did he do that? The author of Acts writes about the events in Antioch in positive terms. However, his account does raise questions. It was written down many years after the event, at a time when the mission among the Gentiles had already become so successful that the number of Jewish Christians was far exceeded by the influx of Gentile Christians. The writer himself belonged to the latter group, as did Theophilus, the man to whom he dedicated both his Gospel and the book of Acts. Moreover he had a tendency to idealize the past and put it in a favourable light, so that the life of the primitive community in Jerusalem even took on a fairy-tale character (Acts 2.41–47; 4.32–37). However, the euphoria did not last long. Very soon the author could not disguise the fact that there were tensions even in the 'ideal' community of Jerusalem: 'Now in those days, when the disciples were increasing in numbers, the Hellenists murmured against the Hebrews because their widows were neglected in the daily ministration' (Acts 6.1). To combat this division within the community the twelve original apostles appointed seven 'deacons', Stephen and his companions (Acts 6.3–6). Probably this new measure brought only temporary relief. Soon new tensions arose both within the primitive community and between the followers of Jesus and the other Jews in Jerusalem. To an increasing degree the Torah was experienced as a problem. The censure was already made of Stephen: 'We have heard him speak blasphemy against Moses and against God' (Acts 6.11). This censure developed into an accusation. Stephen was arrested, interrogated and stoned (Acts 7.1–53). As a result of all this, the division within the primitive community took on the character of a schism: 'And on that day a great persecution arose against the church in Jerusalem; and they were all dispersed throughout the region of Judaea and Samaria' (Acts 8.1). The further fortunes of these 'dispersed' ones have already occupied us earlier.[6]

Considering the tensions in Jerusalem which have been sketched out, it seems highly improbable that the surprising developments within the community of Antioch made no impact at all. Here, too, the commandments of the Torah will have been experienced as a stumbling block. Did the situation get too much for Barnabas? He need not have been ashamed if it did. The questions raised by the crossing of boundaries in Antioch, indicated above, were very complicated. Barnabas could use support. It is not strange that in these difficult circumstances he went in search of the man whom he knew from Jerusalem, a man who had perhaps made an impression on him and whom he regarded as a kindred spirit, because he too was a Diaspora Jew. So Barnabas undertook the journey from Antioch to Tarsus – the distance between the two cities could be covered in several days. His quest was successful. He found Paul, and Paul proved ready to go with him to Antioch. It was the beginning of a new episode in the life of the 'independent' apostle.

Conflict between Peter and Paul[7]

Antioch could be regarded as a testing ground for the early
Christian communities. The problems and tensions which
emerged in the Syrian metropolis would quickly repeat themselves in numerous other cities in the regions around the
Mediterranean Sea. A large Jewish minority had already been
living in Antioch for centuries. Unfortunately we do not know
to which religious parties and trends the Antiochene Jews
belonged. From the fact that there were different synagogues
we could cautiously infer that there were also adherents of
Phariseeism and perhaps representatives of the different
Pharisaic schools. As has already been said, the Jewish religion
was also attractive to non-Jews in Antioch. There were
proselytes, and others who showed a close interest.

Into this community, which was certainly not without
tensions and conflicts, a new element came from outside: the
'dispersed' fugitives arriving from the south, who called themselves followers of Jesus. They had left Jerusalem because after
the stoning of Stephen, also through the zeal of those like
Saul/Paul, things had become too hot for them. Earlier it proved
that there were already contacts between the Christian communities in Antioch and Jerusalem. We can safely assume that
there were also the same contacts between the Jewish communities in the two cities. The consequences can easily be guessed.
Oppositions which had already produced great tensions in
Jerusalem transplanted themselves as it were northwards and
will also have caused trouble in Antioch. How was the local
Jewish community to react to other Jews who were fugitives
because they called themselves sympathizers with a man who
had been stoned as a blasphemer in Jerusalem? Already existing
tensions increased further, and became confusion and chaos
because of the successes that the Christian preaching achieved
in the circle of non-Jews. It is not inconceivable that these non-
Jews also included men and women who had earlier been
attracted to the Jewish synagogue, but who for various reasons
had not taken or had not felt able to take the decisive step to

Judaism. Who was in a position to bring some order to this chaotic situation?

In his letter to the community of the Galatians Paul recalls a striking event. It took place in Antioch and gives us some insight into the complicated circumstances which prevailed then: 'But when Cephas (= Peter) came to Antioch I opposed him to his face, because he stood condemned. For before certain men came from James, he ate with the Gentiles; but when they came he drew back and separated himself, fearing the circumcision party. And with him the rest of the Jews acted hypocritically, so that even Barnabas was carried away by their hypocrisy' (Gal. 2.11–13).

Although it was written some time later, Paul's account of the event still bears traces of his emotions and of a bewilderment and anger that he can hardly suppress: 'even Barnabas – for a long time my true friend and travelling companion! – was carried away by their hypocrisy' (Gal. 2.13). Not without reason Paul recalled this tragic conflict with his apostolic colleague at a crucial moment in his letter. He had rounded off the defence of his unique apostolate – not from men nor through a man, but through Jesus Christ, and God the Father' (Gal. 1.1) – and used the confrontation with Peter as an occasion to give an extended account, based on scripture and tradition, of the scope and significance of the Torah for those members of the community who had not been born Jews and thus had not been circumcised (Gal. 2.15–4.31). What significance do the commandments of the Torah still have? Must Gentile Christians also be circumcised? Do they need to observe the food laws, sabbath commandments, etc.? The questions were pressing in the community of the Galatians, but they already played a role in Antioch earlier.

Peter's behaviour offended Paul. His verdict on the event could not be clearer: 'But when I saw that they (= Peter, Barnabas and others) were not straightforward about the truth of the gospel . . .' (2.14a). By his own account, Paul then accused his fellow-apostle 'before them all' of half-heartedness and inconsistency: 'If you, though a Jew, live like a Gentile and not like a Jew, how can you compel the Gentiles to live like Jews?' (Gal. 2.14b). It is regrettable that we know this conflict only in Paul's interpretation. It would be good if here, too, we could apply the principle of giving a hearing to both sides, but for lack of information that is not possible. Moreover, the readers of the letter will have little difficulty in understanding Paul's annoyance. Peter's behaviour was ambivalent. One does not expect that from a man who in the Gospels is described as prince of the apostles. Clearly he had a prominent position within the circle of the twelve disciples, and after Easter and Pentecost that was initially also the case in the primitive community in Jerusalem (Acts 1.15–22; 2.14–40; 3.11–26; 4.8–12).[8]

His behaviour in Antioch raises yet more questions if we connect it with a passage which is to be found only in the Gospel of Matthew: 'Jesus said to him: "Blessed are you, Simon bar Jonah, for flesh and blood has not revealed it to you, but my Father in heaven. I tell you, you are Peter, and on this rock I shall build my community, and the gates of Hades shall not overcome it. I shall give you the keys of the kingdom of heaven, and what you bind on earth shall also be bound in heaven, and what you loose on earth shall also be loosed in heaven' (Matt. 16.17–19). These words of praise cannot be applied to Peter's actions in Antioch. There he was no rock, and proved not to be capable of coming forward with authority and providing leadership for a community in confusion. In all probability the words in the Gospel of Matthew are of a later date. They will even have been added to the Gospel later, when the need arose to link the offices to the circle of the first twelve disciples. That Peter was assigned a special position here was obvious, given his prominent role in this circle.[9]

In Antioch, Peter was put in a difficult position. His behaviour aroused the wrath of Paul, but his action cannot be said to be incomprehensible. The local situation was complex: a Christian community composed of Jews and a rapidly growing number of non-Jews. Which religious culture was to gain the upper hand? Was the Christian community in the first place a continuation of the Old Testament-Jewish tradition – a new messianic sect *within* Judaism? Or would this limit Christian faith too much? In answering questions as deep as this, much creativity and wisdom was required of the leaders of the early Christian community. Jesus had not left any clear instructions in this area. His life had largely been lived in a Jewish country. Encounters with non-Jews were the exceptions to the rule (Matt. 8.5–13; 15.21–18). Consequently the evangelists did not discuss circumcision as a problem.

We may assume that all this was grist to Peter's mill. In the primitive Jerusalem community he was not among the supporters of Stephen. When these fled and were dispersed, he remained in Jerusalem with the other apostles (Acts 8.2). Later he did go outside the city. On his travels, in Joppa on the coast he came into contact with Cornelius, who has already been mentioned, a Gentile, the centurion of the Italian cohort (Acts 10.1–48). Peter baptized the soldier because he had discovered that 'the gift of the Holy Spirit was also poured out on the Gentiles' (Acts 10.45). On his return to Jerusalem it proved that his action did not earn him the thanks of others: 'The apostles and the brethren who were in Judaea heard that the Gentiles also had received the word of God. So when Peter went up to Jerusalem, the circumcision party criticized him, saying: "Why did you go to uncircumcised men and eat with them?"' (Acts 11.1–3). According to the author of Acts, Peter had no difficulty in rejecting this censure in a forthright way. At the end of his argument his opponents were completely convinced that he was in the right: 'When they heard this they were silenced. And they glorified God, saying, "Then to the Gentiles also God has granted repentance unto life"' (Acts 11.16).

It cannot escape any attentive readers of the Bible that there is a world of difference between the attitude of Peter in Acts and the way in which Paul describes his actions to the letter to the Galatians. How can we explain the fact that the self-confident apostle, who had no difficulty in Jerusalem in persuading his opponents to change their mind, could not stand up to opposition in Antioch and also seemed to have forgotten all the arguments? Here we come up against a problem which has already occupied us earlier: in many cases the author of Acts and the apostle Paul do not have the same view of events in the past. Both writers prove to have their 'interests'. That will also be the case here. Paul thought it desirable to take a stand, and therefore he had an interest in depicting the appearance of Peter in negative terms. By now we have come to know the author of Acts as a man who idealized the past. Peter, who had difficulty in finding his way in the complex situation of early Christianity, in Acts became a true rock, an apostle with almost 'papal' status.

In Antioch Peter was still hesitating. What was he to do? Thanks to the successful missionary activity, the local Christian community had become very variegated: Jewish Christians and a growing number of Gentile Christians. According to Paul's view of the event, initially Peter had no objection to sitting at one and the same table and sharing a meal with the 'Gentiles' (= Gentile Christians, Gal. 2.12). As is well known, the commandments of the Torah on eating are very strict. The result is that a pious Jew may not eat just anything, and must also be very careful about sitting at the same table as others. According to the evangelist, Jesus was vigorously criticized because 'he ate with toll collectors and sinners' (Mark 2.16). For this reason he was accused of being 'a glutton and a drunkard' (Matt. 11.19). Peter ventured to go even a step further. Jesus already ate with Jews who risked getting lost (Luke 15), 'the lost sheep of the house of Israel' (Matt. 15.24). In Antioch Peter took his place at a table at which Gentiles were sitting: Gentile Christians, to be sure, brothers and sisters of the community of Jesus Christ, but from a Jewish standpoint uncircumcised and thus also unclean. Can and may a Jew – even a Jewish Christian – take a place at the same table with these people and enjoy a meal? Initially Peter thought that he could answer this question in the affirmative. However, he changed his mind. Paul claimed to know the reason: at a given moment 'some people from James' arrived in Antioch and then Peter became afraid, and 'began to draw back and separated himself, fearing the circumcision party' (Gal. 2.12). It is not an exaggeration to say that the tension is still tangible in this text. Peter found himself between two fires and did not know which side to choose. What role had the Torah to play in the life of the Christian community? Peter ventured on new ways, but allowed himself to be drawn back by 'some people from James'. According to the view of the apostle Paul they represented the wing within early Christianity which was firmly convinced that the Torah had not lost any of its significance.

A meeting at Jerusalem

Even after the conflict between Peter and Paul, the discussion about the value of the Torah began to occupy people within the early Christian community intensely. A broad gulf developed above all between the primitive community of Jerusalem and the mixed Christian community of Antioch. Closer reflection was desirable and necessary. The author of Acts gives a fascinating account of this important meeting of leading apostles, held in Jerusalem towards the end of the 40s (Acts 15.1–21). It is remarkable that there is no reference whatsoever to it in the letters of Paul. In the first instance one can only be amazed at the apostle's silence. As a delegate from the community in Antioch he was one of those who took part in the deliberations in Jerusalem. Moreover the problem on the agenda was very close to his heart, and during his missionary journeys around the world of the Gentiles he was constantly confronted with this sort of question. In the letter to the Galatians Paul felt compelled to defend his surprising view of the significance of the commandments of the Torah – in particular the precepts relating to circumcision – with the force of 'scriptural' arguments. Nowhere in this letter does he refer to the compromise proposal which was accepted at the meeting in Jerusalem after long discussions. Was he writing before the meeting in question, or after further reflection, and in the course of time could he no longer accept the compromise that had been achieved?

There is no mistaking the fact that there are parallels

between the conflict between Peter and Paul in Antioch and the event which formed the immediate occasion for the meeting of apostles in Jerusalem. 'But some men came down from Judaea and were teaching the brethren, "Unless you are circumcised according to the custom of Moses, you cannot be saved"' (Acts 15.1). Again the question of the significance of the Torah is central to a Christian community which is composed of a mixture of Jewish Christians and Gentile Christians. The stand-point of the men from Judaea is unambiguous and clear: the Torah is the way to be observed not only by Jews but also by Gentile Christians.

According to the account of the event in Acts, the view of the men from Judaea caused a commotion in Antioch. Because above all Paul and Barnabas were fiercely opposed these views, it was resolved to send them along with some others to Jerusalem as delegates from the community (Acts 15.2). For various reasons the two apostles will have viewed the journey with mixed feelings. Once Barnabas had come from Jerusalem to Antioch as a delegate from the primitive community. Now he was making the same journey in the opposite direction as a delegate of the community in Antioch. At all events he must have been a man to whom one could venture to entrust such responsible tasks with confidence. For Paul, above all the return to Jerusalem will have been an emotional event. Long ago in this city he had been brought up at the feet of Gamaliel in the finer points of the Pharisaic interpretation of scripture and tradition (Acts 22.1–3), and the beginning his career as a passionate zealot for his ancestral traditions lay there (Gal. 1.14). After his Damascus experience he had returned to Jerusalem. As I remarked earlier, it seems unclear precisely when he arrived there. Opinions are divided. According to the author of Acts, Paul travelled directly to Jerusalem after his over-hasty departure from Damascus (Acts 9.23–30). The apostle himself had another view of the course of events; he claimed to have travelled to Jerusalem only three years later. Clearly he cherished no plans to settle there again. His stay was of short duration: fifteen days (Gal. 1.18–20).

Paul was now travelling to Jerusalem for the second time. By now the former persecutor of the Christian community had become an authoritative man in the circle of followers of Jesus Christ. He goes to Jerusalem as a delegate of the influential community in Antioch. He also writes in his letter to the Galatians about a second visit to the city where he had once been brought up in the Pharisaic tradition: 'Then after fourteen years I went up again to Jerusalem with Barnabas, taking Titus along with me. I went up by revelation; and I laid before them (= the men of note, the leaders of the primitive community) the gospel that I preached to the Gentiles' (Gal. 2.1–2). Anyone who reads the texts from Galatians and Acts side by side will discover both agreements and differences. Barnabas is mentioned in both passages. Paul also reports that he was accompanied by Titus, whom he introduces as a Gentile Christian, an uncircumcised Greek (Gal. 2.3). The author of Acts does not conceal the fact that 'some of the others' travelled with Paul and Barnabas to Jerusalem (Acts 15.2), but he does not mention the name of Titus here. Indeed one looks for this name in vain in Acts. That silence is surprising, because Paul made no secret of the fact that Titus played a mediating role in the sharp conflict that he had with the community in Corinth. In his second letter to that community, Paul sometimes speaks with great respect about Titus and is grateful to him for the way in which he put an end to the disputes and was able to achieve reconciliation between the parties (II Cor. 2.12–13; 7.6–7; 8.6, 16–24). In this framework the name of Titus could have been mentioned with honour in Acts. It has already been striking that the author of this book of the Bible had a tendency to idealize the past. In his view of the first decades of church history there was simply no place for the appearance of a man like Titus. Anyone who is unwilling to recognize any conflicts will also not want to pay any attention to a man who was able to resolve a serious conflict along peaceful lines. For Titus personally it is regrettable that he suffered this fate. Of course he finally gained his 'monument' in the New Testament, a letter of Paul addressed to him personally: 'to Titus, my true child in a common faith' (Titus 1.4). The doubt of contemporary scholars about the authenticity of this writing does not detract from the value of this token of honour.

In his letter to the Galatians Paul gives the reason for his journey to Jerualem as: 'I went up by a revelation' (Gal. 2.2). The motivation in Acts has a less 'exalted' character. The community in Antioch sent Paul and Barnabas as their delegates to Jerusalem. However, the differences indicated do not force us to conclude that Acts and Galatians are talking about different journeys to Jerusalem.[10] I already remarked earlier that even Paul could not escape looking at the past from a particular perspective. In the letter to the Galatians his prime concern is to emphasize his independence as powerfully as possible (Gal. 1.11). He has been called by God and therefore in what he does he is in no way dependent on the first apostles (Gal. 1.17) and thus also on the leaders of the community of Antioch. It was not other people who sent him on his way, but God, by means of a 'revelation'. In the same way, on the road to Damascus, through a kind of apocalyptic vision he came to the insight that the crucified Jesus had been raised from the dead by God (Gal. 1.12).

There is an account of the meeting in Jerusalem in Acts (Acts 15.1–21). The decisions are reported at such length that one is inclined to think that the author of this book of the Bible had access to the minutes of the meeting. That will not have been the case, but it does not diminish our admiration for the fascinating way in which the course of the meeting is described. The tone of the discussion is set by participants who – like Paul – came from the Pharisaic party. Unlike the apostle, they did not want to deviate from the Torah in any way and stated in reference to the Gentile Christians that 'it is necessary to circumcise them, and to charge them to keep the law of Moses' (Acts 15.5). It would be going too far to report the whole of this interesting debate. What is important for us is the result of the discussions. After Paul and Barnabas had given their views (Acts 15.12), James spoke. He enjoyed great authority in the circle of the primitive community, not least because he was

known as 'the brother of the Lord' (Gal. 1.19).[11] In his letter to
the Galatians Paul suggests that James was one of the defenders
of the view that no exception whatsoever might be made to
the validity of the commandments in the Torah for Gentile
Christians. His supporters in Antioch are said to have persuaded no less a figure than Peter to change his mind here. Thus
indirectly they were also responsible for the conflict in principle
between Paul and the influential apostle who suddenly proved
to be a hesitant and uncertain 'rock' (Gal. 2.11–14).

In the description of the meeting in Jerusalem in Acts,
James's standpoint seems less immovable. During the discussions he plays the role of reconciler and he is the one who
finally drafts a compromise that is subscribed to with more or
less difficulty by all present: 'Therefore my judgment is that we
should not trouble those of the Gentiles who turn to God, but
should write to them to abstain from the pollutions of idols and
from unchastity and from what is strangled and from blood'
(Acts 15.19–20). For Gentile Christians that is enough. It is a
minimum: anyone who is not satisfied with that and wants
more is told by James with surprising terseness in the compromise proposal that the Torah of Moses is read aloud in the
synagogue each sabbath (Acts 15.21).

Shortly after the end of the meeting Barnabas and Paul,
accompanied among others by Judas and Silas, returned to
Antioch in high spirits. They were instructed to make the
following report about their mission: 'It has seemed good to the
Holy Spirit and to us to lay upon you no greater burden than
these necessary things: that you abstain from what has been
sacrificed to idols and from blood and from what is strangled
and from unchastity' (Acts 15.29).

Evidently the conflict thus ended with a solution which was
satisfactory to all concerned. In all probability the reality was
less rosy. The phenomenon is age-old and still to be found in
our day: sometimes the ink on which the text of an agreement
has been written is barely dry than differences of opinion of the
interpretation of decisions taken lead to new disputes. Did that
also happen after the meeting in Jerusalem? The joy over the

compromise was soon tempered by the account of a new conflict which put an end for ever to the close collaboration between Barnabas and Paul (Acts 15.35–41). According to Acts they had no difference of opinion over the outcome of the discussions in Jerusalem. However, Barnabas and Paul had a disagreement over John Mark. He had come from Jerusalem (Acts 12.12, 15) and accompanied Paul and Barnabas on the first missionary journey which they undertook from Antioch (Acts 13.1–4). While they were still on the way, John Mark resolved to return to Jerusalem (Acts 13.13). One can only guess at the reason for his decision. The book of Acts is sober in its account on this point and contents itself with a mention of John Mark's premature departure. In the course of church history people have often been dissatisfied with this silence. Thus the Greek church father Chrysostom relates that the poor John Mark became homesick and longed for his mother, who lived in Jerusalem. This is an attractive and even touching thought, but is completely uncertain. According to Acts, this premature departure of John Mark was the cause of the break between Barnabas and Paul. When they were making plans for a new journey, Barnabas indicated that he would again like to take John Mark with him. Paul opposed this: 'And there arose a sharp contention, so that they separated from each other; Barnabas took Mark with him and sailed away to Cyprus, but Paul chose Silas and departed, being commended by the brethren to the grace of the Lord. And he went through Syria and Cilicia strengthening the communities' (Acts 15.39–41).

The sharp conflict between Barnabas and Paul forms an enigmatic episode from the first years of church history. It is surprising that the author of the book of Acts is not silent about it, as he was over other conflicts within the early Christian community. Why did he devote attention to a vigorous difference of opinion which at first sight seems to take place above all in the private sphere? I find it difficult to avoid the impression that there must have been more to it than that. In the letter to the community at Colossae we find the name of a certain Mark, who proves to be a nephew of Barnabas (Col. 4.10). If this

Mark were the same person as the John Mark mentioned earlier, the family relationship could explain why Barnabas was better disposed to his relative than Paul. But I still find it strange that the author of the book of Acts, who had a tendency to keep quiet about disputes and difficulties within the early Christian community or to attach less importance to them, thought it necessary to pay attention to the conflict between Paul and Barnabas. It seems to me that we must take serious account of the possibility that the tragic alienation of the two men had a deeper cause. Initially they were of a like mind. They understood each other well and valued each other. Both came from the Diaspora and for this reason attached great importance to the preaching of the gospel in the Gentile world. It was impossible for the two of them to mistake the consequences that crossing this frontier would have in connection with the meaning of the Torah for Gentile Christians. It is conceivable that their views gradually began to differ on that important point. Paul gradually developed a daring vision of the Torah – especially in the letter to the Galatians. Paul also mentions Barnabas's name in the fascinating passage about his conflict with Peter in Antioch – and not in a positive sense: 'even Barnabas was carried away by their hypocrisy' (Gal. 2.13). At that moment was their unanimity destroyed – temporarily or definitively? Like Peter, Barnabas too allowed himself to be persuaded to change his mind by men from James's circle who had come from Jerusalem to Antioch (Gal. 2.11–14). So Paul's criticism of Peter also applies to Barnabas. Furthermore it is evident from the letter to the Galatians that Paul had meanwhile abandoned the compromise agreed on in Jerusalem. He went in search of a 'scriptural' solution to the problems which had arisen. That is indeed the reason why in this letter Paul pays no attention to the decisions taken in Jerusalem. For him they were no longer valid. In his view, recent developments and his own reflection on the significance of the Torah for Gentile Christians had made the decisions of the Jerusalem assembly an obsolete phase in the developments within the early Christian community.

In his letter to the Galatians Paul writes about meetings with the original apostles – the 'pillars' (Gal. 2.9) – but the content of these discussions took on another character. The question of circumcision arises only through an incidental remark: 'But even Titus, who was with me, was not compelled to be circumcised, although he was a Greek' (Gal. 2.3). It is impossible to misunderstand the hint: his opponents who were causing a commotion in the communities of Galatia must not think that they could refer back to the apostles in Jerusalem. Paul himself can bear witness that the apostle did not require Titus, a Gentile Christian, to be circumcised. The rest of the discussions between the delegation from Antioch to which Paul, Barnabas and indeed Titus belonged and the apostles in Jerusalem were about a fair distribution of the mission fields: 'we (= Paul and his supporters) should go to the Gentiles and they (Peter and his supporters) to the circumcised' (Gal. 2.9).

The apostle to the Gentiles

Jesus was a Jew. In accordance with the commandments of the Torah (Lev. 12.3) he was circumcised on the eighth day (Luke 2.21). He grew up in Nazareth. At the age of around thirty he began to travel around in Galilee (Luke 3.23). In all probability, his followers were also Jews (Mark 3.13–19). Readers of the four Gospels can hardly escape the impression that the activities of Jesus took place primarily within the framework of Jewish tradition. Mention is made of encounters with non-Jews, but they were the exception rather than the rule (Matt. 8.5–13; Mark 7.24–30). On such an occasion Jesus himself had a surprising confrontation with a women from the region of Tyre and Sidon. She asked Jesus to heal her daughter. According to the evangelist Matthew Jesus reacted in a negative way to this request: 'I have been sent only to the lost sheep of the house of Israel' (Matt. 15.24). Did Jesus' mission indeed remain almost exclusively limited to the Jewish people? In the light of the later success of the Christian preaching in the Gentile world it is difficult to answer this question in the affirmative. Moreover we are in good company. To all appearances the writer of the Gospel of Matthew wrestled with the same problem.[12] He took from one of his sources – the Gospel of Mark – the story about the non-Jewish woman who sought Jesus' help (Mark 7.4–30). The sentence quoted earlier about 'the lost sheep of the house of Israel' is the most important difference that Matthew has introduced into the text of Mark. In this way he underlined Jesus' divergent view towards non-Jews. However, from the later course of the Gospel it proves that this was not the last word about Jesus' relation to the Gentiles. In his account of the birth of Jesus it is Matthew who pays considerable attention to the surprising coming of 'wise men from the East' (Matt. 2.1–12). He is also the one who adds the words *Galilee of the Gentiles* to a quotation from scripture (Matt. 4.15). Jesus took refuge in that Galilee after the arrest of John the Baptist (Matt. 4.12–17). Finally it is also Matthew who makes his Gospel end with a grandiose scene: 'Jesus came to them and said: "All authority in heaven and on earth has been given to me. Go therefore and make disciples of all nations, baptizing them in the name of the Father, and of the Son and of the Holy Spirit, teaching them to observe all that I have commanded you; and lo, I am with you always, to the close of the age"' (Matt. 28.18–20).[13]

When Matthew wrote these words – the famous 'mission command' – around the year 80, the missionary journeys of Paul already lay some time in the past. Nowhere in his letters does the apostle refer to the impressive final chord of the Gospel of Matthew. His missionary zeal is not aroused by this command. In all probability he never heard these words. The evangelist attributed them to Jesus some years later. In his letter to the Galatians Paul himself gave the following explanation of his 'call'. 'But when he who had set me apart before was born and had called me through his grace, was pleased to reveal his son to me, in order that I might preach him among the Gentiles . . .' (Gal. 1.15–16).

The text quoted gives us some insight into the exciting, complicated world of the apostle. The Diaspora was his birthplace, but he also went to Jerusalem to be instructed in scripture and tradition. He stood out as a passionate zealot. As an apocalyptist he was not hopeful about the future of this world. After the apocalyptic vision, he knew that he had been 'called' as an apostle, a man with a special mission. In the letter to the Galatians Paul was not afraid of referring back to the call visions of Old Testament prophets like Isaiah and Jeremiah when he described his calling (Isa. 49.1; Jer. 1.5). For Paul, who was a man from the Diaspora and an apocalyptist, the world was greater than the limits of Jewish land and Jewish tradition. His 'prophetic' call strengthened this conviction: 'I send you as a light to the nations; my salvation must extend to the corners of the earth' (Isa. 49.6).[14] The people of Israel is indeed central in the prophetic preaching, but that in no way implies that the Gentiles are excluded for ever: 'On this mountain the Lord of hosts will make for all people a feast of fat things, a feast of wine on the lees, of fat things full of marrow, of wine on the lees well refined. And he will destroy on this mountain the covering that is cast over all peoples, the veil that is spread over all peoples' (Isa. 25.6–7). Paul thought that he could see the fulfilment of everything that the prophets dreamed of. Through the resurrection of the crucified Jesus by God the messianic time had already dawned. It was high time – the time was short! (I Cor. 7.29) – to make the Gentile world aware of this and to invite it to take part in God's feast.

6

The first letter to the Thessalonians

The beginning of the second missionary journey

In the previous chapter I discussed at length the meeting of the apostles in Jerusalem. The description in the book of Acts does not give the impression that Paul played a major role in it (Acts 15.1–21). Together with Barnabas he belonged among those who attached great importance to the spread of the gospel among the Gentiles (Acts 15.12). The compromise proposal did not come from Paul, but from James (Acts 15.13–21). At least according to the author of Acts, the apostle to the Gentiles did not make any substantial contribution to theological reflection on the meaning of the commandments of the Torah. This silence makes us think, because it can be inferred from Paul's letter to the Galatians that he had found a 'scriptural' solution to this complicated question. Why was this view not explicitly expressed at the time of the meeting in Jerusalem? Why was Paul silent? Or has the author of Acts made him be silent because he preferred the compromise proposal to reporting a controversial view? It is of course also possible that Paul went deeper into this question and came to define his own viewpoint only at a later stage. My preference is for this relatively 'simple' explanation.

The meeting in Jerusalem is of crucial importance for Paul's biography. After that he became more independent. The author of Acts does not say so in as many words, but given the consequences, it seems very likely that he regarded the meeting of apostles as a turning point in the history of early Christianity. From this moment he turns his attention completely to the activities of Paul. The role of the main character in the first part, Peter, seems finally to have been played out. His name is not mentioned again. It would not be out of place to entitle the second part of Acts 'The Missionary Journeys and Further Fortunes of the Apostle Paul'.

After the discussions in Jerusalem Paul returned to Antioch, still in the company of Barnabas. However, their collaboration would rapidly come to a tragic end. As was described earlier, John Mark was the direct occasion for the conflict (Acts 15.37–38). The ways of Paul and Barnabas parted for good. Accompanied by John Mark, Barnabas went to Cyprus. Paul saw himself compelled to chose a new travelling companion. He found one in the person of Silas. That is striking, for this Silas had previously travelled with Paul and Barnabas from Jerusalem to Antioch as a delegate from the Jerusalem community. Acts calls him 'a man of reputation' (Acts 15.22). Together with Silas, Paul then travelled to Syria and Cilicia (Acts 15.39–40).

On the way, presumably in Lystra, a man joined this travelling company who may be counted as one of Paul's closest colleagues, Timothy. The author of Acts introduces him in the following way: 'a disciple . . . the son of a believing Jewish woman and a Greek father' (Acts 16.1). His appearance in Acts is a surprise. He crops up as it were from nowhere, but he is called a disciple. A passage in one of Paul's letters gives a satisfactory explanation of this course of events. The apostle refers to Timothy as 'my beloved and true child in the Lord' (I Cor. 4.17). This report fits well with the account of Acts. During his first missionary journey, which he had undertaken still in the company of Barnabas, Paul will already have been in Lystra (Acts 14.6). His stay there lasted some time (Acts 15.7) and ended with a stoning which he miraculously survived (Acts 15.19–20). During this visit Timothy will have become a follower of Jesus Christ through Paul's preaching.

The description of the meeting between Paul and Timothy in Acts contains a second surprise: 'Paul wanted Timothy to accompany him, and he took him and circumcised him because of the Jews who were in those places, for they all knew that his father was a Greek' (Acts 16.3). After the extended account of the discussion about circumcision at the time of the meeting of the apostles in Jerusalem (Acts 15.1–21) Paul's actions may be said to be quite remarkable. Why did he have Timothy circumcised? In doing so, did he dissociate himself from the compromise which had been arrived at in Jerusalem shortly beforehand on James's initiative? It seems certain that the answer to this question must be no. At the meeting of the apostles, circumcision as such was not central, but rather the problem whether *Gentile* Christians also had to be circumcised (Acts 15.1,5). Timothy came from a mixed marriage: he had a Greek father and a Jewish mother. According to Jewish tradition Timothy was therefore completely Jewish and should have been circumcised at birth. Clearly this had not happened, and on the instructions of Paul that 'neglect' was now made good. By doing this Paul showed his faithfulness to the Torah. A Jewish follower of Jesus Christ was and remained a Jew, and must not go through life without being circumcised. The compromise which resulted from the meeting in Jerusalem applied only to Gentile Christians (Acts 15.19–21). I shall come back to the question whether Paul later began to think differently about these problems, in a discussion of his letter to the Galatians.

The description of the course of the first part of the second missionary journey in Acts has some striking features. Evidently the journey did not always go as Paul and his companions had planned. The Spirit intervened and sent them straight through Asia Minor in a westerly direction to the coast, to Troas: 'And they went through the region of Phrygia and Galatia, having been forbidden by the Holy Spirit to speak the word in Asia. And when they had come opposite Mysia, they attempted to go into Bithynia, but the spirit of Jesus did not allow them; so, passing by Mysia, they went down to Troas on the coast' (Acts 16.6–9). For Luke, no doubt is possible: the journey took place in accordance with the divine plan. On the way to the ultimate goal – Rome – the gospel will now for the first time cross the frontier between Asia and Europe. The vision that Paul receives is quite plain: 'A man of Macedonia was standing beseeching him and saying, "Come over to Macedonia and help us"' (Acts 16.9). So God called Paul and his companions to cross over to Greece: 'And when he had seen the vision we immediately sought to go on into Macedonia, concluding that God had called us to preach the gospel to them' (Acts 16.10).

There is virtually nothing in the letters of Paul about the surprising diversion in the itinerary. It is therefore natural to presuppose that in the first place we have Luke's view of the way that the preaching of the gospel had taken. Before his ascension Jesus is said to have spoken the following words to his disciples: 'When the Holy Spirit comes upon you, you shall receive power and be my witnesses in Jerusalem and throughout Judaea and Samaria, and to the ends of the earth' (Acts 1.8). For this reason the Spirit drove the apostles on and compelled them to go further and further away from Jerusalem and Jewish territory. Paul will not have disagreed with this view. He too saw it as his task to cross frontiers. In his letter to the community in Rome he shared his plan to travel further to Spain (Rom. 15.24). Furthermore Paul was convinced that his life had been determined by God 'from my mother's womb' (Gal. 1.15). At the beginning of his letter to the community in Thessalonica he expresses this conviction: 'For we know, brothers and sisters beloved by God, that he has chosen you; for our gospel came to you not only in word, but also in power and in the Holy Spirit and with full conviction. You know what kind of men we proved to be among you for your sake' (I Thess. 1.4–5). Thus Paul and Luke, each in his own way, expressed their belief that the Spirit of God gave direction to their lives and 'guided' the preaching of the gospel.

The community of Thessalonica

After sailing from Troas, Paul and his companions landed on the other side of the Aegean, in Neapolis in Greece, and then travelled to Philippi on the Via Egnatia, the most important east-west link in that part of the Roman empire (Acts 16.11–12). I shall consider the events during his stay in this Roman colony in the chapter in which Paul's letter to the Philippians has a central place.

From Philippi the journey continued along the Via Egnatia to Thessalonica (Acts 17.1), from of old an administrative centre and also the most important port of Macedonia, with a favourable position on a crossroads of trade routes. Acts relates that the city had a synagogue: 'And Paul went in, as was his custom, and for three weeks he argued with them from the scriptures, explaining and proving that it was necessary for Christ to suffer and rise from the dead' (Acts 17.2–3). Anyone who reads this passage closely cannot fail to note that the content of Paul's preaching is in striking agreement with the words which the risen Lord is said to have spoken to the disciples on the Emmaus road: 'Did not the Christ have to suffer this to enter into his glory?' (Luke 24.26). Jesus also spoke to his disciples later in the same spirit: 'He said, "Thus it is written, that the Christ should suffer and on the third day rise from the dead, and that repentance and forgiveness of sins should be preached in his name to all nations' (Luke 24.46–47). A comparison of the passages mentioned leads to the conclusion that the words which Paul is said to have spoken in the synagogue in Thessalonica were put into his mouth by Luke.

Whether the apostle was in fact accustomed to visit the local synagogue on the sabbath cannot be discovered from his letters. Presumably it was natural for him to do so, and we can confidently believe Luke's statements which indicate that Paul repeatedly appeared in synagogues (Acts 17.10; 18.4,19; 19.8). As yet there was no question of a schism between Judaism and Christianity. Moreover, the synagogue formed an ideal meeting place, not least for Paul, who saw it as his task to bring Gentiles into contact with the gospel of Jesus Christ.

The account in the book of Acts about the difficulties that Paul encountered, particularly in Thessalonica, is an apt illustration of his 'strategy'. It is known that the synagogues in the Diaspora were not exclusively visited by Jews. That was because the Jewish faith was very attractive to non-Jews. Some people in fact went over to Judaism in the course of time; others remained associated with the local Jewish community out of sympathy and interest. Against this background the account in the book of Acts of the dramatic event in Thessalonica is evocative and illustrative: 'And some of them were persuaded and joined Paul and Silas, as did a great many of the devout Greeks and not a few of the leading women. But the Jews were jealous, and taking some wicked fellows of the rabble, they gathered a crowd and set the city in an uproar' (Acts 17.4–5). The success of Paul's preaching among the non-Jewish visitors to the synagogue led to jealousy and even to fierce opposition to him. The consequence was that the apostle felt compelled to end his stay in Thessalonica rapidly. In the small hours he left for Beroea (Acts 17.10–12).

The first letter to the community of Thessalonica[1]

According to Acts, Paul initially expected a friendlier reception in Beroea than in Thessalonica. There too he went to the local synagogue and took the opportunity to preach his message (Acts 17.10–11). Again he had success: 'Many of them therefore believed, with not a few Greek women of high standing as well as men' (Acts 17.12). Unfortunately this idyllic situation did not last very long. After a short time the Jews in Thessalonica got wind of developments in Beroea. They did not hesitate to travel to Beroea and there too organized opposition to Paul (Acts 17.13). Again the apostle had little alternative than to travel on. Thus he eventually arrived in Athens (Acts 17.15). Considering the circumstances which led him to travel to the world city, this could be called a flight rather than a well-considered planning of his missionary activities. It is difficult to say precisely how long Paul remained in Athens. The account in Acts gives the impression that his stay was of relatively short duration (Acts 17.16–34). In the first instance he waited in this city for Silas and Timothy, who had been left behind in his rapid journey to Beroea. However, before they arrived there,

Paul travelled on to Corinth. Finally the reunion with his fellow-workers took place in the great port (Acts 18.5).

From the letter to the community of Thessalonica it seems that Paul's initial plan was to return to Macedonia as soon as possible. He regretted very much that he had not succeeded in doing this. The apostle himself gave the following striking explanation: 'We wanted to come to you – I, Paul, again and again – *but Satan hindered us*' (I Thess. 2.18). The description of the situation in Acts presumably explains how the passage in italics is to be interpreted. The opposition of the Jews from Thessalonica for the moment made it impossible for him to pay a new visit to the young Christian community there. Paul is fierce in this letter. Anxiety about the welfare of the community led him to make some very sharp statements. He identified the opposition of the Jews in Thessalonica with the work of Satan.

Finally he resigned himself to the fact that he could not come to Thessalonica in person. So he sent Timothy, 'our brother and God's servant in the gospel of Christ' (I Thess. 3.2). Timothy did what Paul himself had wanted to do with all his heart: 'to establish you in your faith and to exhort you that no one be moved by these tribulations. You yourselves know that this is to be your lot. For when we were with you we told you before-hand that we were to suffer tribulation; just as it has come to pass and as you know' (I Thess. 3.2–4). The text indicates Paul's concern for the community. He felt especially respon-sible for it. It is significant in this context that he regarded it as a child of whom he was both the mother and the father: 'We were gentle among you, like a mother cherishing her own children' (I Thess. 2.7); 'For you know, like a father with his children, we exhorted each one of you and encouraged you and charged you to lead a life worthy of God, who calls you into his own kingdom and glory' (I Thess. 2.11–12).

After a while Timothy sent optimistic reports about the community to Paul (I Thess. 3.6–10), in all probability at the beginning of Paul's stay in Corinth, which has been mentioned earlier (Acts 18.5). Paul was especially grateful for these opti-mistic reports. Evidently he was even surprised by them. That is less strange than it might seem, for two themes are central to the letter: 1. tribulations which the community suffer; and 2. confusion about the speedy coming of the Lord.

The two themes are not separate, but need to be interpreted in relation to each other. Both in his vocabulary and his view of the future, Paul shows that he is still an apocalyptist. Completely in the spirit of apocalyptic thought, he put the opposition which he met with from the Jews in the framework of the cosmic struggle between good and evil: Satan was again preventing him from coming to Thessalonica (I Thess. 2.18). He described the difficulties which he met with and which were also shared by the community as 'tribulations': 'And you became imitators of us and of the Lord, for you received the word in much tribulation, with joy inspired by the Holy Spirit' (I Thess. 1.6; cf. 3.3, 7). In both Jewish and early Christian apocalyptic literature 'tribulations' are among the lot that the pious who continue to believe in God must undergo: 'For in those days there will be such tribulation as has not been from the beginning of the creation which God created until now, and never will be' (Mark 13.19).

The following disputed passage must also be interpreted against this apocalyptic background: 'Brothers and sisters, you became imitators of the Christian communities of God which are in Judaea: for you suffered the same things from your own countrymen as they did from the Jews, who killed both the Lord Jesus and the prophets, and drove us out and displease God and oppose all men by hindering us from speaking to the Gentiles that they may be saved – so as always to fill up the measure of their sins. But God's wrath has come upon them at last' (I Thess. 2.14–16). Are these fierce, anti-Jewish words really from the pen of the *Jew* Paul? It seems to me that there is no convincing argument for regarding this passage as a later addition. These words take on meaning and significance if they are explained in the context of Paul's life and thought.[2] He is sharp, and goes a long way, but he is not 'antisemitic'. The ways of Judaism and Christianity have not yet definitively parted. Therefore his polemic is uttered *within* the limits of the Jewish tradition. Here Paul is making use of well-known traditional motifs like the murder of the prophets (Matt. 23.29–39).[3] Once we note the opposition that the apostle endured from the Jews in Thessalonica it has to be accepted that his tone is sharp. Moreover this was not the first time that Paul clashed with Jews who were opposed to his missionary activities. However, we also need to understand the attitude of the Jews who did not want to be convinced. Paul carried his past around with him all his life. After his experiences near Damascus, friends had become enemies and supporters opponents. Most of the members of the early Christian community in Jerusalem had reservations about the man whom they had learned to fear. The Jews who had admired his zeal and had collaborated with him had since then regarded him as an apostate. For these reasons they treated him with more passion than the other members of the early Christian community. The polemical tone of the passage can be explained, but it is certainly not to be praised. The apostle never again expressed himself as sharply as this.

For an apocalyptist like Paul, the current 'tribulations' were the convincing proof that the great break in history, the definitive intervention of God, was at hand. It is typical of Paul's 'new' thought that in this letter he interprets this great moment in the history of the world above all 'christologically': 'Jesus who delivers us from the wrath to come' (I Thess. 1.10); 'For what is our hope or joy or crown of boasting before our Lord Jesus at his coming? Is it not you?' (I Thess. 2.19); 'So that he may establish your hearts unblameable before our God and Father, at the coming of our Lord Jesus with all his saints' (I Thess. 3.13); 'For this we declare to you by the word of the Lord, that we who are alive, who are left until the coming of the Lord, shall not precede those who have fallen asleep' (I Thess. 4.15); 'May the God of peace himself sanctify you wholly; and may your spirit and soul and body be kept sound and blameless at the coming of our Lord Jesus Christ' (I Thess. 5.23).

Clearly Paul had succeeded in communicating his tense apocalyptic expectation to the members of the community during his stay there. His letter makes it clear that in so doing he had sometimes thoroughly confused the community and had raised more questions than he had given answers. For the apostle, this did not mean that he 'de-apocalypticized' his preaching. He did not want to do that, nor was he able to. He was an apocalyptist and he did not deny his message: 'For you yourselves know that the day of the Lord will come like a thief in the night. When people say "There is peace and security," then sudden destruction will come upon them as travail comes upon a woman with child, and there will be no escape' (I Thess. 5.2–3).[4]

Considering the questions which have already required our attention, it should be tentatively concluded that the earliest letter of Paul's that we possess is somewhat disappointing. The work contains little information about the situation within the community of Thessalonica. Theologically the apostle could be accused of a degree of one-sidedness. Has the apocalyptic vision of the future made such an impact on the members of the community that other topics are not discussed or are relegated to second place as being less important? The composition of the Christian community in Thessalonica cannot have been very different from that in other cities in Asia Minor, Macedonia and Greece: a mixed company of men and women of different backgrounds, Diaspora Jews and Gentiles who had perhaps been involved with the local synagogue as 'godfearers'. Was the significance of the Torah also being discussed in Thessalonica? How did the integration of the various 'blood groups' go? This kind of question will also have occupied people there. Paul writes little or nothing about such issues.

In a discussion of Paul's 'christology', this letter plays only a marginal role. The apocalyptic expectation is central, and only in that framework are some remarks made which can shed some light on the apostle's thought about the significance of Jesus Christ. His starting point was the nearness of the 'wrath'. Thanks to the apocalyptic vision that he had on the way to Damascus, he had become convinced that he no longer need to fear this 'wrath'. Aroused, he summed up his hope briefly as follows: '. . . and to wait for his son from heaven, whom he raised from the dead, Jesus, who delivers us from the wrath to come' (I Thess. 1.10).

It is reasonable to ask how Paul imagined this deliverance. In the text quoted above, he does not look to the past, but forward to the near future. Jesus will save us from the 'wrath' because we may expect him from heaven. His coming is near, because he will come like a thief in the night (I Thess. 5.2). God's wrath certainly cannot be averted, but not everyone will be affected by it: 'For God has not destined us for wrath, but to obtain salvation through our Lord Jesus Christ, *who died for us so that whether we wake or sleep we might live with him*' (I Thess. 5.9–10). The clause in italics adds a new thought to what has gone before. Through his coming Jesus will save us from the 'wrath', but he has also 'died for us'. Earlier in the letter Paul wrote a sentence which contains a comparable thought: 'For since we believe that Jesus died and rose again, even so, through Jesus, God will bring with him those who have fallen asleep' (I Thess. 4.14). In death and resurrection Jesus has 'gone before' believers. So he also saves from the 'wrath'. Because Jesus has 'gone before' us, Paul can also write that he has died 'for us'. It can be inferred from these summary christological statements that the apostle had not (yet?) developed any 'doctrine' in which the thought of representation or vicarious suffering stood at the centre.

Paul did not write a second letter to Thessalonica which has been preserved. The canonical second letter to the Thessalonians is not by him. An anonymous author at the end of the first century drafted a writing which had to resemble a letter of Paul in order to make the first letter to the Thessalonians 'innocuous'. We may be grateful that this unknown Christian only partly succeeded in his aim.

7

Correspondence with the community in Corinth (I)

From Corinth to Ephesus

Acts reports that Paul lived for eighteen months in the port of Corinth (Acts 18.11). During that stay, after some time he again came into conflict with the Jews. They brought him before the judgment seat of Gallio, the Roman proconsul of Achaea. Their accusation ran: 'This man is persuading men to worship God unlawfully' (Acts 18.13). According to the Jews in Corinth Paul was making efforts to disseminate religion without 'law', i.e. without Torah. The accusation does not sound strange to the readers of Acts. Around ten chapters earlier it was related that Stephen was accused of a similar offence: 'We have heard him speak blasphemous words against Moses and God' (Acts 6.11) – 'this man constantly speaks blasphemous words against this holy place and the law' (Acts 6.13). Stephen is stoned as one who transgresses the commandments of the Torah (Acts 7.1–53). The following sentence is indelibly stamped on the memory of all readers of Acts: 'and Saul was consenting to his execution' (Acts 8.11). The same man is now being accused in Corinth by Jewish activists – 'zealots', as Paul once was – for following in Stephen's footsteps. Did they have right on their side? Some verses later the author of Acts gives a surprising answer.

There was no verdict in Corinth, for the simple reason that Gallio refused to pronounce judgment in a matter which he thought did not concern him and in which moreover he was not particularly interested (Acts 18.12–17). This Gallio is particularly important for the life of Paul. From an inscription found in Delphi we can infer that he lived in Corinth from May 51 to May 52. The conflict with the Jews came to a climax at the beginning of Gallio's residence in the city. That would mean that Paul travelled from Corinth in the summer of 51, in which case he must have arrived eighteen months earlier, at the beginning of the year 50.[1]

The events in Corinth were not isolated. From the moment that Paul set foot in Greece, his preaching provoked opposition. In Philippi he ended up in prison (Acts 16.4–40), the Jews in Thessalonica forced him to leave the city; and that also happened in Beroea (Acts 17.1–14); in Athens the philosophers on the Areopagus either reacted with scorn or were uninterested (Acts 17.15–34); and in Corinth he again came up against fierce opposition from the synagogue. This time, however the description in the book of Acts does not give the impression that Paul departed rapidly. He said farewell to his sympathizers 'after staying many days longer' (Acts 18.18). Nevertheless, I find it difficult to escape the impression that the hostile attitude of Jewish opponents was the reason for Paul's change of plans. That happened to him often. It has already proved earlier that his itinerary was not firmly fixed. Repeatedly he had to adapt it, and he saw himself compelled to improvise, because he was confronted with unforeseen circumstances. What was the local situation? Would he receive hospitality? Was his preaching successful? Was he opposed by Jews or by others who interpreted his appearance as a threat? The author of the book of Acts holds the Spirit responsible for the detours in the itinerary (Acts 16.6–7). In his letter to the community of Thessalonica Paul suggested that his plans were sometimes thwarted by evil powers; thus it was Satan who had prevented him from visiting this community a second time (I Thess. 4.18).

From Corinth Paul travelled eastwards by ship. Now he was accompanied by Priscilla and Aquila (Acts 18.18). He had got to know this couple at the beginning of his stay in the Greek port: 'There he met a Jew named Aquila, a native of Pontus, lately come from Italy with his wife Priscilla, because Claudius had commanded all the Jews to leave Rome' (Acts 18.1).[2] In the work of the Roman historian Suetonius (75–150) the following statement may be found about the 'edict' of the emperor Claudius (41–54): 'He (= Claudius) drove the Jews out of Rome because they constantly caused disorders on the instigation of Chrestus.' Who was this Chrestus? There is some consensus among New Testament scholars over the answer to this question. The name Chrestus (= the good, a customary name for a slave) will have been a corruption of Christ (= the anointed). The mistake is both understandable and significant. In the Graeco-Roman world an 'anointed' played no role in a religious context. If the unrest among the Jews in Rome was in fact caused by differences of opinion over the question whether Jesus was the Messiah, we need not be surprised that the Roman historian thought that he could attribute the cause of the dispute to a slave who was perhaps called Chrestus, as were so many slaves at that time. The confusion of names shows something of the social conditions within the Roman empire. Crucifixion was regarded as an extraordinary humiliating punishment. Those who might boast of being a Roman citizen – like Paul (Acts 16.36–39) – were not executed in such a brutal way. That was almost exclusively the fate of slaves and rebels.

The emperor Claudius probably issued his edict against the Jews in 49.[3] A short time later, at the beginning of 50, Paul met Aquila and Priscilla in Corinth. This was a happy 'coincidence', which had favourable consequences for the preaching of the gospel. The difficulties that Paul had experienced from the Jewish side successively in Philippi, Thessalonica and Beroea made him decide to travel via Athens to Corinth. The edict of Claudius forced Aquila and Priscilla to leave the city of Rome and they too sought their salvation in the great Greek port. According to the Acts of the Apostles Paul made friends with the couple. He lived with them. The bond was good and close. They were kindred spirits and colleagues: 'And because he was of the same trade he stayed with them, and they worked, for by trade they were tentmakers' (Acts 18.3). It is striking that no remark can be found anywhere from which it could be inferred that Priscilla and Aquila were converted to Christianity by Paul's preaching. They were clearly already followers of Jesus Christ. Evidently Christian preaching had reached Rome at a relatively early stage.[4] When Paul approached the city almost ten years later, after many wanderings and vicissitudes he was welcomed by members of the Christian community: 'When Paul saw them he thanked God and took courage' (Acts 28.15).

Paul's journey from Corinth eastwards was very soon interrupted for a short time by a mysterious interlude. Acts relates that the company took ship, 'after he (= Paul) had cut his hair at Cenchreae, for he had taken a vow' (Acts 18.18).[5] An extended description of the Nazirate can be found in the book of Numbers. Here is the passage: 'When either a man or a woman makes a special vow, the vow of a Nazirite, to separate himself to the Lord, he shall separate himself from wine and strong drink; he shall drink no vinegar made from wine or strong drink, and shall not drink any juice of grapes or eat grapes, fresh or dried. *All the days of his separation no razor shall come upon his head; until the time is completed for which he separates himself to the Lord, he shall be holy; he shall let the locks of hair of his head grow long*' (Num. 6.1–5)

Did Paul take such a vow? There is no reason to answer this question negatively. He had enjoyed a Jewish upbringing and from his youth was familiar with scripture and tradition. The apocalyptic vision that he had on the way to Damascus opened his eyes and made him a follower of Jesus Christ. Nevertheless Paul remained a Jew body and soul. He lived in two worlds, and in all his thinking and creativity tried to link the two worlds together. Scripture and tradition did not lose their authority. Some commandments of the Torah proved stumbling blocks, but for the 'Christian' Paul, too, the Torah as such was a source of inspiration and joy in life. He had grown up in this spiritual world and he devoted himself with all his strength to preserving it. Even afterwards he was not ashamed that he had been passionately zealous 'for the traditions of my forefathers' (Gal. 1.14).

Against this background it is not strange that Paul was inspired by the custom described in Numbers. Did he need it because in Greece in particular he had come into conflict with Jews several times? Did he also want to show by his outward appearance – long hair, behaviour, the refusal of drink, etc. – that he was still observing the commandments of the Torah? We do not know for certain, but there is hardly any other explanation for his behaviour. The report in Acts that Paul had his hair cut in Cenchreae because of a vow is strange. Why there and not in Jerusalem (cf. Acts 21.23)? The regulation in the book of Numbers is that in special circumstances it is possible to end the vow prematurely: 'if a man very near to the Nazirite dies very suddenly beside him, and he defiles his consecrated head, then he shall shave his head on the day of his cleansing; on the seventh day he shall cleanse it' (Num. 6.9). Was that perhaps the reason? For lack of adequate information, it is impossible to give a satisfactory answer to this question. From the conclusion of Paul's letter to the community in Rome we may infer that Paul's stay in Cenchreae was meaningful for other reasons. There he met a woman who was dear to him: 'I commend to you our sister Phoebe, a deacon of the church at Cencreae, that you may receive her in the Lord as befits the saints, and may help her in whatever she may require from you, for she has been a helper of many and of myself as well,' he wrote later at the end of the letter to the Romans (Rom. 16.1).

How did the journey continue after this strange stop? The author of Acts relates the sequel in summary statements. Paul travelled by sea eastwards from Corinth, with Antioch in Syria as his final destination. On the way he paid a short visit to Ephesus. The biblical text gives us too little information to get a good picture of the situation. Paul travelled on, but Priscilla and Aquila did not accompany him further on his journey. One can only guess at the reasons. There is no mention of disagreement or dispute in this case. In his letters Paul wrote positively about this friendly couple. He called them 'my fellow-workers in Christ Jesus, who risked their necks for my life, to whom not only I but also all the communities of the Gentiles give thanks' (Rom. 16.3–4). Through their dedication to the gospel they had gathered a house community around them (Rom. 16.5; I Cor. 16.19).

Paul's second missionary journey came to an end when he landed in Caesarea and went from there to Antioch (Acts 18.22). The author of Acts pays remarkably little attention to this episode from Paul's life. The text raises many questions. Who accompanied him on this part of the journey? Why did Paul not go up to Jerusalem? Did he not think it important to make contacts with the original community and the first apostles? The author of Acts does not make it possible for us to produce a satisfying reconstruction of events. Paul stayed 'some time' in Antioch and then 'departed and went from place to place through the region of Galatia and Phrygia, strengthening all the disciples' (Acts 18.23). Thus began his third missionary journey.

Tensions in Ephesus

In the first chapters of Acts an idyllic picture is painted of the original community in Jerualem: 'the company of those who believed were of one heart and soul' (Acts 4.32). Very soon, however, it becomes clear that even Luke cannot conceal the fact that forces were at work within the early Christian community which threatened its unity (Acts 6.1–7).

We assume that Paul began his third missionary journey in 52/53. Around twenty years had passed since the death of Jesus on the cross. Much had happened and much had changed in this time. The Christian faith had crossed the frontiers of Jewish territory and Jewish tradition. The successful preaching of the gospel by Paul and his fellow-workers, by Peter, Barnabas, Thomas and others, was beginning to bear fruit. But this success also had its shadow side. Paul inspired men and women, but his person was controversial. He was not accustomed to concealing his opinion. He had not only a sharp mind but an equally sharp tongue. He could bind people to himself, but he also made many opponents. His past continued to pursue him. He was not beyond criticism and posed a stumbling block in his contacts both with Jews and with members of the early Christian community. That was to an important degree due to his earlier way of life as a 'zealot'. Many people in the early Christian community found it very difficult to receive him in love (Acts 9.26). For the majority of the Jewish community he had become a deserter and an apostate.[6]

During this third missionary journey Paul encountered new developments within the early Christian communities: internal tensions as the result of differences of insight into theological and ethical themes. We need not be surprised at this course of events. Even in the initial phase of Christianity it can already be said that the tradition of faith was variegated. Paul was a Diaspora Jew, and so too was Barnabas. They knew the world outside Jewish territory. Men like Peter and James had a different background. They had grown up in Galilee. All brought along their personal experiences and insights when they became followers of Jesus Christ. It is not strange that conflicts arose – as between Paul and Peter in Antioch (Gal. 2.11–14). Even the compromise which was resolved on at the meeting of apostles in Jerusalem (Acts 15) did not put a final end to the discussion. The spread of the 'Jewish' gospel in the pagan world caused new problems, and sowed confusion and division within the early churches. From what follows it will emerge that it was these very tensions and conflicts which forced Paul to make his views and insights known by letter.

The Acts of the Apostles tells a story which illustrates this admirably. At the end of his second missionary journey Paul paid a short visit to Ephesus. After his departure, 'Apollos, a Jew from Alexandria, an eloquent man, well versed in the scriptures' (Acts 18.24) arrived in the same city. Apollos regarded himself as a follower of Jesus, but he had little factual knowledge (Acts 18.25). Priscilla and Aquila took pity on him and 'expounded to him the way of God more accurately' (Acts 18.26). The passage about Apollos again shows that within the span of still less than twenty years the Christian faith had spread with amazing speed along the coasts of the Mediterranean: Antioch in Syria, Rome in Italy and Alexandria in Egypt.[7] Paul was preceded by numerous unknown preachers.

After a while Apollos left the city of Ephesus and went from Asia Minor to Greece. How did the learned Jew from Alexandria fare after that? Passages in Paul's letters indicate that the author of Acts has again been led astray by the desire to present the past in rosier colours than it really had. Apollos had gained so much support in the community of Corinth that he was put at the same level as the best-known apostles. Paul writes: 'What I mean is that each one of you says, "I belong to Paul", or "I belong to Apollos", or "I belong to Cephas", or "I belong to Christ!"' (I Cor. 1.12; 3.22). Paul protests sharply against these parties (I Cor. 3.4–8). He did so while Apollos was with him in Ephesus (I Cor. 4.6). Despite repeated urging by Paul, Apollos did not prove immediately ready to return from Ephesus to Corinth (I Cor. 16.12). From all this it appears that he was an influential and authoritative man who was capable of winning men to himself and who was accustomed to go his own ways and make his own decisions.

During his third missionary journey Paul arrived in Ephesus, while Apollos had already gone to Greece and was meanwhile active in Corinth (Acts 19.1). This time too Paul went through the regions of Galatia and Phrygia (Acts 18.23). There he gradually found himself on familiar ground. His second stay in Ephesus lasted for some time. In the first instance Acts reports that Paul appeared openly in the local synagogue for three months (Acts 19.8). Gradually difficulties also arose there. They led to Paul leaving and holding meetings in the hall of Tyrannus. The situation continued. Acts speaks of a period of two years (Acts 19.9–10). This report is striking, because it gives the impression that the tensions between the synagogue and the Christian community in Corinth had become so great that an actual schism had developed. This had its consequences. Paul again got into more difficulties (Acts 19.13–20). Although he had plans to travel further and cross over to Macedonia and

Greece, he stayed in Ephesus and sent two of his colleagues, Timothy and Erastus, on in advance (Acts 19.22).

The author of Acts forces his readers to read between the lines. Behind some of the reports there is a 'world' of tensions and conflicts. Paul faced a difficult dilemma. He wanted to travel on. He had received reports from Corinth which made him fear the worst. His presence seemed urgently needed. However, the situation in Ephesus was such that he thought that he could not abandon the local community at that moment. After mature consideration he remained and sent two of his colleagues on ahead. From what happened later it will prove that this was a sensible decision and that both men were able to do good work. At the end of the first letter to the community of Corinth there is a passage which provides some clarification: 'I will visit you after passing through Macedonia, for I intend to pass through Macedonia, and perhaps I will stay with you or even spend the winter, so that you may speed me on my journey, wherever I go. For I do not want to see you now just in passing; I hope to spend some time with you, if the Lord permits. But I will stay in Ephesus until Pentecost, for a wide door for effective work has opened to me and there are many adversaries' (I Cor. 16.5–9). Paul wanted to go to Corinth, but he could not leave Ephesus yet, since he had adversaries there . . . Well, meanwhile he had also got them in Corinth!

The community of Corinth

Paul knew Corinth well. During the second missionary journey he had lived and worked there for eighteen months (Acts 18.11). To understand the content of his letters to the community we need to form a picture of the city. Here it immediately becomes evident that there could be a world of difference in the surroundings in which the gospel was preached in the initial phase of church history. With a single exception, Jesus remained within the frontiers of Jewish territory. The sphere of his work was limited: the area around the Sea of Galilee. There were a number of small towns here: Capernaum, Tiberias, Magdala,

Chorazin, Bethsaida. The population consisted of Jews and non-Jews. Aramaic was spoken, and also Greek. The Gospels suggest that Jesus did not feel called to give his full attention to the salvation of *non*-Jews. Inspired by his apocalyptic vision, Paul opted for another course. For him as a Diaspora Jew it was less difficult to cross the frontiers of Jewish territory. His journeys through Asia Minor and Greece brought him to great Greek Hellenistic cities.[8] If Jews lived there, they formed a small minority. This situation was not alien to Paul. His birthplace Tarsus had such a profile. So he will not have been completely surprised by what he saw in cities like Thessalonica, Philippi, Athens and Corinth. He had seen a great deal, but it is not rash to suppose that it was the last of these cities which made the most impression on him.

In the time of Paul Corinth was a large and very busy city.[9] Its walls surrounded an area which was two and a half times the size of Athens. Its situation can be described as ideal. Corinth lay at a crossroads of important trade routes, both by land and by sea. Because Corinth had two important harbours, it was also a very cosmopolitan city, a melting pot of races, religions and philosophical schools. Excavations have shown that in this period there was also a Jewish synagogue, the place where a small Jewish minority met.

Corinth was destroyed by the Romans in 146 BC in revenge for a vigorous rebellion by the population against the Roman expansionist drive. A beginning was made on the rebuilding of the city on the orders of Julius Caesar in 44 BC. In the following decades, Corinth experienced a period of great economic prosperity. When Paul was living there, he could have seen the consequences of the prosperity with his own eyes: wealth and luxury, numerous imposing buildings and temples. His stay lasted eighteen months. He clearly felt at home in the great port. Perhaps Corinth reminded him of Philippi. Both cities had been founded as Roman colonies.

Corinth was big, varied and colourful. The ports gave the city status and international fame. In addition Corinth was the administrative centre for the province of Achaea (in fact the whole of southern Greece). Moreover it offered its inhabitants and visitors a wide range of religious opportunities. We know that it had a Jewish synagogue. This building will certainly not have been striking. However, some impressive temples dedicated to the Greek goddess Aphrodite attracted attention.[10] Historians from this time speak without reserve about large numbers of prostitutes, including male prostitutes, who worked in these temples. The phenomenon of temple prostitution was customary in the ancient word and was regarded as unfashionable or immoral only by a few. So we need not be surprised that Paul writes at length about 'immorality' in his letters to the community of Corinth (I Cor. 5–7). How radical a change to his life did a pagan have to make if he wanted to become a Christian? Was he forbidden from that moment once and for all to go to the temple prostitutes?

More can be said. Corinth was not just a busy port and an important administrative centre. Its inhabitants came from many regions. On leaving their birthplaces they had not left behind their ideas of God and religious customs, as they had left behind hearth and home. Their faith accompanied them on their journey and formed the basis of their existence in the city which they had chosen as their new home. The consequence was that in Corinth there was a wide range of religious opportunities. The Greek goddess Aphrodite was worshipped, and alongside her also the goddess Isis, who had an important place in the Egyptian pantheon. It is said of Isis that 'she gave the same power to women as to men',[11] a striking expression, which could explain why women do not seem to have wanted to play a subordinate role in the Christian community of Corinth (I Cor. 11.2–16; 14.34–36).

Naturally adherents of the same religions sought one another. They joined together and formed communities which met at appointed times. In Corinth there was a great variety of such religious 'associations'. As well as differences there were also similarities. Archaeological discoveries have shown that the members usually met one another at communal cultic meals. Readers especially of Paul's first letter to the community of Corinth know that these customs also caused problems within the early Christian community (I Cor. 8–11).

Corinth had much to offer not only its inhabitants but also its visitors. It was a busy city, and much money could be earned through this business. The consequences were predictable and even became visible in the Christian community. Some people lacked nothing, whereas others lived in poverty. The blatant contrasts between rich and poor posed a direct threat to the unity of the community in Corinth, as will emerge later.

How many letters did Paul write to Corinth?

From the text quoted earlier in the last chapter of the first letter it can be inferred that Paul was living in Ephesus when the correspondence with Corinth had reached an important phase (I Cor. 16.5–9). At all events it is certain that the 'canonical' first letter was not really the first letter which Paul wrote to the community of Corinth. That is evident from the following passage: 'I wrote to you in my letter not to associate with immoral people' (I Cor. 5.9). The discussion had clearly already been begun some time earlier, precisely when we cannot say. Making and maintaining contacts between Ephesus and Corinth was no great problem. There were intensive trade relations between the two cities. Paul travelled by ship from Corinth to Ephesus and later Apollos went in the opposite direction (Acts 18.24–26; 19.1). While Paul was staying in Ephesus, disquieting reports reached him about problems within the early Christian community in Corinth. We need not look far for the causes. Temple prostitution was 'normal'. But was it also normal for members of the Christian community? At all events, in that earlier letter Paul will have discussed 'immorality'.

It is possible that this letter has not been completely lost. In the second 'canonical' letter to Corinth there is a passage which does not fit into the argument well. Paul is arguing for 'room', for himself and for others (II Cor. 6.13; II Cor. 7.2). Suddenly he interrupts this argument and takes up a completely different subject: 'Do not be mismated with unbelievers. For what partnership have righteousness and iniquity? Or what fellowships has light with darkness? What accord has Christ with Beliar? Or what has a believer in common with an unbeliever? What agreement has the temple of God with idols? For we are the temple of the living God' (II Cor. 6.14–16). In this sharp passage Paul shows that he is not a man who strives for reconciliation and unity. He bluntly argues for a radical 'division of the spirits'. In a later letter he will make more qualifications. Reactions from the community made him see that he had to moderate his standpoint. Some members of the community were married to 'unbelievers'. Did the statement 'be not mismated with unbelievers' mean that they had to abandon their partners? Paul hastens to explain that they need not draw this consequence from his words (I Cor. 7.12–16).

The sentences quoted show unambiguously that the apostle was a 'dualistic' thinker. In this passage an apocalyptist is speaking who has divided the world into two camps: light or darkness, good or evil, elect or lost, truth or lie, God or Satan. There is no 'twilight zone' in this radical thinking. Paul did not stand alone in this. The fragment of his letter to the community of Corinth shows a striking degree of affinity with notions of the Essenes from Qumran. Their view too was in principle 'dualistic'. They had turned their back on the world and withdrawn into the wilderness. Although they were priests, they avoided the temple in Jerusalem and regarded their own community as the new Jerusalem. Paul later drew this line of thought through the Christian community.[12]

In his summary of fundamental oppositions the apostle not only set light against darkness but also Christ against Beliar. This is striking. The figure of Beliar/Belial does not occur elsewhere in the letter of Paul. However, it does occur in the Qumran writings. Beliar/Belial was one of the 'eschatological enemies' of the Essenes.[13] Paul knew this expectation and brought it up to date in his letter to the community of Corinth. So he created an 'anti-Christ'. Now does this mean that the apostle was dependent on Qumran, or that the passage cited inexplicably found its way into a letter by Paul as an 'erratic Essene block'? It seems to me unnecessary to draw such far-reaching conclusions. The Qumran community deliberately chose isolation, but that does not mean that its ideas were so esoteric that they could not be found anywhere else than in their own writings. Pharisees and Essenes were in a sense kindred spirits. Paul was a Pharisee. He studied in Jerusalem for some time and with some pride regarded himself as a passionate zealot for the Torah. When he was informed about the difficulties in Corinth, in the first instance he opted for an unambiguous standpoint. In his desire for clarity he was not afraid to speak 'dualistically', in the spirit of the 'separated' Qumran community. From the sequel to the discussion it will prove that such 'sectarian' arguments were not welcomed by everyone in a cosmopolitan city like Corinth.

Paul and the Corinthian community engaged in an intensive correspondence.[14] That was necessary because there were many problems and emotions were running high. As an illustration, here is a passage from the second 'canonical letter': 'But I call God to witness against me – it was to spare you that I refrained from coming to Corinth. Not that we lord it over your faith; we work with you for joy, for you stand firm in your faith. For I made up my mind not to pay you another painful visit' (II Cor. 1.23–2.1). Paul would have liked to travel to Corinth again, but he did not think it sensible to go. An early visit ended up in great disappointment. This was the 'painful visit'. He wanted to spare himself, and also the community, a repetition. In this situation the apostle again took up his pen and wrote an emotional letter, which alas was no more successful in improving personal relations. Shortly after the passage quoted above Paul mentions openly and honestly the dramatic circumstances in which he had written: 'I wrote to you out of much affliction and anguish of heart and with many tears, not to cause you pain but to let you know the abundant love that I have for you' (II Cor. 2.4). He thought this important, because later he came back to it once again: 'For even if I caused you pain with my letter, I do not regret it (though I did regret it); for I see that that letter grieved you, though only for a while. As it is, I rejoice, not because you were grieved, but because you were grieved into repenting' (II Cor. 7.8–9). Relations were thoroughly damaged: a visit that failed and a letter that did more harm than good. This letter was written before the second 'canonical' letter, but cannot possibly be identical with the first 'canonical' letter to Corinth. That writing does not give the impression that it was written 'with tears'.

The course of events can now be reconstructed as follows. During his stay in Ephesus Paul wrote a letter to Corinth in which he discussed the problem of 'immorality' . This letter is lost, but it is possible that a fragment of it has been preserved in II Cor. 6.14–7.1. The community reacted to this letter. It presented Paul with a series of questions, and probably also made it clear to him that his radical viewpoints were not appreciated by everyone. Paul now began really to think and conceived an extensive reply: the first letter to the Corinthians. The effect must have disappointed him, for the letter went down badly in Corinth and he received unfavourable reactions. Thereupon Paul travelled from Ephesus to Corinth, with the negative result mentioned above. The author of Acts is silent about this 'interim visit', and that does not surprise us. After his return to Ephesus Paul again resolved to write a letter. Meanwhile emotions had risen. He indeed wrote 'with tears'.

The 'tearful letter' has not been preserved as a whole. But we can discover the content of at least part of it. In all probability it is even contained in the New Testament, where it functions as the concluding chapter of the second 'canonical' letter (II Cor. 10–13). It is impossible to say how it got there. Any reader of II Corinthians can see that this possibility is worth considering. To begin with, Paul writes calmly and is in control. At the beginning of the tenth chapter his tone suddenly changes radically. He becomes sarcastic and speaks out fiercely against his opponents. He is so carried away with his emotions that he finds it difficult to control himself.

Titus brought the 'tearful' letter to Corinth. His mission had more effect than Paul's unsuccessful 'interim visit'. The mood in the community of Corinth improved. After Paul could leave his imprisonment in Ephesus, he went to Macedonia. There he met Titus, who brought with him positive reports from Corinth. In Macedonia Paul finally wrote the second 'canonical' letter to prepare for his visit.

To conclude this section it is worth pausing for a moment to consider the role that individual colleagues of Paul played in the conflict. Paul's own correspondence did not bring the conflict to an end. During his stay in Ephesus he began to make plans to travel further: 'Now after these events Paul resolved in the spirit to pass through Macedonia and Achaea (= Corinth) and go to Jerusalem, saying, "After I have been there I must also see Rome." And having sent into Macedonia two of his helpers, Timothy and Erastus, he himself stayed in Asia for a while' (Acts 19.21–22). In his first 'canonical' letter Paul discloses that he deliberately sent Timothy to Corinth: 'That is why I sent to you Timothy, my beloved and faithful child in the Lord, to remind you of my ways in Christ, as I teach them everywhere in every community. Some are arrogant, as though I were not coming to you' (I Cor. 4.17–18).

Timothy's mission did not have the success envisaged. It can be inferred from the second 'canonical' letter that Paul himself then travelled to Corinth. Also without success, it seems. Thereupon he resolved for the moment not to pay any further visit to the city so as not to provoke his opponents needlessly (II Cor. 1.23–2.1). However, contact between Paul and the community was not broken off for good. Paul wrote his 'tearful letter'. After his departure from Ephesus he met up with his colleague Titus in Macedonia, who brought him favourable news (II Cor. 2.12–13; 7.6–7). Evidently the 'tearful letter' had had a favourable effect, and perhaps so had Titus' visit.

The Christian community of Corinth

During his second missionary journey Paul had lived in Corinth for eighteen months. He knew the city well and during that time he will also have got to know many people. He had worked there successfully. A Christian community had come into being which seemed to be viable. How large that community was is impossible to say. In a cosmopolitan port like Corinth it will hardly have been conspicuous: one of the many religious communities in which the city was so rich. After Paul's departure others had continued the work. Apollos belonged to this group (Acts 19.1).

Honesty compels one to concede that the historian is virtually groping in the dark. Little can be said with certainty about the composition of the Christian community in Corinth. The city had a synagogue, but we do not know how large the Jewish community was at that time. The book of Acts relates that Crispus, the ruler of the synagogue, came to believe and so did a certain Titus Justus. Two things are said about him: he 'feared God' – in other words he was a pagan who felt attracted to the Jewish faith – and he lived next to the synagogue (Acts 18.7–8). Considering the population of Corinth, it would not be wrong to suggest that the Christian community was a mixed one, both Jews and pagans, and in addition with great differences within the latter group; there were pagans who had already been attracted long before by faith in the God of Israel and who felt a tie to the local synagogue, and there were pagans who lacked this 'preparation'. It seems probable that the composition of the community in Corinth will not have differed greatly from that of other communities in Asia Minor and Greece.

One thing become very clear from the two 'canonical' letters: the community at Corinth did not form a unity. Already at the beginning of his first letter Paul states this problem emphatically: 'I appeal to you, brothers and sisters, by the name of our Lord Jesus Christ, that all of you agree and that there be no dissensions among you, but that you be united in the same mind and the same judgment. For it has been reported to me by Chloe's people that there is quarrelling among you, my brothers and sisters. What I mean is that each one of you says, "I belong to Paul", or "I belong to Cephas", or "I belong to Christ" ' (I Cor. 1.10–12). Paul is very concerned about that lack of unity. He repeatedly touches on the theme (I Cor. 3.1–9; 10.23–11.1; 11.17–34). With all his creativity he sought images and ideas which could underline the need to form a close unity (I Cor. 12.12–31).

Anyone who has spent some time looking at the composition of the population of Corinth will not be surprised at this lack of unity within the Christian community. How could people with such different social and religious backgrounds ever form a community? It was impossible for such unity to come about in a few years. Decades are needed for such a process, and perhaps even different generations. The community included Jews who had visited the synagogue regularly from their youth. The commandments of the Torah were central to their lives and they regarded temple prostitution as an abominable consequence of the worship of idols. By contrast, other members of the Christian community – both men and women – had until recently thought it normal at particular times to pay a visit to a temple of Aphrodite and on these occasions to have sexual intercourse with one of the many prostitutes. Within a relatively short time both groups had become part of one community: the one regarded temple prostitution as quite reprehensible and condemned it from the bottom of their hearts, whereas for the other it was a religious custom which they had never previously thought offensive.

There were also oppositions in the social sphere. Corinth was experiencing a period of prosperity and some were profiting from it more than others. It was inevitable that differences between rich and poor should penetrate the Christian community. They threatened its unity and put its ongoing existence at risk. Paul's eyes were open to his danger. He reacted sharply and emotionally. That is evident not least from the passage in which he criticizes the irregularities during the celebration of the 'Lord's Supper'. In order to give force to his words he refers back to an old, venerable tradition: 'I myself received from the Lord the tradition which in turn I have handed on to you' (I Cor. 11.23).

The content of the first letter to Corinth

Paul faced a difficult task. The reports which reached him from Corinth made him anxious. However, he was in Ephesus, and it was impossible for him to make the long journey to Corinth immediately. He resolved to write a letter, as he had done earlier (I Cor. 5.9). In that letter he had discussed 'immorality', but evidently without much success. The new questions which reached him largely centred on the same theme. That was not surprising, since, as we have already noted, the community of Corinth was in an extremely complicated situation. Opinions were divided, especially over the question whether 'immorality' was acceptable. Paul will have been aware that he had to discuss a controversial question. Whatever opinion he defended, he could reckon on opposition. In fact that also applied to the other points that were put to him (I Cor. 7.1): questions about marriage and divorce, confusion over eating meat offered to idols, his apostolate, the place of women within the community, disorders during the celebration of the Lord's Supper and other disorders during the meetings of the community, and finally belief in the resurrection of the dead.

The questions which reached Paul from Corinth mainly determined the content of his letter. It is worth pausing for a moment over this. It gives us some insight into the way that the apostle worked. In church history and the history of dogma his writings have gained the status of theological treatises, the first products of a systematic reflection on Christian faith, which have become the basis for Christian dogmatics. The result was that in the long run it was forgotten that Paul had written *real* letters. He corresponded with communities in Asia Minor, Greece and Italy. They presented their problems to him, orally or in writing, and he reacted to them, sometimes by letter, sometimes by sending one of his colleagues, and once he himself resolved to go personally to see what the situation was and so put things in order.

Because Paul wrote real letters, it is not surprising that his writings prove to be largely conditioned by time and place. He answered questions about concrete and topical problems. The original readers will have been grateful to him for this, even if they did not agree with everything that he wrote in them. In the course of time this advantage turned into a disadvantage. For later generations Paul's letters were increasingly writings from a distant and grey past. The problems discussed in them were no longer their problems. Society changed, and there were far-reaching changes even within the Christian community. Old questions disappeared and new ones appeared. But at an early stage of church history Paul's writings became authoritative, and they were included in the canon of the New Testament without much opposition. That produced a marvellous paradox: letters conditioned by place and time were given eternal validity. Today, many centuries later, we still read his letters, though we can no longer accept his view of things like marriage, sexuality and the place of women in both the community or society, nor do we want to. We are confronted with questions which are no longer relevant to us and are therefore hardly of any interest: circumcision, eating meat offered in sacrifices and temple prostitution.

Paul's first letter to the community of Corinth is largely conditioned by time and place. Ethics is central. In both exegetical and systematic literature it is not unusual to make a comparison between Paul's two longest letters: I Corinthians and his letter to the community in Rome. Both letters have no less than sixteen chapters. Such a comparison almost always comes out to the disadvantage of I Corinthians.[15] The consequence is that everyone in search of Paul's theology is inclined to concentrate on the letter to the community of Rome, in the expectation that they will find more to their purpose there than in the writing with which we are concerned at the moment. Ethical questions are central to I Corinthians. By contrast, the letter to the community of Rome was not to limit itself to an extensive discussion of problems bound up with a particular time and place. In that writing Paul is said to have left us his theological 'testament'. Indeed, it is said to be no longer conditioned by place and time but to cross the frontiers of contextuality and as such to form a firm basis for systematic reflection on the Christian faith.

However customary these views may be, there is reason to treat them with some scepticism. In the course of church history, theology has been divided into a number of disciplines, like biblical criticism, systematic theology and practical theology. Then within systematic theology a distinction is made between the history of dogma, dogmatics and ethics. From the present and the past we can learn that the letter to the Romans has been primarily of interest to dogmatic theologians. They are less interested in the content of I Corinthians. The extensive ethical discussions leave little room for a profound systematic reflection. Would Paul himself subsequently have regretted that? The apostle cannot be forced into a modern scholarly straitjacket. In his mind, theology was not yet divided into different disciplines. He was as much a biblical scholar as a practical theologian. He passionately expounded the scriptures, but always did so with an eye to the unity and building up of the community. For him dogmatics and ethics were not yet separate disciplines. The ups and downs in the community were high on his list of priorities not only when he wrote to Corinth. That was also the case when he sent his letter to the Christian community in Rome. There were also tensions in Rome, above all between members of the community who were Jewish and those who had come to believe in Jesus Christ as pagans.

Paul was primarily a 'practical' theologian. There is no systematic discussion of theological themes in any of his letters. What he was concerned about was not teaching but life. That is why his 'theology' is so difficult to describe. He did not systematically and skilfully develop a coherent theological view which he tried to apply within the different communities, regardless of the situation. The first letter to the community of Corinth shows how much ethics had priority. And, I hasten to add, the *unity* of the community. Paul's view of the problem of eating meat offered in sacrifices illustrates that. There was a great division over this question in Corinth. Presumably pagan Christians will have had less difficulty with it. They were accustomed to eat such meat. However, for Jewish Christians it was a great problem, Because of the food laws they were emphatically forbidden to eat meat that had been consecrated to idols. Paul will have understood this standpoint. He respected it, but he also relativized it: 'Hence, as to the eating of food offered to idols, we know that an idol has no real existence and there is no God but the One' (I Cor. 8.4). In other words, if there are no idols then there cannot be any meat that has previously been offered to idols!

The argument is both simple and pertinent. Was it sufficiently persuasive to convince opponents? It is evident from the same letter that Paul was aware that he could not persuade everyone to change their minds: 'Eat whatever is sold in the meat market without raising any question on the ground of conscience. For the earth is the Lord's and everything in it. If one of the unbelievers invites you to dinner and you are disposed to go, eat whatever is set before you without raising any question on the ground of conscience. But if someone says to you, "This has been offered in sacrifice," then out of consideration for the man who informed you, and for conscience' sake – I mean his conscience, not yours – do not eat it' (I Cor. 1.25–29).

The community of Corinth was in itself a house divided. Paul knew that, and it caused him great concern. After the usual introduction (opening and thanksgiving, I Cor. 1.1–3 and 4–9) he immediately addressed this problem: 'What I mean is that each of you seems to have his own slogan, "I belong to Paul", or "I belong to Apollos", or "I belong to Cephas", or "I belong to Christ!"' (I Cor. 1.12; cf. 3.4 and 3.22). For want of sufficient information it is impossible to get a clear picture of the differences. There is every indication that Paul refused to take sides, but held the whole community responsible for the difficulties that had arisen. He saw as the root of the evil the claims which the Corinthians made about themselves. They thought themselves 'wise' . They had a monopoly of 'wisdom' This attitude was not intrinsically surprising. The inhabitants of Corinth could boast of living in a city which had much to offer: economically, but also in the sphere of religion. We can ask how far they found the gospel that Paul preached completely new. They were already religious. There was a synagogue for the Jews and the pagans could visit a large number of temples. Some believed in the existence of one God, while others were attracted by a 'pantheon', a rich world of gods and goddesses. Many Corinthians had joined one of the numerous faith communities. They were accustomed to share meals of a cultic character with those of a like mind.

There is an argument as to whether in the time of Paul *Gnostic* ideas had already made their way into cities like Corinth.[16] That is not impossible. Its inhabitants came from all points of the compass. The Egyptian goddess Isis was worshipped alongside the Greek goddess Aphrodite. Thus two old and venerable traditions of wisdom came together and influenced each other, wisdom which gives people 'knowledge' and insight to become a 'spiritual' person. It is not impossible that some members of the Christian community in Corinth thought that they had already reached that 'spiritual' level (I Cor. 2.13–16).

Paul was an emotional man. He was fully aware of the problems in the communities and he sought solutions to them with all his creativity. However, sometimes he could react so sharply that he got people's backs up. In the first letter to the community in Corinth, too, he did not spare the feelings of his readers. It also emerges from other letters that often he was not afraid to make use of ironical and sometimes even sarcastic remarks: 'For consider your call, brothers and sisters; not many of you were wise according to worldly standards, not many were powerful, not many were of noble birth' (I Cor. 4.26). After all those centuries the words still sound unpleasant to us. What did the apostle want to achieve with these remarks? In the first part of the letter he is concerned to unmask the lofty pretensions of the Corinthians and criticize them. There is wisdom and wisdom. Not everything which presents itself as 'wise' is really 'wise'.

Over against the wisdom of human beings the apostle places

the wisdom of God. In his view there is no comparison between these two 'wisdoms': 'Where is the wise man? Where is the scribe? Where is the debater of this age? Has not God made foolish the wisdom of the world? For since in the wisdom of God, the world did not know God through wisdom, it pleased God through the folly of what we preach to save those who believe' (I Cor. 1.20–21). In a way which we find hard to follow, in this part of his letter Paul plays with the terms 'wisdom' and 'folly'. Divine wisdom is different from human wisdom. Therefore the apostle can write about the 'folly of preaching'. Precisely what did he mean by that?

Lofty pretensions, exalted ideals, profound thoughts and philosophical speculations – these were not unknown to the Corinthians. It seems legitimate to suppose that they inter-preted the Christian faith as a welcome supplement to the wisdom that they already knew. They regarded themselves as 'spiritual'. Who had taught them this 'wisdom'? Apollos perhaps? According to Acts he came from Alexandria (Acts 18.24). To a still greater degree than Corinth, Alexandria was a melting pot of religions and philosophical currents. Paul did not let himself be diverted into a polemic against Apollos. He suggested that the Egyptian had continued the work that he had begun: 'I planted, Apollos watered, but God gave the increase' (I Cor. 3.6). Paul belittles himself to make God great, but at the same time he also relativizes Apollos's contribution: 'So neither he who plants nor he who waters is anything, but only God who gives the growth. He who plants and he who waters are equal, and each shall receive his wages according to his labour. For we are fellow workers for God; you are God's field, God's building' (I Cor. 3.7–9).

Paul expresses himself in unmistakable terms. In his view the great problem in the community in Corinth was that some people felt themselves far superior to others both materially and spiritually. He radically opposed this notion. He called on those who thought a great deal of themselves to be humble (I Cor. 4.6–21). All those who thought that they could already be counted 'spiritual' were told to their bewilderment – and perhaps also fury: 'But I, brothers and sisters, could not address you as spiritual, but as of the flesh, as babes in Christ. I fed you with milk, not solid food, for you were not ready for it; and even yet you are not ready, for you are still of the flesh, for you are still living a sinful life' (I Cor. 3.1–3). Paul does not mince his words. Sometimes the truth is hard to hear.

Paul contrasted the 'arrogance' of the Corinthians with humility; over against their lofty pretensions he pointed to the realities of parties and divisions; over against their boasting about their own wisdom he emphasized God's wisdom, which they were inclined to see as folly. Through these comparisons Paul produced a statement which has became extremely important for the history of theology and the church: 'For Jews demand signs and Greeks seek wisdom, *but we preach a crucified Christ*, a stumbling block to Jews and folly to Gentiles, but to those who are called, both Jews and Greeks, Christ the power of God and the wisdom of God. For the foolishness of God is wiser than men, and the weakness of God is stronger than men' (I Cor. 1.22–25). On the basis of this text, in the course of church history the thought has developed that Paul's view could adequately be described as a *theologia crucis*, a theology of the cross. More than any other New Testament author he is said to have given the cross a central place in his preaching.[17] A sentence which he wrote a few lines later in this letter seems completely to confirm this interpretation: 'I decided to know nothing among you except Jesus Christ and him crucified' (I Cor. 2.2).

Anyone who takes the time to look in a concordance will soon discover that this conclusion is being drawn too quickly. The words 'cross' and 'crucify' occur remarkably little in Paul's letters. That also applies to I Corinthians. Only in the first chapters does he several times make use of them (I Cor. 1.13, 17, 18, 23; 2.2, 8). He does not return to them later in this long letter. There is therefore reason to ask how far it is right to describe the apostle's thought as a 'theology of the cross'. Moreover, at the end of I Corinthians Paul writes at length about the *resurrection* (I Cor. 15). Thus the problem is clear:

cross or resurrection? Or better, how did Paul see the relation between cross and resurrection?[18]

It may be regarded as certain that Paul did not become a follower of Jesus Christ because he was convinced by the account of his suffering and death on the cross. He will have noted this with mixed feelings. Perhaps it moved him, but it also shocked and scandalized him. As an inhabitant of the Roman empire he knew that the death penalty could be inflicted in a cruel way. Rebels and runaway slaves were crucified. It is not impossible that on some occasions – willingly or unwillingly – Paul witnessed such an abhorrent execution. Even in the letters which he wrote after his Damascus experience he still writes in negative terms about the cross: it is a curse (Gal. 3.13), a scandal and a folly (I Cor. 1.23). Paul will have remembered all too well that once he had been 'zealous' against the followers of Jesus Christ, the crucified man whom God was said to have raised from the dead. His abhorrence did not disappear, even after the vision on the way to Damascus that overwhelmed him and brought a decisive change to his life. For him the cross remained an offensive symbol, however, with his understanding that a dimension had been added to it. After that Paul could think and speak about the cross and the crucified one only in the form of a paradox. He came to discover that God had raised the crucified one from the dead (Gal. 1.12,15). In that period of history numerous people were put to death in that humiliating way. They died and their names – with one single exception, Spartacus – were forgotten for good. Jesus' words and deeds did not end in the tomb but lived on. God raised him from the dead. Through the vision near Damascus Paul began to interpret the cross from a new perspective. It remained a curse and folly, but – paradoxically – it also became a blessing and the proof of God's wisdom and power.

Paul wrote 'contextual' theology. At the beginning of I Corinthians he did not formulate his doctrine of the soteriological significance of the cross.[19] We look in vain in this part of the letter for words and phrases like 'reconciliation' and 'he died for our sins'. There were other reasons why the apostle thought it necessary to pay explicit attention to the cross and the crucified one. As we have already noted, the community in Corinth was split by oppositions, because many people were inclined to think 'highly' of themselves. Paul deliberately set 'the scandal' of the cross over against this spiritual 'arrogance'. The Christian faith is not a new, interesting and attractive form of wisdom. In human terms it is a 'foolish' faith, because the cross is a 'foolish' symbol. People who think themselves 'spiritual' must be prepared to accept that they are followers of a man who died a contemptible death on the cross. For this reason Paul writes the following passage in the first part of the letter: 'Consider your calling, brothers and sisters; not many of you were wise by worldly standards, not many were powerful, not many were of noble birth; but God chose what is weak in the world to shame the strong, God chose what is low and despised in the world, even things that are not, to bring to nothing things that are, so that no human being might boast in the presence of God. He is the source of your life in Christ Jesus, whom God made our wisdom, our righteousness and sanctification and redemption; therefore as it is written, "Let him who boasts, boast of the Lord"' (I Cor. 1.26–31).

'Arrogance' leads to tensions and division. Paul did not approve of this development at all. Rather, he was concerned that the oppositions within the community of Corinth had resulted in some apostles being played off again one another: himself, Apollos and Cephas (I Cor. 1.12; 3.4, 22). Their names were misused as slogans by competing parties. Paul tried to turn the tide. In his view apostles were not 'big noises' in the church hierarchy, nor leaders of parties within the community. He assigned himself and others a different role: 'This is how one should regard us, as servants of Christ and stewards of the mystery of God' (I Cor. 4.1). Later in his argument Paul is unmistakably carried away by his emotions. He becomes ironical: 'For I think that God has exhibited us apostles last of all, like men sentenced to death, because we have become a spectacle to the world, to angels and to men' (I Cor. 4.9). And even sarcastic: 'We are fools for Christ's sake, but you are wise in Christ. We are weak, but you are strong. You are held in honour but we in disrepute' (I Cor. 4.10). He ends by summing up the difficulties that the apostles must put up with in the service of the preaching of the gospel: 'To the present hour we hunger and thirst, we are ill-clad and buffeted and homeless, and we labour, working with our own hands. When reviled, we bless; when persecuted, we endure; when slandered, we try to conciliate; we have become, and are now, as the refuse of the world, the offscouring of all things' (I Cor. 4.11–13). It seems legitimate to ask whether the apostle did not gradually allow himself to be carried away by his emotions. How convincing was this complaint? In Corinth the letter was received with mixed feelings. That had not led Paul to moderate his tone on this point. In a subsequent letter he would give a kind of summary of the difficulties of his apostolate. He then does that at great length, but he sounds less aggrieved and therefore more self-confident and more persuasive (II Cor. 11.21–29).[20]

As has been said, the greater part of I Corinthians is devoted to ethical questions. That makes the letter an attractive document, which after so many centuries gives us some insight into the problems with which an early Christian community was confronted in a Greek city. Temple prostitution was a 'normal' phenomenon. Paul condemned this practice. He had already done so in an earlier letter (I Cor. 5.9), and in I Corinthians he repeated this condemnation in unmistakable terms (I Cor. 5.1–13). In contrast to the eating of meat offered in sacrifices the apostle wanted to make his opposition on this point quite clear. He based his radical rejection of immorality on the notion that followers of Christ no longer had complete control over their bodies: 'The body is not meant for immorality but for the Lord, and the Lord for the body' (I Cor. 6.13). The apostle believes that the relationship between Christ and the human body is so close that immorality must be completely ruled out. That is evident from the following argument : 'God not only raised the Lord but will also raise us by his power. Do you not know that your bodies are members of Christ? Shall I therefore take the members of Christ and make them members of a

prostitute? Never. Do you not know that he who joins himself
to a prostitute becomes one body with her? For, as it is written,
"The two shall become one." But he who is united to the Lord
becomes one spirit with him' (I Cor. 6.14–17). Paul's conclusion was that immorality had to be regarded as one of the most
serious sins. The body was not involved in other transgressions,
but this sin literally and figuratively went through marrow and
bone: 'Shun immorality. Every other sin which a man commits
is outside the body; but the immoral man sins against his own
body. Do you not know that your body is a temple of the Holy
Spirit within you, which you have from God? You are not your
own; you were bought with a price. So glorify God in your
body' (I Cor. 6.18–20).

The readers of Paul's letters are constantly surprised by
the way in which he argued. It is clear that he was not afraid to
be original and that his style of writing has a more or less
'fidgety' character. In the passage in which he gives his view of
immorality there are a couple of passages which were meant to
support his assertions, but which are of such a different order
that they could easily go on to live a life of their own in the
history of the church and dogma. At the end of the quotation
given above come the words, 'You were bought with a price' (I
Cor. 6.20). Paul will use such terminology once again in this
letter (I Cor. 7.22). He wrote the words to make it clear to the
community of Corinth that they belonged to Christ body and
soul. Just as a slave was 'bought with a price' by his owner and
therefore was his possession, so the members of the community
in Corinth were the 'property' of Christ.[21]

The image is clear in the content of Paul's argument. Over
the centuries, however, the words 'bought at a price' took on
another sense, and were read in the light of the classic doctrine
of the atonement. However, in my view those who think that
the classic doctrine of the atonement is already present in
embryo in the text of I Corinthians seem to me to be asking too
much of the metaphor which Paul used in the above texts.[22]

After discussing the question of prostitution, the letter now
comes to marriage.[23] The order is not illogical. The inhabitants

of Corinth came from all points of the compass and therefore the Christian community, too, will have been a variegated society. It included among its members men and women, Jews and non-Jews, Greeks and barbarians, Egyptians and Romans. And they all brought their own morals and customs with them. Paul's view is surprising. Considering his Jewish background one might expect him to be a convinced advocate of marriage and family. However, that was not the case. The following sentence could hardly be clearer: 'It is good for a man not to touch a woman. But because of the temptation to immorality, each man should have his own wife and each woman her own husband' (I Cor. 7.1–2). Paul himself was either unmarried or no longer married. He saw that as an advantage rather than as a disadvantage: 'I wish that all were as I myself am. But each has his own special gift from God, one of one kind and one of another. To the unmarried and the widows I say that it is well for them to remain single as I do' (I Cor. 7.7–8).

Paul did not regret being unmarried. He had his hands free for preaching the gospel: 'I want you to be free from anxieties. The unmarried man is anxious about the affairs of the Lord, how to please the Lord. But the married man is anxious about worldly affairs, how to please his wife, and his interests are divided' (I Cor. 7.32–34). Moreover, we might summarize Paul's argument as saying that it makes little sense to engage in marriage, for 'the time is short' (I Cor. 7.29). Paul's negative evaluation of marriage is also influenced by his apocalyptic world view. Paul was no ascetic. He did not radically reject sexuality and marriage. This is indicated by the following sentences: 'The husband should give his wife her conjugal rights, and likewise the wife her husband. For the wife does not rule over her own body, but the husband does; likewise the husband does not rule over his own body, but the wife does. Do not refuse one another except perhaps by agreement for a season, that you may devote yourself to prayer; but then come together again, lest Satan tempt you through lack of self-control' (I Cor. 7.3–5). Paul called on the members of the community in Corinth not to divorce, even if their partners had not become followers of Christ (I Cor. 7.10–24). In short, the apostle's view can be described as follows: those who marry do well, and those who do not do better (I Cor. 7.38).[24]

The community in Corinth was a house divided in itself. Paul had to operate carefully. He did so, but he could not prevent the conflict coming to a head. New letters proved necessary. The whole correspondence between Paul and the Corinthians proves how concerned he was for the welfare of the communities which he had visited on his travels. It has to be said that it was also not in the nature of the apostle to make things too easy for himself. He thought freedom a great good, but warned against people who in their appeal to freedom took no account of the views of others. For this reason, in I Corinthians he could make two statements which in fact contradict each other: 'All things are lawful for me, but not all things are helpful. All things are lawful for me, *but I will not be enslaved by anything*' (I Cor. 6.12). Some chapters later Paul returns to this statement: 'All things are lawful, but not all things are helpful. *All things are lawful, but not all things build up. Let no one seek his own good, but the good of his neighbour*' (I Cor. 10.23–24).

Paul's thoughts constantly move between these two 'poles'. The consequence is that it is sometimes difficult to follow him and get a clear picture of his own insights. In Corinth there was a difference of opinion over eating meat offered to idols.[25] Paul saw how important this matter was. He came up with a solution which could be described as laconic, but which was not lacking in creativity and profundity. His view is that in fact there is nothing against eating meat which has been offered to idols. At any rate, those who do not believe in the existence of idols – in connection with the Old Testament Jewish tradition a follower of Jesus Christ should also reject this superstition – could buy and eat that meat without hesitation (I Cor. 8.4–6). There are no idols, so there cannot be any meat offered to idols either. Did Paul realize that not everyone was in a position to subscribe to this original notion? He goes on to ask understanding for such people: 'However, not all possess this knowledge. But some, through being hitherto accustomed to idols, eat food as really offered to an idol, and their conscience, being weak, is defiled' (I Cor. 8.7). What is to be done in such a situation? Paul radically cuts through the knot: 'Therefore if food is a cause of my brother's falling, I will never eat meat, lest I cause my brother to fall' (I Cor. 8.17).

The situation within the early community in Corinth put great demands on Paul's patience and 'theological inventiveness'. That also applied to the role which he himself played. He had a high opinion of his own apostolate. He regarded it as unique. Certainly he had not belonged to the group of disciples of Jesus, but nevertheless he could claim that he had 'seen the Lord' (I Cor. 9.1). The vision on the way to Damascus had changed his life decisively. It emerges from the letter to the Galatians which he was to write some time later that he felt himself to be a free man, called by God, and for this reason independent of others, even from the apostles in Jerusalem (Gal. 1.11–24). In I Corinthians he similarly emphasized his freedom: 'Am I not free?' (I Cor. 9.1). But he does not stop there; he qualifies his statement as follows: 'For though I am free from all men, I have made myself a slave to all' (I Cor. 9.19). What is the background to this readiness to be of service? The answer is in fact simple: 'to win as many people as possible to Christ'. What comes next illustrates this statement: 'To the Jews I became as a Jew, in order to win Jews; to those under the law I became as one under the law – *though not being myself under the law* – that I might win those under the law. To those outside the law I became as one outside the law – *not being without law towards God but under the law of Christ* – that I might win those outside the law. To the weak I became weak, that I might win the weak. I have become all things to all men, that I might by all means save some. I do it all for the sake of the gospel, that I may share in its blessings' (I Cor. 9.20–23).

Paul was evidently not ashamed of appearing to be a chameleon. He had the capacity to adapt himself relatively easily to other circumstances. He could do so because he was 'a man of two worlds', a Diaspora Jew who knew the Graeco-Hellenistic world but had also enjoyed instruction in Jerusalem from the influential Pharisaic scriptural scholar Gamaliel (Acts 22.1–13). However, those who still have the picture of the apostle as a zealot in their heads will be surprised at the sentences I have put in italics. Was Paul personally really no longer 'under the law'? He goes on to qualify this statement: he was not without the law of God, for he stood 'under the law of Christ'. This passage is highly significant for the development of his thought. It is the first time that he speaks critically about the Torah. He does not develop this notion further in I Corinthians. But he does in Galatians and finally in his letter to the community in Rome.

Paul was utterly devoted to the preaching of the gospel. Even after his Damascus experience he remained a 'zealot'. He risked everything, his whole existence: 'I do it all for the sake of the gospel, that I may share in its blessings' (I Cor 9.23). Paul had travelled a great deal and seen much. Great importance was attached to sport and games in the Graeco-Roman world. The celebration of sporting heroes did not begin in our time, but was already there in antiquity. 'Games' were held in many places, especially in Greece, at fixed times – like the Olympic Games – and attracted a large public. The winners of various events received many marks of honour. Unfortunately we do not know whether Paul was ever present at them, but he certainly knows how much effort the sportsmen needed to make to win first place. He compares his own dedication to the spread of the gospel with these sporting achievements: 'Do you not know that in a race all the runners compete, but only one receives the prize? So run that you may obtain it. Every athlete exercises self-control in all things. They do it to receive a perishable prize, but we an imperishable. Well, I do not run aimlessly, I do not box as one beating the air; but I pommel my body and subdue it, lest after preaching to others, I myself should be disqualified' (I Cor. 9.24–27).[26]

Moreover the world of sport can teach us that while a great deal of effort is needed to come first, it is often even more difficult to hold on to this first place over a lengthy period. Those in high positions can fall far. Paul warns his readers in very much the same words: 'Therefore let any one who thinks that he stands take heed lest he fall' (I Cor. 10.12). The apostle was not a dull writer. He had a rich variety of images and ideas. He compared his efforts to proclaim the gospel with the contest over first place in sport. He also illustrated the effort that it can take to continue to be 'first' in events from the journey of the people of Israel through the wilderness (I Cor. 10.1–13). Without hesitation Paul made a giant leap in historical, cultural and religious terms. The achievements of sportsmen were an inspiring example. Paul used the conduct of Israel during the journey through the wilderness as a warning: 'Now these things are warnings for us, not to desire evil as they did' (I Cor. 10.6). Some became idolaters (Ex. 32.6), others engaged in immorality (Num. 25.1–18), tempted the Lord (Num. 21.5–6) and murmured against him (Num. 16.41–49). After his summary of the misdeeds of the people of Israel, the apostle concludes: 'Now these things happened to them as a warning, but they were written down for our instruction, upon whom the end of the ages has come' (I Cor. 10.11).

Those in first place have a good deal to lose. Those who are exalted can fall a long way. Those who want to be part of the elect people of God need to demonstrate this claim in their lives. Paul made a bold comparison. To back up the example that he chose, he developed the surprising thought that Christ had already been present in the history of the people of Israel in a hidden way: 'I want you to know, brothers and sisters, that our fathers were all under the cloud, and all passed through the sea, and all were baptized into Moses in the cloud and in the sea, and all ate the same supernatural food and all drank the same supernatural drink. For they drank from the supernatural rock which followed them, *and that rock was Christ*' (I Cor. 10.1–4). Thus Christ was already present in the journey of the people of Israel through the wilderness, but that does not mean that no one else was lost. Therefore the history of Israel is a warning to the Christian community: 'Nevertheless with most of them God was not pleased; for they were overthrown in the wilderness' (I Cor. 10.5).

Paul's style amazes modern readers. How did he come to arrive at the thought that Christ played a role in the history of the people of Israel? The clause in italics – *and that rock was Christ* – has also inspired theologians down the centuries to a 'christological' interpretation of the Old Testament. Not only are prophetic texts said to contain countless references to the coming of Christ in the New Testament, but at the same time Christ is said already to be present in the Old Testament in a hidden way.[27] Did Paul already interpret the Old Testament in a consistently 'christological' approach? This question can only be answered with qualifications. In the first place it has to be pointed out that Paul did not yet know the difference between Old and New Testament. For him *scripture* was 'undivided': the books of the Hebrew Bible. All the books that are known to us? It is certain that the 'Torah and prophets' were generally accepted as authoritative. There was less unanimity over the extent of the third part of the Tenach.[28] Certainly in using the word 'scripture' Paul will never have thought of something like the New Testament. It did not exist, nor would he have thought it necessary for it to be written. 'The end of the ages' had come (I Cor. 10.11).

Paul's striking remark about 'Christ as the rock in the wilderness' was not the result of a theological reflection on the relationship between the two Testaments. The apostle was a brilliant man, but even those who are highly gifted have their limits. He would have had to look at least a century into the future to see the basis for such reflection. But even had he been in a position to do this, presumably he would not have wanted to believe his eyes. He lived in the conviction that the end of the world was near (I Cor. 7.29). Considering this situation, Paul's thought was very strongly orientated on everyday practice. He wanted to warn the community of Corinth, and used the journey of the people of Israel through the wilderness as a deterrent. In order to give force to his comparison he suggested that the people of Israel was already accompanied by Christ, but even the presence of 'the rock in the wilderness' did not provide protection for everyone against idolatry and godlessness.

Paul thought that he knew for sure that idols did not exist (I Cor. 8.4). Unfortunately, however that did not mean that there was no idolatry either. Paul knew better. The cities in the Greek-Hellenistic world were in general richly blessed with a large number of temples. Corinth was no exception to this rule. The city was famous for its temples. Religion was flourishing. New religious movements were greeted with joy. In the first instance the early Christian community, too, will have been regarded as an interesting curiosity. For some new members, the borderline between Christian faith and their former way of life was difficult to draw. Why should they suddenly no longer be able to pay a visit to the temples which had fulfilled such an important function in their existence as soon as they became members of the Christian community?

Paul did not hesitate to issue a warning: 'Therefore, my beloved, *flee* idolatry' (I Cor. 10.14). Paul writes 'flee' with good reason; the dangers were enormous. Evil was sticking its head up everywhere. 'Temptations' were lurking everywhere, not only in the temples but also in the many religious meals which were held in Corinth. It was natural to presuppose that 'eating the Lord's Supper' (I Cor. 11.20) was in fact little different from taking part in these other meals. Why should one suddenly avoid these communal tables? Paul vigorously opposed this thought: 'You cannot drink the cup of the Lord and the cup of demons. You cannot partake of the table of the Lord and the table of demons' (I Cor. 10.21). The apostle has explained why that is ruled out in a striking passage which preceded this statement: 'The cup of blessing which we break, is it not a participation in the body of Christ? Because there is one bread, we who are many are *one body*, for we all partake of the one bread' (I Cor. 10.16–17).

The term 'one body', which I have put in italics, proves to be of central significance for what follows. Paul did not regard participating in the Lord's Supper as a voluntary matter. Those who had once opted for this 'table' had to keep away from other 'tables'. The Lord's Supper implied 'community' in two senses: community with Christ and community with one another. Those who thought that they might draw the boundaries less sharply and at different 'tables' forgot themselves and were guilty of 'idolatry' (I Cor. 10.14). The Christian community is not a voluntary club of like-minded people but forms 'one body'. With this image the apostle gave a fresh description of an 'ideal' community: of one mind and closely bound to Jesus Christ.[29] He will work out the consequences of his thought later in the letter. Then he describes the Christian community consistently as 'the body of Christ' (I Cor. 12.27). For that reason he can conclude this part of his letter like this: 'Be followers of me, as I am of Christ' (I Cor. 11.1).

Paul was doubtless aware that within the community at Corinth reality hardly corresponded to the ideal, if at all. Parties threatened to tear the community apart. There was rank and status, high and low, on the religious, the economic and the social level. Paul had probably known this for a long time. Corinth was a city with a very mixed population: rich and poor, intellectual and illiterate, 'wise' and 'stupid'. He could have expected the tension easily to come to a head, but in all probability the reports on the course of events in the community were more shocking than he had ever imagined. Indeed Paul got into more and more of a state. The course of events during the celebration of 'the Lord's Supper' in the community in Corinth gave him every occasion for bewilderment and indignation.[30]

Paul's reports are not so clear and detailed that it is possible to get a complete picture of the situation. In the first place he says that the internal division can be seen in a shameful way during meetings of the community (I Cor. 11.17–19). The celebration of the Lord's Supper was evidently preceded by an ordinary meal. Members of the community brought their own food to it from home. The difference in rank and status became painfully clear, and there was little or no sign of a readiness to share. 'For in eating, each one goes ahead with his own meal, and one is hungry and another is drunk' (I Cor. 11.21). Paul's criticism is pointed. He scornfully tells the community: 'Do you not have houses to eat and drink in? Or do you despise the community of God and humiliate those who have nothing?' (I Cor. 11.22).

The 'ordinary meal' was followed by the Lord's Supper. There was a clear difference between the two meals, but obviously it was impossible to avoid the atmosphere at the second part of the meeting being unfavourably influenced by the unpleasantness that had taken place earlier. Were some members of the community really aware of how much damage they were doing? Whereas at first they took no notice of their brothers and sisters who had less money and possessions, they thought that they could join them at the Lord's Supper. Paul's bewilderment was great. That is evident from what he goes on to say. Finally to give force to his words, he appealed to the early Christian tradition. He rarely did that (cf. I Cor. 15.1–3). That on this occasion he resorted to such a 'word of power' shows his indignation: 'For I received from the Lord what I also delivered to you, that the Lord Jesus on the night when he was betrayed took bread, and when he had given thanks he broke it, and said, "This is my body which is for you. Do this in remembrance of me." In the same way also the cup, after supper, saying, "This cup is the new covenant in my blood. Do this, as often as you drink it, in remembrance of me"' (I Cor. 11.23–25).

Paul himself did not compose these words himself. On this occasion he did not conceal his dependence on the early Christian tradition. A comparison with 'the words of institution' in the three Synoptic Gospels shows that the text in I Corinthians is related to the description of the 'institution' of the Lord's Supper in the Third Gospel (Luke 22.14–20). Mark and Matthew have a good deal in common, but they differ notably from Luke and thus also from Paul (Mark 14.22–25; Matt. 26.26–29). Because I Corinthians is earlier than the three Synoptic Gospels, this letter contains the first *written* statement of the 'words of institution of the Lord's Supper'. That does not automatically mean that Paul's text will contain the authentic words. The New Testament in fact knows two traditions: Mark and Matthew on one side and Paul and Luke on the other. Which tradition is more likely to be authentic? There is no consensus in the scholarly discussion.[31] For different reasons a majority opts for Paul; however, my preference is for Mark/Matthew.[32] They have an *older* tradition, which cannot be called authentic either, but is closer to the original words than the texts in I Corinthians and the Gospel of Luke. In my view simplicity has priority over complexity. Mark and Matthew relate the event. They do so soberly and virtually without theological interpretations. Thus they do not know the invitation to repeat 'the eating of the bread' and 'the drinking of the cup'. The Gospel of Luke contains an exhortation which is closely related to the text in I Corinthians: 'Do this in remembrance of me' (Luke 22.19). This notion is also felt to be of essential importance in the early Christian tradition on which Paul proves to be dependent (I Cor. 11.24, 25).

In the community of Corinth it was customary to meet regularly at the Lord's Supper: 'For as often as you eat this bread and drink the cup, you proclaim the Lord's death until he comes' (I Cor. 11.26). It is impossible to say how often the community met for this purpose. The problems that had arisen suggest that it met often. Weekly meetings certainly cannot be ruled out. In this way the Christian community would have fitted in well with habits and customs familiar to the inhabitants of Corinth. Many who became followers of Jesus the Christ had previously been members of religious associations in which a regular communal meal had also had an important place. There is no doubt that a distinction must be made between the 'eucharistic practice' in Corinth and the common meals which according to Acts characterized the atmosphere of the early Christian community in Jerusalem: 'And day by day, attending the temple, they broke the bread in someone's house with glad and generous hearts' (Acts 2.46).

Paul drew no comparisons, nor did he pass judgment in principle. His prime concern was that the Corinthians should be aware of what they were doing when they took their places at the Lord's table: 'Whoever, therefore, eats the bread or drinks the cup of the Lord unworthily sins against themselves the body and blood of the Lord. Let each examine himself before eating the bread and drinking the cup. For anyone who eats and drinks without discerning the body eats and drinks judgment upon himself' (I Cor. 11.27–29). In the course of church history these words became detached from the specific context of the community in Corinth and began to lead a life of their own. For centuries, especially in the world of Reformed Protestantism, they functioned as serious warnings, and in some circles they still function in this way. Many people did not dare to take a step in the direction of the Lord's Supper. As a result they avoided the eucharist. They preferred to be certain rather than uncertain whether they were drinking judgment upon themselves. Paul's words gradually took on a sombre, threatening and macabre tone and got 'stuck' in the memory of many generations: 'whoever unworthily . . . sins against the body . . .' (I Cor. 11.27).

Did Paul mean them like this? The question deserves a well-considered answer. The development in later Reformed Protestantism would have amazed him. But that does not mean that for Paul 'eating the Lord's Supper' was without risk. He certainly meant the sentences quoted as a warning. However, for him the focal point did not lie on the individual, inner life of faith but on everyday practice, on the rank and status within the community and the fact that some lived in prosperity and others suffered want. In this pericope the image of 'the body' has an ambiguous meaning. Again it proves that the apostle was a creative thinker. The body of Christ, in bread and wine, is to be found *on* the Lord's table, but the Christian community has gathered *around* this same table as the body of the Lord. Paul's urging 'to discern the body' does not just relate to the event on the table but also – and no less – to the body *around* the table. This 'ambiguity' was essential to Paul's thought. That emerges once more from a sentence which is as clear as could be: 'That is why many of you are weak and ill, and some have died' (I Cor. 11.30). We do not know how this 'accusatory' sentence was received in the community of Corinth. It is conceivable that this remark of Paul's was not received gratefully and perhaps also became a cause of the difficulties which were soon to arise.

To round off his discussion of the problems which had arisen during the celebration of the Lord's Supper, Paul also gave the following advice: 'So then, brothers and sisters, when you come together to eat, wait for one another – if any one is hungry, let him eat at home – lest you come together to be condemned. About the other things I shall give directions when I come' (I Cor. 11.33–34). After all the emotion, the tone is suddenly strikingly peaceful. In the end Paul tried not to make the conflict worse than it already threatened to be. However, it emerges from his correspondence with the community that his attempts to bring about reconciliation soon came to grief because of differences of opinion. Even the celebration of the Lord's Supper was overshadowed by the fact that great social differences – rich–poor – did not disappear from the scene when the community met (I Cor. 11.17–22). Paul thoroughly abhorred all this: it was in flagrant conflict with his view of the Christian community. This was no voluntary 'club', no association of like-minded people, no group of individuals who were not interested in the welfare of the other members. There is every appearance that Paul's thoughts would develop further as he wrote. The celebration of the Lord's Supper in particular forges the community together into an indissoluble unity: 'Because there is one bread, we who are many are one body, for we all partake of the one bread' (I Cor. 10.17). According to Paul, this 'one body' can be described as *the body of Christ* (I Cor. 12.27).[33]

Unity and division, these are the words which govern Paul's thoughts about the community: 'Now there are varieties of gifts, but the same Spirit; and there are varieties of service, but the same Lord; and there are varieties of working, but it is the same God who inspires them all in everyone' (I Cor. 12.3–6). Paul was not against differences, but they were not to pose a threat to the unity of the community. The unity precedes the difference – and not the other way round. The apostle clarified his view of the unity of the community with the help of the image of the body: 'For just as the body is one and has many members, and all the members of the body, though many, are one body, so it is with Christ. For by one spirit we were all baptized into one body, Jews or Greeks, slaves or free – and all were made to drink of one spirit. For the body does not consist of one member but of many' (I Cor. 12.12–14). A body is built up of many members, but nevertheless it forms one whole. None of the separate parts may cherish the thought that they are more important than others: 'If the whole body were an eye, where would be the hearing? If the whole body were an ear, where would be the smell?' (I Cor 12.17–18). Evidently Paul attached great importance to the metaphor of the body. It was difficult for him to move away from it, and he never tired of rephrasing his thoughts time and again: 'As it is, there are many parts, yet one body. The eye cannot say to the hand, "I have no need of you," nor again the head to the feet, "I have no need of you." On the contrary, the parts of the body which seem to be weaker are indispensable, and those parts of the body which we think less honourable we invest with the greater honour, and our unpresentable parts are treated with great modesty, which our more presentable parts do not require' (I Cor. 12.20–24).

In the last sentences Paul develops the image so far that to some degree it begins to become embarrassing. Paul was no prude. The 'wise' and distinguished members of the community in Corinth will have heard the words with growing irritation and presumably they will have understood the hint. In the apostle's view it is not in the spirit of the crucified Christ – 'be followers of me, as I am of Christ' (I Cor. 11.1) – to look down on one another and to scorn others because they have less money or influence or because they have less 'wisdom'. The basis of unity within the community of Christ is love. That Paul saw things this way emerges unmistakably from the way in which he has structured I Corinthians 12–14. He abruptly breaks off his argument about unity to introduce a surprising hymn of praise to love (I Cor. 13). To all appearances this Pauline hymn of praise was not created by Paul himself.[34] The apostle made grateful use of a text which already existed. He did that often (e.g. I Cor. 15.3–4; Phil. 2.6–11).

The hymn of praise has a 'traditional' – pre-Pauline –

character. That explains the remarkable fact that no connection is made in any way between love and Christ. So Paul did not draw on a specifically Christian source. Because of his broad cultural and religious background he was familiar with texts in which the praise was sung of the pre-eminence of 'virtues' like wisdom and truth. These texts did not occur only in Greek Hellenistic writings but also in early Jewish wisdom literature. To illustrate that, here is a passage from the deutero-canonical work The Wisdom of Solomon, composed some time before the beginning of our era in the Diaspora Judaism of Alexandria in Egypt, which had a Hellenistic orientation:[35] 'For she is a breath of the power of God, and a pure emanation of the glory of the Almighty; therefore nothing defiled gains entrance into her. For she is a reflection of eternal light, a spotless mirror of the work-ing of God, and an image of his goodness. Though she is but one, she can do all things, and while remaining in herself she renews all things; in every generation she passes into holy souls and makes them friends of God, and prophets; for God loves nothing so much as the man who lives with wisdom. For she is more beautiful than the sun and excels every constellation of the stars. Compared with the light she is found to be superior, for it is succeeded by the night, but against wisdom evil does not prevail. She reaches mightily from one end of the earth to the other, and she orders all things well '(Wisdom 7.25–8.1)

Paul's religious and cultural background was many-sided. That emerges once more from the 'hymn of praise' to love, which has to serve as the basis of his plea for the unity of the community. It is typical of the apostle's creativity that at this moment in the letter he has taken up a text which must have been sounded familiar to his wisdom-loving readers in Corinth. This time, however, it is not wisdom or truth which is central, but love: 'Earnestly desire the higher gifts. And I will show you a still more excellent way' (I Cor. 12.31). Many things are important in human life, but one thing bears the crown: 'So faith, hope, love abide, these three; but the greatest of these is love' (I Cor. 13.13).

The hymn of praise to love does not fail to have its effect. It sheds new light on what has gone before and puts what is to come in a 'loving' framework. Paul knew what he was doing. The community in Corinth is torn apart by divisions: parties, rank and status; boasting of one's 'own wisdom' coupled with contempt of those who think differently. The gatherings of the community are disfigured by this and become chaotic. Everyone thought that his or her ideas and convictions were more important than those of others. Paul did not spare the community: 'If therefore the whole community assembles and all speak in tongues, and outsiders or unbelievers enter, will they not say that you are mad?' (I Cor. 14.23). Love leads to tolerance, creates space for others and results in order – 'for God is not a God of disorder but of peace' (I Cor. 14.33).

Beyond doubt Paul meant the call to order in the community well, but abuse is lurking. Indeed that has happened for centuries. Women have been given a subordinate role in church history with an appeal to a remark of Paul's: 'As in all the communities of the saints, the women should keep silence in the communities. For they are not permitted to speak, but should be subordinate, as even the law says. If there is anything they desire to know, let them ask their husbands at home. For it is shameful for a woman to speak in the community' (I Cor. 14.33–35). The text is quite clear. But it does not fit. Some time later Paul would write in his letter to the Galatians: 'There is neither Jew nor Greek, there is neither slave nor free, there is neither male nor female; for you are all one in Christ Jesus' (Gal. 3.28). The apostle was not at all a misogynist. He spoke appreciatively of Phoebe, deacon of the community at Cenchreae (Rom. 16.1) and of the couple Prisca/Priscilla and Aquila (Rom. 16.3–4). There is nothing to suggest that he thought that these and other women should keep silent and might not play a role in the early Christian community. Therefore we must consider why he reacted in a different way in his letter to the community in Corinth. There are two possible explanations: (a) women had more of a say in Corinth than elsewhere and that was going too far for Paul; (b) this passage was not written by him but added later; the verses could be removed without damaging the argument.[36] I prefer the latter solution. Even if we opt for the former solution, it needs to be recognized that these words are so 'contextual' – bound up with the specific context in the community of Corinth – that it is impossible for them to lay any claim to eternal validity.

Faith-hope-love (I Cor. 13.13). The praise of love has been sung, the implications of Christian faith have been largely presented – but what may a Christian hope for? Paul was an apocalyptist, and it was not difficult for him to live in the expectation that the time could be short (I Cor. 7.29). But what would happen after that? For Paul this question was easy to answer. His apocalyptic background and conviction put the words into his mouth: 'For the Lord himself will descend from heaven with a cry of command, with the archangel's call, and with the sound of the trumpet of God. And the dead in Christ will rise first; then we shall be caught up together with them in the clouds to meet the Lord, and so we shall ever be with the Lord' (I Thess. 4.16–17). Anyone familiar with apocalyptic thought would not have been surprised at the combination of 'the coming of the Lord' and 'the resurrection of the dead' (cf. Dan.12.1–3; Matt. 25.31–46).

The community in Corinth was a mixed one. It consisted of Jews and Gentiles. Whether the Jewish members of the community were familiar with apocalyptic thought is by no means certain – we cannot rule out the possibility that to a large degree they were influenced by Hellenism – but we can assume that those who had no Jewish background were surprised when for the first time they were confronted with Jewish-apocalyptic notions. Paul thought it wise to devote some attention to this problem. The key sentence is: 'Now if Christ is preached as raised from the dead, how can some of you say *that there is no resurrection of the dead?*' (I Cor. 15.12). In the preceding verses he has started from the early Christian tradition which he also knew as venerable tradition and which he had in turn handed down: 'For I delivered to you as of first importance what I also received, that Christ died for our sins in accordance with the scriptures, that he was buried, that he was raised on the third day in accordance with the scriptures' (I Cor. 15.3–4).[37] In what follows, within this framework Paul seems to pay little or no intention to the 'soteriological' significance of the death of Christ. He mentions a long list of eye-witnesses to appearances: 'Last of all, as to one untimely born, he appeared also to me. For I am the least of the apostles, unfit to be called an apostle, because I persecuted the church of God. But by the grace of God I am what I am, and his grace towards me was not in vain. On the contrary, I worked harder than any of them, though it was not I, but the grace of God which is with me' (I Cor. 15.8–10). This text is worth quoting from a biographical point of view. Paul too knows that he is an eye-witness of the risen Lord, in a different way from his fellow apostles, but basically nevertheless not inferior to Peter and his sympathizers.

God raised the crucified Christ from the dead. The vision on the way to Damascus opened Paul's eyes to a new reality. It will have overwhelmed him, but deep down it was not alien to him as an apocalyptist. However, on his way through Asia Minor and Greece he repeatedly came up against the problem of making the apocalyptic belief in the resurrection clear to non-Jews. According to the author of Acts, the conversation between Paul and the philosophers on the Areopagus ended on that point: 'Now when they heard of the resurrection of the dead, some mocked, but others said, "We will hear you again about this"' (Acts 17.32). It can easily be inferred from the last sentence that a continuation of the discussion clearly never took place.

In his conversation with the community in Corinth Paul thought that he could start from the common confession that God had raised the crucified Christ from the dead. Everything rests on this basis: 'If Christ is not risen, then our preaching is vain and your faith is in vain' (I Cor. 15.14). The apostle then reacted violently against such conclusions: 'But in fact Christ has been raised from the dead, *the first fruits of those who have fallen asleep*' (I Cor. 15.20). Christ's resurrection is not an 'incident', a unique event which will never be repeated. Paul deliberately used the term 'firstfruits' to indicate that Easter had its consequences. Just as the first fruits announce that the harvest is approaching, so the resurrection of Christ is the guarantee that the resurrection from the dead is not a fiction, but will take place soon (I Cor. 15.22).

The apocalyptist Paul then goes on to develop his expectation of the future. He already did that in his letter to the community of Thessalonica. Anyone who compares the two works on this point will again discover that the apostle's view was not always clear. Thus he does not speak anywhere in I Corinthians of a 'meeting in the air'. When the Lord comes, the dead will be raised. All the dead? The texts mentions only 'those who belong to Christ' (I Cor. 15.23). And then? 'Then comes the end, when he delivers the kingdom to God the Father after destroying every rule and every authority and power' (I Cor. 15.24). Again Paul betrays his apocalyptic background here. It seems that he was thinking of two periods, two worlds: first the kingship of Christ and then the kingship of God: 'When all things are subjected to him, then the Son himself will also be subjected to him who put all things under him, that God may be everything to everyone' (I Cor. 15.28). In Paul's apocalyptic view it is ultimately God, not Christ, who stands at the centre. The end will become reality when God's definitive victory has been realized.[38]

At the end of this long letter Paul introduced yet another 'diaconal' theme: the collection for the community of Jerusalem. That is also mentioned in the book of Acts and a connection is made with a severe famine in Jewish territory under the reign of the emperor Claudius: 'And the disciples determined, every one according to his ability, to send relief to the brethren who lived in Judaea; and they did so, sending it to the elders by the hand of Barnabas and Saul' (Acts 11.29–30). It can be inferred not only from Acts (12.25; 24.17) but also from Paul's own letters that Paul conscientiously fulfilled this task (Rom. 15.26–28; II Cor. 8–9; Gal. 2.10). It does not seem rash to suppose that he saw it not only as a proof of concrete help and love of neighbour but also of unity and solidarity between believers with a pagan background and those who came from Judaism. Thus the collection symbolized Paul's own position: the man of two worlds, who was indefatigably occupied in reconciling and uniting these two worlds.

8

The first letter to the community in Philippi

In prison in Ephesus

After sending his letter to the community in Corinth, Paul got into increasing difficulties in Ephesus (Acts 19.23–40). The book of Acts does not relate that the end of his stay in the city the apostle landed up in prison for some weeks or perhaps months. But Paul does refer to that in a passage at the end of his first letter to the community of Corinth: 'What do I gain if, humanly speaking, I fought with beasts at Ephesus?' (I Cor. 15.32). There is a long summary in the second letter to Corinth of all the difficulties that Paul had to put up with because of his preaching of the gospel (II Cor. 11.22–29). In that connection he writes: 'with far greater labours, far more imprisonments, with countless beatings and often near death' (II Cor. 11.23). We know from Acts that Paul spent a night in prison in Philippi (Acts 16.19–40) and that he was imprisoned in Caesarea (Acts 23.23–26.32). From there he was taken by ship to Rome, where he wanted to give an account of himself to the emperor (Acts 27–28). Given the difficulties which arose in Ephesus from Paul's appearance, imprisonment in this city is certainly within the realm of possibilities. In these difficult circumstances he saw an opportunity to write a letter to the community of Philippi. Paul makes no secret of the fact that he wrote this letter in prison and sent it from there (Phil. 1.7, 13–14).

The unity of the letter

There has been hardly any difference of opinion about the authenticity of the letter to the Philippians in New Testament scholarship over recent decades. There is a widespread view that there is no reason to doubt Paul's authorship. However, there has been a good deal of discussion about the *unity* of the letter. No one who reads the text of the whole writing closely can fail to note that the 'tone' suddenly changes decisively at the beginning of the third chapter. In the first verse of this part nothing seems to have happened. The sentence 'Finally, brothers and sisters, rejoice in the Lord' (Phil. 3.1) recalls similar exhortations to joy and gladness in the preceding chapters of the letter (Phil. 1.4, 25; 2.17–18, 28). However, in the second verse of the third chapter the apostle very abruptly goes over to another theme and addresses his readers with words of warning: 'Look out for the dogs, look out for the evil-workers, look out for those who mutilate the flesh' (Phil. 3.2).

What is going on? Why has the gladness disappeared, to give way to a fierce polemical tone? The reader faces a riddle and exegetes feel compelled to try to give this an acceptable explanation.[1] It is impossible to attain complete certainty. What incident has led Paul suddenly to express himself in these fierce words? It is conceivable that after writing the invitation 'Rejoice in the Lord' he laid down his pen because he was disturbed or for some other reason was not in a position to write more. When he took up his pen again later, something had happened to change his mood radically, and he wrote the warnings which are in striking contrast to the cheerful tone in the first chapters of the letter.

Exegetes who argue for the unity of the letter usually argue in this direction. However, this can hardly be said to be a satisfactory solution. The content of Chapter 3 cannot be explained simply by a change in mood. More has happened. Paul had received reports which indicated that opponents were confusing the community in Philippi. For this reason his tone changed and he began to write polemic.

It is impossible to discuss the question at length in this book. Anyone who wants to sketch a picture of the life and thought of Paul must accept some restrictions. Choices have to be made. A great deal can be said about the unity of the letter to the community of Philippi,[2] but at some point a decision has to be arrived at. After carefully weighing up the arguments for and against, I go along with exegetes who conclude that the canonical letter to the Philippians is in fact a compilation of two letters (letter A and letter B) which Paul wrote to the community in Philippi. Letter A consists of the first two chapters (Phil. 1.1–3.1) and is continued with a short interruption in Chapter 4 (Phil. 4.2–7, 10–23); letter B can be reconstructed from the remaining verses of the canonical writing (Phil 3.2–4.1 and 4.8–9). In the discussion of the content of the two letters it will become clear why I think the above choice in the discussion on the unity of the letter is a responsible one.

Paul and the city of Philippi

During his second missionary journey Paul paid his first visit to the city of Philippi in Macedonia. His stay there was short but tumultuous (Acts 16.12). The author of Acts proves to be well informed when he describes Philippi as a Roman 'colony'. After the campaign which had taken place in the immediate vicinity of the city in 42 BC, the victor, Antony, gave it this status. From this time, above all veterans from the Roman legions and farmers from Italy settled here. The consequence was that this city in Macedonia had taken on a typically Roman character.[3]

Paul was not put off by this. The description in Acts of events in Philippi shows that the apostle was in an excellent position to adapt to local conditions. At an early stage of his stay in the city he quickly got into difficulties. He was arrested and had to spend the night in prison (Acts 16.19–40). And in the Roman colony he did what he usually tried to avoid on other occasions: with appropriate pride he said that he was a Roman citizen. He was immediately released and treated with respect (Acts 16.35–40). It is striking that the Roman citizenship did not prevent him from leaving Philippi as quickly as possible after his stay in prison. We already saw earlier that the notion that Paul's missionary journeys ran according to a carefully prepared plan has little if anything to do with reality. Perhaps he aimed at Christianizing the whole of the then known world. To his disappointment he will have had to recognize that his careful planning was constantly thwarted by unexpected events. This gave his missionary journey the character of a constant 'flight forwards'. In retrospect it could be said that in this way he did after all reach his destination, albeit by strange detours and surprising routes.

Paul's first visit to Philippi was of short duration and was full of incident. But a Christian community came into being in this city. Perhaps some inhabitants of the Roman colony were easily persuaded by the preaching of a man who could also boast of being a Roman citizen. In any case it is striking that there were close links between Paul and the community in Philippi. At the end of letter A he recalls the support which he received from them: 'And you Philippians yourselves know that in the beginning of the gospel, when I left Macedonia, no church entered into partnership with me in giving and receiving except you only; for even in Thessalonica you sent me help once and again' (Phil. 4.15–16). Paul returns to this fact again in his second letter to the community in Corinth: 'Did I commit a sin in abasing myself so that you might be exalted, because I preached God's gospel without cost to you? I robbed other churches by accepting support from them in order to serve you. And when I was with you and was in want, I did not burden anyone, but my needs were supplied by the brethren who came from Macedonia. So I refrained and will refrain from burdening you in any way' (II Cor. 11.7–9). Why at this particular moment the 'brethren from Macedonia' gave him financial support and he was also ready to accept their gifts is a problem which remains difficult to resolve.

As we discovered earlier, it seems very likely that Paul was imprisoned in Ephesus. The book of Acts does not mention this, but it does relate in detail the difficulties caused by Paul's appearance in the city (Acts 19.1–40). For lack of information we cannot say with certainty how long the apostle was deprived of his freedom. We could conclude from some reports in the letter to the community of Philippi that we should think of a period of weeks rather than days. Probably history also repeated itself here: after being released, Paul hastily left the city. Again the difficulties which arose were a signal for him to depart and seek his salvation elsewhere. The author of Acts describes the parting in attractive words, but readers have slowly become suspicious: 'After the uproar ceased, Paul sent for the disciples and, having exhorted them, took leave of them and departed for Macedonia' (Acts 20.1).

The content of letter A

During his imprisonment in Ephesus Paul wrote letter A to the community of Philippi. The question of the occasion for this letter can be answered relatively easily. There was no indication of theological differences of opinion. No ups and downs within the community gave occasion for anxiety. Indeed the content of the letter is characterized by words like 'joy', 'happiness' and 'gratitude'. From his cell Paul sent a cheerful, happy letter to the community of Philippi. He did that not to gladden the Philippians with the profundity of his theological insights but to express his gratitude for the support that he had received during his imprisonment. The next sentence speaks volumes in this connection: 'It is right for me to feel thus about you all, because I hold you in my heart, for you are all partakers with me of grace, both in my imprisonment and in the defence and confirmation of the gospel' (Phil. 1.7). A certain Epaphroditus played an important role in maintaining contact between the community in Greece and the apostle in prison in Ephesus. Paul describes him in a few words: 'I have thought it necessary to send to you Epaphroditus, my brother and fellow worker and fellow soldier, and your messenger and minister to my need' (Phil. 2.25).

Because his gratitude was the direct occasion for writing the letter, Paul did not think it necessary to discuss specific theological themes at length. At all events it is clear that the apostle still lived in the expectation of the speedy coming of the Lord. The subject is not central to Letter A to the community of Philippi, as it was in the first letter to the community in Thessalonica. But the thought that 'the day of Christ' is near and now determines what Christians do is certainly present in this writing (Phil. 1.6, 10; 2.16). We have come to know Paul as an apocalyptic. He remained one all his life. That does not mean that his thought was static. Rather, the opposite was the case. Here too he was a child of his time. The apocalyptic literature which has been preserved is characterized by a great variety in images and ideas. The apocalyptist wrote contextual theology. The world changed. The 'signs of the times' needed to be interpreted anew.

Paul had a sharp mind and a lively spirit. Apocalyptic thought offered him the possibility of expressing his belief in the coming of Christ. He always looked in great expectancy for the definitive intervention of God in world history. His vision on the way to Damascus had not brought any fundamental change here, but a new aspect had been added. Since then his life and thought had been largely determined by the expectation of the speedy coming (again) of Christ. He looked forward to it. It made him cheerful and excited. He knew that he was a sinner, but in his letters we can find hardly any trace of fear of the judgment, which according to apocalyptic dogma was to be an essential part of the dramatic event at the end of times. Paul did not look to the future with anxiety, because he had come to discover that the judgment had already become reality in the crucified Christ. He did not develop this strange, fascinating thought further in the letter to the community of Philippi. He only did that later in his letters to the Galatians and the community of Rome.

Paul was a hopeful man. Even in prison he did not allow his cheerful mood to be spoilt by sombre feelings. Full of longing, he awaited the coming of Jesus Christ. It is impossible to penetrate deeply into the psyche of the apostle, but it does not seem too rash to presuppose that the parousia of the Lord must have had a special significance. Doubtless he looked forward to the encounter with the risen Lord with even more expectation than his fellow apostles. Peter and his companions had followed Jesus on his journey through Jewish territory. They had their memories of his words and actions. In this circle Paul occupied a place apart. He sarcastically described himself in his summary of eye-witnesses to the resurrection as 'one born out of due time' (I Cor. 15.8). For the moment he had to be content with a vision. Of course, it had radically changed his life, but it remained a vision. Therefore Paul was inclined to direct his gaze more to the future than to the past. A passage occurs in the letter to the community of Philippi which indicates that he himself found it very difficult to wait patiently: 'For to me to live is Christ, and to die is gain. If it is to be life in the flesh, that means fruitful labour for me. Yet which I shall choose I cannot tell. I am hard pressed between the two. *My desire is to depart and be with Christ,* for that is far better. But to remain in the flesh is more necessary on your behalf' (Phil. 1.21–24).

The day of Christ will not be long in coming. However, for Paul it cannot come quickly enough, and he himself would like to take his farewell to 'be with Christ'. He had an intense longing for his meeting with the Lord. Sometime the apostle makes it very difficult for the readers of his letters. This is at moments when his longing becomes so great that he no longer directs his gaze towards the future but already in the present makes a direct link between himself and Jesus. He also did this in a surprising sentence which immediately precedes the text quoted above: 'It is my eager expectation and hope that I shall not be at all ashamed, but that with full courage now as always *Christ will be glorified in my body,* whether by life or by death' (Phil. 1.20). In later letters the apostle will develop this surprising view further. The one who had never met the earthly Jesus now felt very closely bound to the crucified and risen Christ (Gal. 2.20).

The first letter to the community of Philippi is characterized by a strong emphasis on paraenesis – advice in the sphere of ethics. There were no specific problems, and therefore Paul addressed his readers in general terms, to inspire them to a Christian way of life: 'Only let your manner of life be worthy of the gospel of Christ' (Phil. 1.27). Again the apostle gives the impression of having chosen his words carefully. He tried to write in such a way that he spoke the language of his readers. Departing from his custom (Phil. 3.17; Rom. 6.4; 8.4; I Cor. 3.3), in the letter to the community of Philippi he did not use the well-known term 'walk' – firmly rooted in the Old Testament Jewish tradition – but a Greek word which did not deny his Roman background and which can be admirably translated 'fulfilling one's civic duties'. This is not just fortuitous. A similar thought recurs in the second letter to the community of Philippi: 'for our citizenship is in heaven' (Phil. 3.20). The author of Acts chose the same word in his description of Paul's defence of himself before the Sanhedrin: 'And Paul, looking intently at the Sanhedrin, said, "Brethren, I have lived before God with a clear conscience about my public behaviour up to this day"' (Acts 23.1). There is no doubt that Paul deliberately chose these terms in his letters to the community of Philippi. The Christians in this city were proud of their Roman citizenship and so too was the apostle. On this basis they had come together and because of that, by using terms which sounded familiar to his readers, Paul could encourage and inspire them to a way of life which corresponded with the demands which may be made on followers of Jesus Christ.

Paul did not write his first letter to the community of Philippi because there were concrete problems which needed a solution. However, the lack of internal conflicts did not prevent the apostle from directly emphasizing how important it was for the community to form a unity (Phil. 1.27). Earlier, the first letter to the Corinthians has shown us clearly that the apostle attached particularly great importance to this aspect. So it is not surprising that he also discusses this theme in later letters (Gal. 3.28). For Paul, the consequences of unity were far-reaching : 'Complete my joy by being of the same mind, having the same love, being in full accord and of one mind. Do nothing from selfishness or conceit, but in humility count others better than yourselves. Let each of you look not only to his own interests but also to the interests of others' (Phil. 2.2–4). If this unity has become a reality, it will transform the community from being a group of ordinary mortals into a community of 'renewed' men and women who will prove to be in a position to make their own interest subordinate to the interests of others.

How important all this was for Paul becomes clear if we look at the impressive 'Christ psalm'[4] which he has included in the letter (Phil. 2.5–11). Theologically, this part makes the letter to the community of Philippi somewhat unbalanced. Up to that moment the tone had been cheerful and the style light. Paul had spent his days in prison trusting in a good outcome. He was not discontented with his stay there. He even thought that he could see it in positive terms in connection with the preaching and dissemination of the gospel: 'I want you to know, brothers and sisters, that what has happened to me has really served to advance the gospel, so that it has become known throughout the whole praetorian guard and to all the rest that my imprisonment is for Christ; and most of the brethren have been made confident in the Lord because of my imprisonment, and are much more bold to speak the word of God without fear' (Phil. 1.12–14). In prison Paul has received support from Philippi, and he is very grateful to the community for that. There were no serious conflicts. The apostle wrote an encouraging letter in which he gave instructions about a Christian way of life in words which were not strange to his readers. Suddenly the tone changes and the readers are confronted with a passage which directs attention to Jesus Christ. Why has Paul chosen this surprising continuation for his argument?

The Christ psalm in Philippians 2 has prompted a great many commentaries in the course of the centuries. Countless publications fill the bookshelves in the libraries of theological faculties.[5] The passage has also played an important role in the history of dogma.[6] Paul could not possibly have suspected that his decision to give this text a place in his letter – in a sense in

passing, as support for his plea for a Christian way of life –
could have such far-reaching consequences down the centuries.
It seems certain, and there is a remarkably wide consensus on
this point in scholarly literature, that the Christ psalm in its
original form was not written by Paul. In Philippians 2.6–11 we
find a strikingly large number of words and expressions which
cannot be found anywhere else in his letters, like the term 'the
form of God', a Greek word which is difficult to translate, and
which can be rendered as 'grasp' or 'think it robbery'; and
finally the thought that 'he emptied himself'.

The last word has yet to be spoken about the origin of the
Christ psalm. There is no doubt that the hymn is Christian in
origin. However, a careful analysis of the text shows the degree
to which reflection within early Christianity is stamped by
the Old Testament-Jewish tradition.[7] The great variety of the
tradition is echoed in the words of the Christ psalm. The
humiliation and suffering of the one 'who was found in the
form of God' has an affinity with (a) the psalms of the righteous
sufferer (Pss. 22; 69; 86)[8] and (b) the song of the suffering
servant in Isaiah 53;[9] his pre-existence seems to be derived from
(c) the talk about the pre-existent wisdom which is already
present in embryo in the Old Testament (Prov. 8.22–30), but is
developed further in Hellenistic Jewish literature from the
intertestamental period.[10]

There is unmistakably 'movement' in the Christ psalm: from
above downwards, from heaven to earth, from God to human
beings, and through being a slave to the absolute nadir: 'He
became obedient to death, even the death of the cross' (v. 8).
Then the way goes upwards again: 'therefore God has also
highly exalted him' (v. 9), so highly that he can be compared
with God: 'and given him a name which is above every name,
that at the name of Jesus every knee shall bow, in heaven, on
earth and under the earth, and every tongue confess that Jesus
Christ is Lord, to the glory of God the Father' (Phil. 2.9–11).[11]
The scheme of *humiliation* (v.8) and *exaltation* (v. 9) is of
crucial importance. That is powerfully emphasized by the
many-sided terminology. Thus humiliation can be described

and interpreted more closely with terms like 'emptying' (v. 7) and 'obedience' (v. 8), while exaltation is expressed in both the 'worship' (v. 10; cf. Isa. 45.23) and the 'confession' that the one who has been humiliated is now, like God, to be addressed as Lord.

The Christ psalm speaks the language of the time. Images and ideas are unmistakably 'contextual'. They represent the thought-world of people of the ancient Near East. The heaven is 'above', human beings live 'below' on the earth, while 'under the earth' the darkness of the kingdom of the dead prevails. The distance is emphasized particularly in Old Testament-Jewish literature: 'The heaven is the Lord's; to men he gave the earth' (Ps. 115.16). There is distance, but also surprising and saving nearness. God comes into contact with human beings. The distance can be bridged. In the deutero-canonical writing The Wisdom of Solomon there is a prayer for wisdom which is put into the mouth of the famous king Solomon centuries after his time: 'O God of my fathers and Lord of mercy, you have made all things by your word, and by your wisdom have formed man to have dominion over the creatures you have made, and rule the world in holiness and righteousness, and pronounce judgment in uprightness of soul. *Give me the wisdom that sits by your throne . . . Send her forth from the holy heavens, and from the throne of your glory send her, that she may be with me and toil, and that I may learn what is pleasing to you*' (Wisdom 9.1–10). Contact is possible between 'above' and 'below', between heaven and earth. God remains in heaven, but through his Spirit, his Word, his Wisdom, he is 'present' among human beings on earth. The author of the Christ psalm has brought the traditional notion up to date. In this way he gives us some insight into the process of reflection within the early Christian community about questions relating to the life and death of Christ.

Who was he, the man from Nazareth? A human being among other human beings? That was certainly true, but after his death and resurrection the early Christian community was soon no longer content with the 'simplicity' of this answer. He was a human being, but he was a special human being. His disciples preserved recollections that he felt close to God. Jesus was a man after God's heart. To express this conviction the power of the Christ psalm resorted to the age-old creation story in Genesis: 'And God created man in his image; in the image of God created he him; male and female created he them' (Gen. 1.27). Jesus was the human being as God had once meant human beings to be at creation: 'He who was found in the form (or as the image) of God' (Phil. 2.6).

The human being after God's image becomes an 'ordinary' human being. That is a deliberate choice. The author of the Christ psalm depicts that in two different ways: (a) 'he did not want to cling on to being equal with God' (v. 6) and (b) 'he emptied himself and assumed the form of a slave' (v. 7). The last sentence admirably emphasizes how radical this event is: 'the form of God' stands over against 'the form of a slave', while 'being like God' is exchanged for 'being like a man' (v. 8). Next there is a real 'hinge' in the hymn: the moment the nadir of the humiliation – the death on the cross – is reached, the exaltation (v. 9) begins, an exaltation which in fact no longer knows any limits, for Christ Jesus is ultimately set alongside God: 'Jesus Christ is Lord'.

We need to consider the question why Jesus chose to be 'like men'. The answer is not easy to give. Why did he humiliate himself and become obedient to death (v. 8)? In thinking through the problem further we do well to realize that the Christ psalm is a *hymn* and not a theological treatise which strives for clarity and completeness. The 'hymnic' language calls for poetic treatment. Not every question can be answered satisfactorily. However, it is certain that the author of the Christ psalm has put the life and above all the death of Jesus in the early Jewish tradition of the suffering righteous. He was the man after God's heart, the righteous one who walked in the ways of the Lord. He appeared as the light in the darkness, as a sign of hope in a world without comfort. Experience had taught that the life of the righteous was quite often hard. The righteous were mocked, scorned, persecuted and sometimes even killed. In the Psalms the righteous lament their distress (Ps. 22; 69). The anonymous prophet who for want of a better name is known in scholarly literature as Deutero-Isaiah, and who knew that the end of the Babylonian exile was near, spoke about the suffering of a righteous man whom he called 'the servant of the Lord' (Isa. 53.11). In the intertestamental period, in a wide circle the suffering of the righteous became an accepted notion which at the same time expresses the inevitability and necessity for that innocent suffering. The righteous *have to* suffer. That is what people do to the righteous (Wisdom 2.10–20). There is no way out except for flight or betrayal of one's own ideals. For this reason, too, the Christ psalm emphasizes 'the obedience' of the righteous 'who had emptied himself' (v. 7). He himself remained faithful to death – and he also hoped and waited for God.

In general the Old Testament-Jewish tradition is reticent in speaking about 'the meaning' of the suffering of the righteous. What significance can this have 'for' others? One of the few answers which are given to this question is to be found in the pericope about the suffering of the servant of the Lord in Isaiah 53. Here are two passages from it: 'He was wounded for our transgressions, he was bruised for our iniquities, upon him was the chastisement that made us whole and by his stripes we are healed' (v. 5); and: 'He bore the sin of many, and made intercession for the transgressors' (v. 12). The suffering of the servant is described as a suffering 'for others'. His suffering does not remain without significance for others and ultimately it can be said that he suffers 'in the place of others'.

Anyone who reads the Christ psalm against the background of Isa.53 will be surprised by the sobriety and restraint with which the significance of suffering is spoken of. The author of the psalm has used motifs from the Old Testament Jewish tradition about the righteous sufferer and the suffering servant, but says little or nothing about what he meaning of this suffering can be for others. He is content to give a sketch of the way of emptying, humiliation, death and exaltation. The exegete of this complicated text is faced with a difficult dilemma. How are we to explain this silence? Is vicarious suffering presupposed, and does it not therefore need to be mentioned explicitly? In the light of the Christian tradition with its strong emphasis on the vicarious suffering and death of Jesus Christ it is natural to say yes to this question. But is it certain that the author of the Christ psalm indeed wanted to see things like this and not otherwise? Because we can no longer ask him, we have no alternative than to interpret the words that he has set down in writing. And no more than that. We shall have to respect his restraint. Of course the later dogmatic reflection on his text did not yet know this restraint.

The 'christology' of the Christ psalm can be briefly summarized as follows. We do not know who the author of the original psalm was. It must have been someone who was at home in scripture and tradition. Given his knowledge of the wisdom literature from the intertestamental period it seems likely that he came from Hellenistic Judaism. In the first place he portrayed Jesus very much in line with the Old Testament Jewish tradition, as a righteous sufferer. Faithful to God and himself, Jesus obediently went the way of suffering. This attitude moved his disciples, made an impression on them and was experienced as 'exemplary'. In this sense it can also be said that Jesus died 'for us'. His way of living, his faithfulness and love, his obedience to the death, challenges us and inspires us to a new and creative humanity. The author of the Christ psalm, nourished by wisdom literature, adds one more element to these thoughts. Jesus died as a righteous sufferer, but that is not the last word about him. In his living and dying his followers have felt able to talk about a special relationship between Jesus and God. He was the man after God's heart, the man who was what God had meant the creation to be. Bearing the image of God – in the form of God' (v. 6) – he emptied himself and entered into solidarity with human beings on earth. In this way he bridged the gap between God and human beings. His 'exaltation' symbolizes that his way of humiliation was not hopeless, but full of perspective.

Paul included this Christ psalm in his letter to the community of Philippi. Why did he do that?[12] There was no direct occasion for doing so. Up to that moment in his argument he had only made sporadic comments about christological themes – his longing to be with Christ is an exception (Phil. 1.23). Paul directed his attention above all to aspects of a Christian way of life. In writings which he subsequently sent to other communities, he never referred back to the words of the Christ psalm. Did he allow himself to be carried away by a text which was – and is! – so impressive that we too are still moved by it? Presumably we should answer yes to this question. We cannot say much with any certainty about Paul's way of working. Remarks in his letters suggest that usually he did not write himself, but dictated (Rom. 16.22). One can only guess at the circumstances in the prison in Ephesus. His stay there will not have been very comfortable. For this reason it does not seem too bold to suppose that Paul also dictated this letter. If that may be the case, then it is difficult to reconstruct his train of thought to any degree.

As we saw, Paul attached great importance to the unity of the Christian community. He wrote his ethical admonitions with an eye to that. Earlier he had made a bold connection between Christ and his own fate. Here is the text again: 'It is my eager expectation and hope that I shall not be at all ashamed, but that with full courage now as always Christ will be glorified in my body, whether by life or death' (Phil. 1.20). The essence of this statement is not easy to fathom, but in any case it is certain that Paul thought that his life had consequences for the proclamation of the gospel of Jesus Christ. In my view that is a good explanation for the sentence 'Christ will be glorified in my body'. The surprising transition from the ethical admonitions to the Christ hymn is also understandable against this background: 'Let this disposition be among you which was also in Christ Jesus' (Phil. 2.5). What disposition was Paul thinking of? In the interpretation of the Christ psalm it became clear that terms like 'humiliation' and 'emptying' are central. Considering that in the previous ethical admonitions Paul had put great emphasis on the unity of the community and unselfish attention

to others, it is not surprising that suddenly – Paul was an impul-
sive man – he quoted the Christ hymn. Perhaps he really sang
the hymn. Because the words were 'in his head', it is not surprising that he quoted the whole hymn, i.e. also the aspects
which can no longer be applied to the community: the humiliation to the death of the cross and the subsequent exaltation.

It becomes clear that we must look in this direction when we
analyse how Paul's argument is continued after the Christ
hymn. Again ethics is central, even with a surprising statement:
'Therefore, my beloved, as you have always obeyed, so now,
not only as in my presence but much more in my absence, *work
out your salvation with fear and trembling'* – it seems as if Paul
is quick to add, to avoid possible misunderstandings – 'for God
is at work in you, both to will and to work for his good
pleasure' (Phil. 2.12–13).

Thus letter A to the community in Philippi ends in great
contentment: 'I have received full payment, and more; I am
filled, having received from Epaphroditus the gifts you sent, a
fragrant offering, a sacrifice acceptable and pleasing to God'
(Phil. 4.18). There is every reason for joy. It is almost beyond
imagining that such words were written by a man who had
already spent some time in prison. Again we must marvel at the
apostle's strength of mind.

No problems. Relations between Paul and the community
were as good as could be. The letter contains few, if any,
passages which could irritate the readers. Soon it would prove
that even the good relationship between Paul and the community of Philippi could be troubled.

9

Letter to Philemon

A second letter from prison

'Paul, a prisoner for Christ Jesus, and Timothy our brother. To Philemon our beloved fellow worker and Apphia our sister and Archippus our fellow soldier and the community in your house: Grace to you and peace from God our Father and the Lord Jesus Christ' (Philemon 1–3). So runs the heading of a short letter which Paul in all probability also wrote in prison in Ephesus. This time too Timothy is also mentioned as a fellow sender (Philemon 1).

The name of Philemon appears only here. We know no more about him. That also applies to Apphia. The apostle calls her 'our sister'. Presumably she was Philemon's wife. They made their house available for meetings of the communities. Paul does not write where that happened, but the name of Archippus, 'our fellow soldier', can give us a clue. At the end of the letter to the community of Colossae a remark is made about someone with the same name: 'And say to Archippus, "See that you fulfil the ministry which you have received in the Lord"' (Col. 4.17). If this is one and the same person, that could indicate that the house community of Philemon and Apphia met in Colossae. The city was in Phrygia in Asia Minor. The distance from Ephesus – just over 100 miles – was such that both correspondence and personal contacts were possible without many problems.

A personal letter

There was a specific reason for writing a letter to Philemon and his people. Paul was trying to put in a good word for Onesimus. His name, too, is mentioned in the letter addressed to the community of Colossae (Col. 4.9). This is another indication that Philemon and his family lived in that city. Paul's shortest letter has a very personal character. There is no doubt that Paul knew the person to whom he was writing. That is evident, among other things, from the conclusion: 'Confident in your obedience, I write to you, knowing that you will do even more than I say. At the same time, prepare a guest room for me, for I am hoping through your prayers to be restored to you' (Philemon 21–22). We do not know whether Paul indeed travelled via Colossae to Troas on his departure from Ephesus. That would have been a substantial detour. It is also conceivable that the apostle felt compelled to change his plans. That sort of thing happened to him often!

Paul introduces his plea for Onesimus as follows: 'Accordingly, though I am bold enough in Christ to command you to do what is required, I prefer to appeal to you, I, Paul, *an old man* and now a prisoner also for Jesus Christ' (Philemon 8–9). By now twenty years had passed since the days when as a young man in Jerusalem he had studied with Gamaliel and had been present at the stoning of Stephen (Acts 7.58). But he certainly cannot yet be called an aged man. He was still in the prime of life. That he nevertheless describes himself as 'an old man' says something about his mood rather than about his real age. From the next part of his life it is quite clear that at least he was an exhausted man, who longed for rest and for the end of his career. He constantly had new plans. Thus some time later he wrote from Corinth to Rome: 'This is the reason why I have so often been hindered from you. But now, since I no longer have any room for work in these regions, and since I have longed for many years to come to you, I hope to see you in passing as I go to Spain' (Rom. 15.22–24).

A special bond had developed between Paul and Onesimus,

'the child whose father I have become in my imprisonment' (Philemon 10). With these words, which could easily give rise to misunderstanding, Paul wanted to make it clear that in prison he had converted Onesimus to the Christian faith. Moreover the sentence suggests that Onesimus too was in prison in Ephesus. Why? From the rest of the letter at all events it can be inferred that difficulties had arisen between Philemon and Onesimus. We can no longer discover precisely what these difficulties were. It is certain that Onesimus was Philemon's slave. The apostle does not say why he had run away from his lord and master and how he had landed up in prison in Ephesus. Had Onesimus fled from Philemon's house? That is the traditional view, and of course it is possible.[1] That often happened. The fate that awaited runaway slaves was sometimes cruel. The Romans punished harshly. Rebels and slaves who had sought freedom in vain were usually mercilessly nailed to the cross.

One of Paul's remarks suggest that Onesimus possibly had possibly cheated his master financially: 'If he has wronged you at all, or owes you anything, charge that to my account. Here is my signature, Paul, I shall pay . . . To say nothing of your owing me even your own self. Yes, brother, I want some benefit from you in the Lord. Refresh my heart in Christ' (Philemon 18–20). This passage is a good example of the personal tone in which the letter is written.

Slavery was a widespread phenomenon in Graeco-Roman society. Here we need to remember that there was also rank and status among slaves. There were slaves who lived as real serfs in complete dependence on their lord and master and in fact had no say whatsoever. But there were also slaves who themselves had possessions and made long journeys on behalf of their masters, for example to conclude important trade agreements. Onesimus could have been such a slave.[2] Clearly he came into conflict with Philemon in the financial sphere. The consequence was that he ended up in prison in Ephesus. There he met Paul.

The letter to Philemon was written at the time of Onesimus's release. The financial conflict will have been resolved. Of course that does not mean that the mutual relationship between master and slave could automatically be restored. In his moving plea Paul puts great emphasis on this aspect: 'I am sending him back to you, sending my very heart. I would have been glad to keep him with me, in order that he might serve me on your behalf during my imprisonment for the gospel; but I preferred to do nothing without your consent in order that your goodness might not be by compulsion but of your own free will. Perhaps that is why he was parted from you a while, that you might have him back for ever, no longer as a slave but more than a slave, as a beloved brother, especially to me but how much more to you, both in the flesh and in the Lord. So if you consider me your partner, receive him as you would receive me' (Philemon 12–17).

Paul's plea will not have failed to have an effect. There is no reason to doubt that Onesimus returned to Philemon's house. However, he did not go home as a penitent sinner or as a runaway slave who on the recommendation of Paul was to be received kindly by his lord and master. The apostle attached great importance to Philemon coming to realize that he might welcome not a slave but a 'beloved brother' into his house. Paul does not consider further who was most to blame for the broken relationship between Philemon and Onesimus. He left the past to be the past. There was no sense in looking back. Thanks to the meeting in prison in Ephesus Philemon has a brother, a new, enthusiastic member of his house community.[3]

Paul and slavery

Does this letter give us some insight into Paul's view of the problem of slavery?[4] He is often criticized for having given a runaway slave in search of freedom the hard command to return to the rule of his lord and master. If that were the case, then the letter would indicate that Paul did not challenge slavery, but in fact sanctioned it. Other exegetes have pointed out that this conclusion is drawn too easily and that it does no justice to the advice which Paul has given in his letter to

Philemon. Certainly he sent Onesimus back to his master, but he does say something important as well: 'no longer as a slave, but more than a slave, as a beloved brother' (Philemon 16). It may then be true that Paul did not perform any revolutionary action which radically changed existing social conditions (cf. Rom. 13.1–7), but he was convinced that there might no longer be any rank and status within the Christian community.

We ask too many questions of this short letter to Philemon if we want to infer from the small number of verses in which Paul is treating a very specific question what the apostle thought about slavery. It is important for us to realize that slavery has had many faces down the ages. To us the phenomenon is in flagrant contradiction to the most fundamental rights of all men and women on earth. Freedom is the greatest good. However strange it may perhaps seem, within certain limits a 'slave' like Onesimus also knew freedom. In exchange for the activities which he engaged in for his master – Philemon was his 'patron' – he was offered protection, security and in due course a peaceful old age. It was regrettable that this had led to a conflict. But that did not mean that social conditions had to be changed once and for all. Onesimus's circumstances would not be improved by that. It was intelligent of Paul that he made an effort not only to restore the relationship between Philemon and Onesimus but even to put it on a higher level.

10

Correspondence with the community in Corinth (II)

Paul departs from Ephesus

At the end of I Corinthians Paul promised his readers: 'I will visit you after passing through Macedonia, for I intend to pass through Macedonia, and perhaps I will stay with you or even spend the winter, so that you may speed me on my journey, wherever I go. For I did not want to see you just in passing; I hope to spend some time with you if the Lord permits. *But I will stay in Ephesus until Pentecost,* for a wide door for effective work has opened to me and there are many adversaries' (I Cor. 16.5–9). His imprisonment in Ephesus was not wholly unexpected. After he had regained his freedom he thought it wise to prepare to depart from the city. Evidently his life was in no immediate danger, for this time there is no mention of a 'flight'. The author of Acts also reports that the apostle made a leisurely departure: 'After the uproar ceased, Paul sent for the disciples, and having exhorted them took leave of them and departed for Macedonia' (Acts 20.1). We know a little more about the journey from a short passage in II Corinthians: 'When I came to Troas to preach the gospel of Christ, a door was opened for me in the Lord; but my mind could not rest because I did not find my brother Titus there. So I took leave of them and went on to Macedonia' (II Cor. 12–13).

At that time Troas was an important port, a crossroads of routes by land and sea. Through excavations we know that ancient Troy is to be situated in the immediate vicinity of Troas.

Did Paul also know that? Did he know Homer's epics? We cannot be sure, but given the fact that he grew up in the Diaspora we cannot rule out the possibility that he did. In the first century of our era the works of Homer had for some time been 'classics' and were widespread in the Graeco-Roman world. Other writers were inspired by them. Without this literature the cultural history of Europe would have taken on a different appearance. Paul, 'the man of two worlds', will not have been completely ignorant of the legendary conflict which had raged on this part of the western coast of Asia Minor in the distant past.

From Troas it was possible to cross over to Macedonia and Greece. Paul knew the voyage. He had also embarked from Troas during his second missionary journey (Acts 16.8–11). On this occasion he had made no attempts to preach the gospel locally. Paul had a 'vision', and subsequently resolved to cross over to Macedonia immediately. Now that he was visiting the city for the second time he tried to make good his 'neglect'. Circumstances seemed favourable. In the passage from II Corinthians quoted above there is a phrase which Paul used often when he experienced that his preaching was successful: 'and the Lord had opened the door for me' (II Cor. 2.13; I Cor. 16.9; cf. Acts 14.27; Col. 4.3; Rev. 3.8). Although things in Troas went as he wanted them to, the apostle was restless there. He had hoped to meet his fellow-worker Titus, but Titus did not turn up. Paul did not have the patience to wait long and after a while resolved to cross over to Macedonia.

Where was Titus? After receiving negative reports about the situation within the community of Corinth he had travelled from Ephesus to Greece. He brought the 'tearful letter' from Paul and also hoped by his efforts to be able to calm things down and restore the damaged relations between the apostle to the Gentiles and the community there. The texts are not clear enough about the absence of Titus and Paul's restlessness. Had the two of them agreed to meet in Troas? The passage from II Corinthians quoted earlier suggests this. Nowhere are we told why Titus did not appear. Paul was disturbed and travelled on to Macedonia. There finally the meeting took place which is described in II Corinthians as follows: 'For even when we came into Macedonia our bodies had no rest but we were afflicted at every turn – fighting without and fear within. But God, who comforts the downcast, comforted us *by the coming of Titus,* and not only by his coming but also by the comfort with which he was comforted in you, as he told us of your longing, your mourning, your zeal for me, so that I rejoiced still more' (II Cor. 7.5–7). It was also thanks to Titus' efforts in Corinth that the air had been cleared. Relations between Paul and the community there had been notably improved. 'Somewhere' on the way to Macedonia the apostle then gratefully wrote another letter to Corinth after the 'tearful letter' already mentioned.

The 'tearful letter'

For what happened next in the fascinating correspondence between Paul and the community in Corinth we must first take a step back into the past. While the apostle was still in Ephesus, the conflict with the Corinthians came to a climax. In this tense situation, presumably before he ended up in prison, the apostle wrote a letter which because of his own description has come to be known by scholars as the 'tearful letter': 'For I write to you out of much affliction and anguish of heart and with many tears, not to cause you pain but to let you know the abundant love that I have for you' (II Cor. 2.4). However, the correspondence indicates that while Paul deeply regretted the course of events, he was still not inclined to change his standpoint: 'For even if I made you sorry with my letter, I do not regret it (though I did regret it), for I see that that letter grieved you, though only for a while. As it is, I rejoice, not because you were grieved, but because you were grieved into repenting; for you felt a godly grief, so that you suffered no loss through us' (II Cor. 7.8–9).

The letter which was 'written with many tears' has not been preserved. However, it is possible that part of it has found its way into the New Testament. From the middle of the nineteenth century, New Testament scholars have discussed the *unity* of II Corinthians.[1] We have already met one of the problems: the part in which Christ and Beliar are contrasted (II Cor 6.15–7.1) is said to come from the 'immorality letter' which Paul wrote before I Corinthians. However, the most striking feature is the abrupt transition between the conclusion of chapter 9 and the beginning of chapter 10. Suddenly the tone changes radically. Whereas in the previous chapters Paul proved conciliatory and gave the impression that the sharp conflict had meanwhile become a thing of the past, from chapter 10 he writes in a remarkably fierce and sarcastic way.[2] Despite a gulf of centuries one is still inclined to pause. The dispute begins to get so fierce that there is a risk that personal relations will be destroyed for good.

Again the exegete faces a dilemma. On the basis of our knowledge of the earliest manuscripts there is no reason to doubt the unity of the letter. But in my view, in this case arguments on the content prove decisive.[3] The differences between the first part and the final chapters are such that we can virtually rule out the possibility that the apostle sent the letter in the form which has become canonical. Anyone who nevertheless thinks it necessary to defend the unity of the letter cannot avoid explaining the remarkable change in Paul's argument. In the history of the exegesis of the text, exegetes have proved remarkably inventive in devising solutions.[4] Usually they start by assuming that there has been a 'dictation pause' for one reason or another. One can only guess at the reason for the pause. Explanations vary a great deal. Some argue that evening had come. It was decided to stop and continue the next morning. However, Paul slept badly, with the inevitable consequences. Others suggest that the dictation pause was caused by the arrival of more, unfavourable news about the situation in Corinth.

Of course it is possible that Paul was disturbed while he was dictating, but even if that were the case it is difficult to imagine that on closer inspection he would not have changed his letter radically. Anyone who begins in a conciliatory tone and ends with fierce polemic knows in advance that he shares the responsibility for bringing the dispute to a head. One does not need to be an expert in psychology to know this. Paul was not, of course, acquainted with this science, but he was intelligent enough to sense this nevertheless. From the letters that we have examined so far we have come to know Paul as a man who knew what he was doing and who felt closely involved in the welfare of the community that he knew. The problem is resolved if we do not treat II Corinthians as a unity. Here it is natural to suppose that chapters 10–13 were written earlier. They were composed at the time when the conflict had reached his height. Paul wrote the rest of the letter later, in the hope of being ale to bring about peace.

If II Corinthians 10–13 is seen as part of the 'tearful letter' sent earlier, a number of inconsistencies seem to disappear and we get a clear picture of the course of events. I have already discussed this question briefly in an earlier chapter. Reports about tensions in the community of Corinth reached Paul in Ephesus. He wrote a letter in which he discussed subjects like immorality and prostitution. The Corinthians reacted with new questions, which compelled him to write a long letter in which he reacted at length to the questions raised. That is the writing which has been incorporated into the New Testament canon as the first letter of Paul to the community in Corinth. In this letter the apostle does not utter very sharp polemic, but on the other hand he leaves no misunderstanding about his views on certain developments within the Corinthian community. New reports from the Greek port disclosed that the reception of the letter had been unfavourable. Thereupon Paul resolved to pay an 'interim visit' to Corinth. That did not prove to be a success.

In this hopeless situation, after his return to Ephesus he wrote an emotional 'tearful letter' which he gave to Titus and in which he announced his third visit. The tone is sharp: 'Here for the third time I am ready to come to you. And I will not be a burden, for I seek not what is yours but you; for children ought not to lay up for their parents, but parents for their children' (II Cor. 12.14). It seems legitimate to ask whether someone who

announces his visit in such a way can count on a happy reception. In this phase of the conflict efforts towards reconciliation
were clearly not yet a high priority for Paul. That also emerges
from a later part in the letter when he again announces his
coming: 'This is the third time I am coming to you. Any charge
must be sustained by the evidence of two or three witnesses. I
warned those who sinned before and all the others, and I warn
them now while absent, as I did when present on my second
visit, that if I come I shall not spare them' (II Cor. 13.1–2).

When Paul wrote and sent the tearful letter, he had planned
shortly to travel to Corinth to put things in order. After that he
changed his plans and for the moment abandoned making a
new visit to the Greek port. In the letter which he wrote after his
departure from Ephesus to Macedonia – and which now for the
sake of convenience I shall call II Corinthians – he explained his
decision not to come as follows: 'But I call God to witness
against me – it was to spare you that I refrained from coming to
Corinth?' (II Cor. 1.23). Who or what persuaded Paul to
change his mind? The question is difficult to answer. His mood
has changed drastically. Did his fellow-workers persuade him
not to bring the conflict with Corinth to a head? Certainly from
the beginning Titus was wise and inclined to reconciliation (II
Cor. 7.7, 13–15). Perhaps Paul received hopeful reports. At all
events, he reflected, and resolved to postpone his journey: 'For
I made up my mind not to make you another painful visit. For
if I cause you pain, who is there to make me glad but the one
whom I have pained?'(II Cor. 2.1)

Why could the conflict between Paul and the community in
Corinth get so heated? In an earlier chapter I pointed out that
the Corinthians had come from all points of the compass. The
mixed population resulted in a mixed community. There were
many parties and unity was a long way off (I Cor. 1.10–17).
There was also rank and status within the community.
Differences between the rich and poor sometimes led to painful
confrontations. Highly educated, literate members of the community often found it difficult to treat as equals their brothers
and sisters who had had virtually no education and had little

culture. Contempt was lurking and it was easy to give way to it. There were very different notions of a Christian way of life. Those who until recently had been accustomed to visiting a temple at various times and having intercourse with a male or female temple prostitute were confronted with the question whether they could still do this as members of a Christian community. In his 'immorality' letter and also in I Corinthians Paul did not conceal his view. In so doing he provoked opposition. The Corinthians were cosmopolitan. They could not easily be persuaded to change their minds by the view of one apostle. And was he really an authentic apostle? Hadn't he written ironically in I Corinthians that compared with the other apostles he was 'one born out of due time' (I Cor. 15.8)?

The 'tearful letter' is a very human document – a special document, which gives us the possibility after so many centuries of catching sight of the human Paul. This work offers few new aspects for those who are exclusively interested in the apostle's theology. The tense situation in Ephesus and the heated discussion with the Corinthians were a serious obstacle in the way of a quiet and balanced community. Paul had his hands full getting rid of misunderstandings and rejecting the criticisms made of his personal activity. If some people still doubt the truth of the statement that he wrote *real* letters, then I suggest that this last trace of hesitation will disappear for good after reading II Cor. 10–13. Those who love profound theology will read these chapters with a feeling of disappointment. Paul was a realist and not a dreamer. One can respect him for not making reality seem more attractive than it was. Thanks to the openness and honesty with which he wrote about his own experience we have some information about the disputes within some early Christian communities in Greece and Asia Minor. The picture that is conjured up may shock us. The beginning of the book of Acts describes an ideal community (Acts 2.41–47), more dream than reality, an idyll which probably never existed, or if it did, existed only for a short time (Acts 6.1–2). Paul knew the reality, and he did not keep quiet about it or disguise it. Human beings remain human, even when they become

followers of Jesus Christ. The beginning of the part of the tearful letter which has been preserved in the New Testament leaves
no doubt about this: 'I, Paul, myself entreat you, by the meek-
ness and gentleness of Christ – I who am humble when face to
face with you, but bold to you when I am away' (II Cor. 10.1).
The Corinthians had accused him of being two-faced. In
personal dealings he was said to have been shy, but when he
had departed and was addressing them by letter, all his shyness
disappeared: 'I would not seem to be frightening you with
letters. For they say, "His letters are weighty and strong, but his
bodily presence is weak, and his speech of no account." Let
such people understand that what we say by letter when absent,
we do when present' (II Cor. 10.9–11).

The words quoted show how personal relations can be
destroyed by misunderstandings. Communication between
Paul and the community in Corinth did not run smoothly.
His appearances were marked by caution and modesty. Evidently he made little impression on the Corinthians. They were
inhabitants of a metropolis, for the most part self-confident,
educated people who called themselves 'wise' and were not
quickly influenced by what others might have to offer. From
Paul's reaction one could infer that he too was treated with a
degree of condescension and even contempt. What has this Jew
from the East to teach us, inhabitants of a great Greek
Hellenistic city with a wide cultural and religious influence, that
we did not know already? In such a situation we can easily
imagine that to begin with, Paul's letters did more harm than
good. Paul had a sharp pen and he rarely minced his words.
Nor did he do so in the tearful letter. His tone is fierce, and
often he allows his emotion to lead him to engage in quite
sarcastic arguments: 'Not that we venture to class or compare
ourselves with some of those who commend themselves, but
when they measure themselves by one another, and compare
themselves with one another, they are without understanding'
(II Cor. 10.12).

As his argument goes on, the sarcasm increases: 'I wish you
would bear with me in a little foolishness' (II Cor. 11.1). Clearly

Paul's opponents judged him to have behaved stupidly, without understanding and foolishly (II Cor. 4.13). This criticism must have hurt him deeply and led him to write a text in which he mocks his opponents by playing the role of fool with feigned conviction: 'I repeat, let no one think me foolish; but even if you do, accept me as a fool, so that I too may boast a little. (What I am saying I say not with the Lord's authority but as a fool, in this boastful confidence; since many boast of worldly things, I too will boast). For you gladly bear with fools, being wise yourselves. For you bear it if a man makes slaves of you, or preys upon you, or takes advantage of you, or puts on airs, or strikes you in the face. To my shame, I must say, we were too weak for that!' (II Cor. 11.16–21).[5]

The last two sentences need explanation. Doubtless they can be regarded as taunts. And Paul certainly meant them as such. From the correspondence, he had learned about the appearance of men who seemed to be preaching another gospel: 'For if some one comes and preaches another Jesus than the one we preached, or if you receive a different spirit from the one you received, or if you accept a different gospel from the one you accepted, you submit to it readily enough' (II Cor. 11.4). The last words contain a direct rebuke to the Corinthians. Paul objected to their having been taken in so easily by his opponents. They had given in to everything that they had been told. Anyone who has followed the correspondence between Paul and the community in Corinth can hardly escape the impression that here the apostle is guilty of exaggeration. Can we really imagine that the Corinthians who had shown themselves to Paul as very self-confident people would have suddenly allowed themselves to be tyrannized by his opponents as though they were immature? There seems no doubt that the apostle is giving a distorted picture of reality. We may criticize him for that. At the same time we can also forgive him and be grateful to him that through this scornful exaggeration he has given us a glimpse into his soul. In this connection the following quotation speaks volumes: 'I feel a divine jealousy for you, for I betrothed you to Christ to present you as a pure bride to her one husband. But I am afraid that as the serpent deceived Eve by his cunning, your thoughts will be led astray from a sincere and pure devotion to Christ' (II Cor. 11.1–2).

Who were these opponents who caused Paul so much sorrow? The question of the identity of his opponents has been one of the most difficult problems to solve in the interpretation of his letters.[6] In the tearful letter Paul first speaks – again full of sarcasm – about 'arch-apostles' (II Cor. 11.5), and then he describes them as 'pseudo-apostles' (II Cor. 11.3). It is not easy to sketch their profile. According to Paul they claimed to be 'apostles of Christ'. The influence that they gained in Corinth suggests that they could present themselves in an authoritative way. It is conceivable that they were Jewish Christians connected with the group of apostles in Jerusalem. In any case their view of Jesus was worth considering – or so many people in Corinth thought. What did Paul really know about Jesus? He had not been a disciple. Did he have the right to the title 'apostle'?

Again Paul's apostolate was under discussion. That did not happen for the first time, nor was it to be the last (Gal. 1.11–12). His past as a persecutor of the early Christian community made him disputed and vulnerable as an apostle. Sometimes he showed some understanding of the criticism of his person (I Cor. 15.9–11), but he refused to be deterred by the wise. He regarded himself as an apostle called by God himself (Gal. 1.15–16). In the 'tearful letter' he defended his apostolate with verve and passion: 'Do you desire proof that Christ is speaking in me? He is not weak in dealing with you, but is powerful in you. For he was crucified in weakness, but lives by the power of God. For we are weak in him, but in dealing with you we shall live with him by the power of God' (II Cor. 13.3–4).

This ongoing, vigorous criticism of his apostolate must have been particularly irritating to Paul. He felt challenged to silence his opponents for good. He did so in a way which may be regarded as a lesson in sarcasm. The passage is so fascinating that I shall quote it in full: 'But whatever anyone dares to boast of – I am speaking as a fool – I also dare to boast of. Are they

Hebrews? So am I. Are they Israelites? So am I. Are they descendants of Abraham? So am I. Are they servants of Christ? I am a better one – I am talking like a madman – with far greater labours, far more imprisonments, with countless beatings, and often near death. Five times I have received from the hands of the Jews the forty lashes less one. Three times I have been beaten with rods; once I was stoned. Three times I have been shipwrecked; a night and a day I have been adrift at sea; in frequent journeys in danger from rivers, danger from robbers, danger from my own people, danger from Gentiles, danger in the city, danger in the wilderness, danger at sea, danger from false brethren; in toil and hardship, through many a sleepless night, in hunger and thirst, often without food, in cold and exposure. And, apart from other things, there is the daily pressure upon me of my anxiety for all the churches. Who is weak, and I am not weak? Who is made to fall, and I am not indignant?' (II Cor. 11.21–29).

Anyone who is capable of writing such an emotional text must have been a warm-blooded and passionate person. Such a person is a grateful object for a biographer to investigate. At the same time many people who now read Paul's letters in the hope of getting some sight of the core of Christian belief, having noted such personal outbursts, will ask what this emotional man can still say to us today and how valuable his theological remarks can still be. In his correspondence with the community in Corinth the apostle took capricious ways. He challenged immorality and prostitutes. He drew sharp lines, but on closer inspection his thought also proved to be capable of being more gentle. The unity of the community was extremely important for him. He said a great deal about it – but not everything. He was tolerant and ready for sacrifice. He recognized the great art of modesty, but at particular moments – less modestly – he put himself emphatically at the centre. The apostle was a special person – not a saint, but a man of flesh and blood.

II Corinthians

Paul begins the letter in a way which betrays that he had not yet forgotten the unpleasant discussion about his apostolate: 'from Paul, an apostle of Christ Jesus by the will of God' (II Cor. 1.1). We all know from experience that forgiving is often less difficult than forgetting. Paul too will go on to defend himself and once again to counter criticisms which had reached him from Corinth: 'Who is sufficient for these things? For we are not, like so many, peddlers of God's word; but as men of sincerity, as commissioned by God, in the sight of God we speak in Christ' (II Cor. 2.17–18).

After the usual 'thanksgiving' (II Cor. 1.3–7), Paul relates 'the difficulties which we encountered in Asia'. In all probability he was referring to the events in Ephesus which have already discussed: 'For we were so utterly, unbearably crushed that we despaired of life itself. Why, we felt that we had received the sentence of death; but that was to make us rely not on ourselves but on God who raises the dead; he delivered us from so deadly a peril, and he will deliver us; on him we have set our hope that he will deliver us again, also with the help of your prayer' (II Cor. 1.8–11). It says a great deal that Paul can describe the difficulties which he had in Asia Minor as 'sharing fully in the suffering of Christ' (II Cor. 1.5). In the next part of the letter he will return to this theme (II Cor. 4.7–12).

As we noted earlier, the correspondence between Paul and the community in Corinth is very personal. In the letter which we are now considering, there are certainly more theological themes than in the previous 'tearful letter', but the apostle discusses them only because he felt that further reflection and deeper thought were necessary. The situation defines the theology and not vice versa. Or, to put it in a more pointed way: Paul's 'biography' had a decisive influence on his theological development. There is no mistaking the fact that at this moment in his life his thought had not been rounded off. What comes next will show us that this was still also the case later.

Paul again allows himself to be diverted into writing about

his own efforts and the sacrifices that he made for the sake of the gospel. Clearly he found it difficult to keep silent about them. However, he understood that he risked repeating himself: 'Are we beginning to commend ourselves again? Or do we need, as some do, letters of recommendation from you?' (II Cor. 3.1). The question is rhetorical and so the answer is clear. Is there still more to be said about that apostolate of Paul? Yes, of course it comes from God, and Paul owes even his skill to none other than God: 'He it is who has qualified us *to be ministers of a new covenant* – it is important to pause here, for the apostle is introducing a notion which he has not previously mentioned so explicitly – he defines this 'new covenant' in the following way: '. . . not in a written code but in the Spirit. For the written code kills, but the Spirit gives life' (II Cor. 3.6).[7]

Paul was a scriptural expert. He knew the scriptures and could also bring together different texts and motifs. With the notion of a 'new covenant' he was doubtless alluding to a well-known text from the book of the prophet Jeremiah: 'Behold the days are coming, says the Lord, when I will make a new covenant with the house of Israel and the house of Judah, not like the covenant which I made with their fathers when I took them by the hand to bring them out of the land of Egypt, my covenant which they broke, though I was their husband, says the Lord. But this is the covenant which I will make with the house of Israel after those days, says the Lord; I will put my law within them, and I will write it upon their hearts; and I will be their God, and they shall be my people' (Jer. 31.31–33).

Here we see Paul the scriptural scholar at work. He stood in the Old Testament-Jewish tradition. He did so in full conviction and did not want things otherwise. But he began to draw conclusions which broke new ground. At least, that is how they have functioned over the course of church history, and they have strongly stimulated the Christian sense of superiority over Judaism.[8] According to the prophet Jeremiah it was God's purpose to make a new beginning and conclude a new covenant with Israel after all the disappointments. Paul now applied this notion primarily to himself: as a follower and preacher of Jesus

Christ he thought that he could regard himself as 'minister of a new covenant'. Could he have been pleased that the way which he took would have dangerous consequences? In my view there is no doubt that the answer to this question must be no. Paul could not as yet have been aware of that and that was certainly not his aim. It is good for us to realize that the apostle lived in a period of history when the schism between Judaism and Christianity still lay hidden in the far distance. He was no soothsayer, but a child of his time, and like everyone else he thought and acted in a way which seems naive in the light of later developments and events. He did not want the schism, but his remarks were one of the reasons why it came about. That is the tragedy of Paul's life, and the consequence of the theological legacy which he left. Thus – involuntarily – he became the man who to the present day has been declared guilty of the rise of two different worlds: Judaism and Christianity.[9]

The fact that Paul had become a follower of Jesus Christ certainly did not mean for him that he should no longer be an Israelite. We cannot attribute to Paul the thought that the church took the place of Israel. Certainly he strongly encouraged that thought – consciously or unconsciously. Theologians who believe that the role of Israel as the elect people of God is played out for good refer, among others, to the passage which follows the words about the new covenant which have been quoted here.[10] In the fire of his arguments Paul draws conclusions which are so far-reaching that even now one wants to warn the apostle to be careful and not to be too hasty. Unfortunately, however, the damage was done centuries ago. The words have not failed to have their effect over the course of church history: 'Now if the dispensation of death, carved in letters of stone, came with such splendour that the Israelites could not look at Moses' face because of its brightness, fading as this was, will not the dispensation of the Spirit be attended with greater splendour? For if there was splendour in the dispensation of condemnation, the dispensation of righteousness must far exceed it in splendour. Indeed, in this case, what once had splendour has come to have no splendour at all, because of the splendour that surpasses it' (II Cor. 3.7–10). Paul does not yet completely abolish the continuity between the old covenant and the new, but – inspired by the works of the prophet, 'I shall put my law within them and write it upon their hearts' – he does place greater emphasis on the contrast between old and new, letter and spirit; and then, as a climax, the ministry of death and the ministry of the Spirit.[11]

In using the term 'ministry of death' Paul intended only to refer to the Old Testament-Jewish tradition. The next part of his argument leaves no doubt about that: 'Since we have such a hope, we are very bold, not like Moses, who put a veil over his face so that the Israelites might not see the end of the fading splendour. But their minds were hardened; for to this day, when they read the old covenant, that same veil remains unlifted, because only through Christ is it taken away. Yes, to this day, whenever Moses is read a veil lies over their minds; but when a man turns to the Lord the veil is removed' (II Cor. 3.12–16).

No one will want to deny that this passage can confuse or even bewilder innocent readers. Were these words written by a man who was still proud of having dedicated himself 'with unbounded zeal' to the veneration of 'the traditions of his forefathers' – see the letter to the Galatians which was written soon afterwards (Gal. 1.12). Or did that slowly become no more than a nostalgic memory? True, a good deal had happened in the meantime. Time was passing. Saul became Paul, he made long journeys, met countless people and had many new experiences. Around twenty years previously, on the way to Damascus, he had the vision that radically changed his life. Twenty years is a respectable part of someone's life. The last visit that Paul had paid to Jerusalem already lay in a distant past. He was a Diaspora Jew and had always remained one despite his years of study in Jerusalem. He felt more at home in Graeco-Roman cities – Tarsus, Antioch, Philippi, Corinth, Ephesus – than on Jewish territory. What role did the Torah play for him in that period? As we have been able to establish so far, he said little or nothing on the subject. We can find one exception to this rule in a wonderful passage in the first letter to the Corinthians: 'To the Jews I became a Jew, in order to win Jews; to those under the law I became as one under the law – though not being myself under the law – that I might win those under the law. To those outside the law I became as one outside the law – not being without law toward God but under the law of Christ – that I might win those outside the law' (I Cor. 9.20–21).

Sometimes it seems that Paul lived in two different worlds even in his thinking: certainly 'not under the law' nor without law towards God but under 'the law of Christ'. Did Paul mean that there were different 'laws'? It does not seem very probable that he answered this question in the affirmative. There is one God and one Torah. Paul thought himself permanently subject to this 'law'. But the same Torah caused him great problems in his encounters with Gentile Christians. That is why he is reacting to this so ambiguously in the passage from I Corinthians quoted above. We would like greater clarity, but Paul did not prove (yet) to be in a position to provide it. However, his thought did not stand still. He was creative and acute. In II Corinthians he took some steps further on the way that he had perhaps embarked on with fear and trembling: now without further ado, over against Moses he set Christ, to whom he gave the title 'Lord' and whom he went on to identify with this Spirit. In this context Paul wrote a sentence which was to prove very important to him later: 'where the Spirit of the Lord is, there is freedom' (II Cor. 3.17).[12]

Paul's thought gradually began to develop along surprising lines. He constantly put the figure of Jesus Christ more in the centre. Later in the letter he called him 'the image of God' (II Cor. 4.4). At the same time Paul again shows that he was an original thinker, sometimes even one who was impossible to follow. In splendid sentences he talks about the difficulties which he has to suffer for the sake of the gospel: 'We are afflicted in every way, but not crushed; perplexed, but not driven to despair; persecuted, but not forsaken; struck down, but not destroyed' (II Cor. 4.8–9). At the beginning of the letter he had already written that he 'shared abundantly in Christ's sufferings' (II Cor. 1.5). Paul's life did not run along existing courses. He was a persecutor and became a preacher. He provoked criticism and opposition. He was admired and hated. He associated the opposition that he faced, the suffering that he had to undergo, with his choice to go the way of Jesus: 'We always carry in the body the *death of Jesus*, so that the life of Jesus may also be manifested in our bodies. For while we live we are always being given up to death for Jesus' sake, so that *the life of Jesus* may be manifested in our mortal flesh' (II Cor. 4.10–11).

It hardly needs demonstrating that these words have set many pens moving in theological discussion.[13] It is remarkable that here Paul, contrary to his custom, does not speak about Christ Jesus or Jesus Christ, but only about Jesus, and then about 'the death of Jesus' and 'the life of Jesus'. The apostle certainly chose these words deliberately. In so doing he was opposing developments within the community in Corinth that disturbed him. Influenced by Gnostic notions. Some people were creating an image of Christ which was so strongly spiritualized and which put so much emphasis on his glorification that the earthly life of Jesus threatened to disappear right into the background. In a similar way, some decades later the author of the Fourth Gospel would emphasize not only the preexistence but also the humanity of Jesus by using a hymn to the Logos: 'Yes, the word became flesh' (John 1.14).

However, in II Corinthians Paul goes one step further. In a surprising way he makes a close connection between his own fortunes and the life and death of Jesus. For this reason too it is not unusual for Paul to be called a 'mystic'.[14] Whether he really was a mystic in fact depends on the definition that is given to the term.[15] Since a consensus seems difficult to achieve, I prefer not to burden the interpretation of the apostle's thought with a term which brings more darkness than light. In my view, a more important question is how Paul could come to make the remarks quoted above. To clarify this it is advisable to look back once again. As we know, the later apostle did not belong to the select circle of the first followers of Jesus. His apostolate rested on a 'revelation'. He encountered the crucified and risen Lord in a vision. It is evident from Paul's letters that he can speak of the consequences of this in different ways. On the one hand he claimed that he had seen Jesus on the way to Damascus (I Cor. 9.1), whereas on the other he emphasized that God has chosen him 'to reveal his son in me' (Gal. 1.15–16). Was that encounter with Jesus 'visible' or was it a 'visionary experience'? From the text mentioned above it proves that Paul can say that it was both. Of course he is not completely clear here. However, we do not do the apostle an injustice if we conclude that for Paul the life and death of Jesus was not exclusively past time. Jesus was not dead like other people who have died. Jesus died, but God raised him from the dead. On the way to Damascus the persecutor arrived at the surprising discovery that the crucified Jesus was alive. Against this background we can understand why Paul presupposed that the life and death of Jesus should be continued in the mortal existence of the man who was chosen by God to become the apostle to the Gentiles. We shall see in the letter to the Galatians that the apostle's thought developed further along these lines.

We have come to know Paul as an apocalyptist. He lived in the expectation of a speedy end to the world. He wrote that quite plainly in his first letter to the community of Corinth: 'the time is short' (I Cor. 7.29). Tribulations are necessary; they can be seen as the 'pangs' which have to precede the birth of the new world. In the end the apostle is not afraid of suffering, for it underlines the certainty that the end is near. The problem now is that in II Corinthians Paul brings other images and ideas forward. It is even difficult to find in his words the apocalyptist that Paul once was. Has he said farewell to apocalyptic? Not so far, but there is no mistaking the fact that he puts the emphasis elsewhere. In the apocalyptic expectation of the future this world stands over against the *new* world that is *to come*. In his last letter to the community in Corinth Paul created another 'break': 'So we do not lose heart. Though our *outer nature* is wasting away, our *inner nature* is being renewed every day. For this light momentary affliction is preparing for us an eternal weight of glory beyond all comparison, because we look not to the things that are *seen* but to he things that are *unseen*; for the things that are seen are transient, but the things that are unseen are eternal' (II Cor. 4.16–18). Is the speaker here Saul the Jewish apocalyptist or Paul the Diaspora Jew, who is at home in the Greek Hellenistic thought of this time? The text quoted[16] makes it clear that Paul was indeed 'a man of two worlds'. His apocalyptic view of human beings and the world will have found little if any echo among the non-Jewish members of the Christian community in Corinth. He will have noted that. Thanks to his broad cultural and religious background, he did not find it difficult to express the gospel in a different way. That also becomes clear from what comes next: 'For we know that if the earthly tent we live in is destroyed, we have a building from God, a house not made with hands, eternal in the heavens' (II Cor. 5.1). The apocalyptist directs his gaze not only to the future but also, full of expectation, above. From there the Son of man and the new Jerusalem will come. Those who are influenced by 'Gnostic' imagery also direct their gaze upwards, but with another intention: 'As long as we are *in this body*, we too groan . . . So we are always of good courage; we know that while we are at home in the body we are away from the Lord, for we walk by faith, not by sight. We are of good courage, and we would rather be away from the body and at home with the Lord' (II Cor. 5.2, 6–8).

Does this indicate that Paul gradually exchanged his apocalyptic expectation of the future for Gnostic ideas about human beings and the world?[17] No simple answer can be given to this question. There is an ocean of literature about gnosis and Gnosticism, and a consensus seems to be an unattainable ideal.[18] Anyone who takes the Gnostic thought of the second/third centuries as a criterion will have to conclude that Paul was not a Gnostic. At the high point of Christian Gnosticism a large number of complicated Gnostic systems were developed. Paul was not a systematic thinker. In contrast to the majority of the later Gnostics he did not draw a distinction between on the one hand the eternal God, high in heaven, who was completely spirit and not matter at all, and on the other hand the creator God, the demiurge, who has to be made responsible for the creation of the earth, the creation of matter, of nature, of animals and human beings. Was the creation good and 'planned' by God or bad and the result of an unfortunate accident? The story in Genesis 1 relates that the creation was 'good' but became bad as a result of the disobedience of Adam and Eve. Paul also subscribed to this thought. In contrast to the book of Genesis the Gnostic view emphasized that creation was bad from the beginning: the divine 'spark' was shut up in the human body as in a prison. How could the divine in human beings be redeemed from that body, unspiritual matter, and find the way back to its origin, to the eternal God? Knowledge (= gnosis) was needed for that, knowledge which had to be given to human beings. How could that happen? Who could give human beings this divine knowledge? Who was in a position to redeem them? It seems that Paul's thought steadily developed in a direction which was determined by this view of human beings and the world, and that later he also began to see the coming of Jesus Christ in this framework as a decisive turning point in history.[19]

To conclude this discussion of II Corinthians we need to consider yet one more important theme: reconciliation or atonement. Hitherto we have not yet encountered the word in Paul's letters. In the light of later dogmatic developments some people may be surprised at this. From the Middle Ages on, 'atonement' began to play an important role in the Christian tradition. To the present day many people are convinced that it is 'the heart of the gospel'. That proves to be the case above all in the Reformation tradition. Those who dare to ask critical questions about the classical doctrine of atonement are soon told that they have crossed a line and departed from the Reformation heritage. In this debate Paul is often cited as an advocate of the said doctrine, but it is very doubtful whether this is right. The term 'reconciliation' occurs relatively rarely in his letters. In II Corinthians he mentions it for the first time. This passage is famous and is one of the most important foundations of the classical doctrine of the atonement.

Paul introduces the theme like this: 'For the love of Christ controls us, because we are convinced that one has died for all: therefore all have died' (II Cor. 5.14). The conclusion that Paul drew is surprising, and from the Christian notion of representation even seems illogical. If Christ has died 'for us' – that is to say, in our place – then we need no longer fear death as a punishment for sins. Evidently Paul's thought did not (yet?) go this far. There is also every reason to ask whether in this text as a matter of course he started from the idea of 'representation'. That does not seem to be directly the case in what follows either: 'And he died for all, that those who live might live no longer for themselves but for him who for their sake died and was raised' (II Cor. 5.15). In this context the 'for us' does not primarily have a soteriological significance – 'he died for our sins' – but rather an ethical orientation – 'they no longer live for themselves'.

It is therefore worth recommending that we do not lose sight of the context of the second letter to the community in Corinth. Much had already happened when Paul wrote these words. Here it is enough to recall the extensive correspondence between the apostle and the community. Paul exerted himself to the utmost to promote unity. He did so among other things with the help of the image of 'the body of Christ' (I Cor. 12–14) and with his splendid 'hymn of praise to love' (I Cor. 13). Was he successful? Presumably not. The Corinthians thought they knew it all and did not learn easily. Paul was a creative person, so it need not surprise us that in II Corinthians he again brought out the theme of 'unity within the community'. A new notion had occurred to him here: the metaphor of reconciliation. To avoid possible misunderstandings, Paul did not use any term which came from a sacrificial cult. Given the many temples in Corinth we cannot rule out the possibility that he thought it sensible not to use such an image, because it could easily lead to misunderstandings. The Greek word for 'reconciliation' which Paul uses in II Corinthians comes from the world of social and interpersonal relations.[20] In every century it happens that for one reason or another people live in tension, quarrel over things, over legacies, and so on. In such a situation 'reconciliation' is necessary, two parties which are alienated from each other must again be 'reconciled', the gulf bridged, the hostility overcome.

To begin with, Paul emphasized that the believer may be *a new person*: 'Therefore, if any one is in Christ, he is a new creation; the old has passed, behold the new has come' (II Cor. 5.17). Is the old apocalyptist speaking again here, who thought he was living in the messianic kingdom? It seems that we must say yes to that question, because the apostle's thought was so agile. The resurrection of the crucified Christ by God is the proof that the old world has disappeared and the new world has dawned. Again Paul is living in two worlds: as a new creation in the messianic kingdom, but at the same time he also knew that the old world had not completely disappeared (Gal. 2.20). Two worlds as it were overlapped. There was the beginning of the new creation, and no one could alter that fact. For it came from God and from no one else: 'All this is from God, who through Christ reconciled us to himself and gave us the ministry of reconciliation; that is, in Christ God was reconciling the world to himself, not counting their trespasses against them, and entrusting to us the message of reconciliation. So we are ambassadors for Christ, God making his appeal through us' (II Cor. 5.17–20). God's love has driven away the enmity and done away with the alienation.[21] Reconciliation between God and humankind automatically leads to reconciliation among human beings.

Paul was a Jew. From his youth he had known that every year God reconciles himself anew with his people (Lev. 16). It is striking that in this passage the apostle does not refer in any way whatsoever to the ritual of the great Day of Atonement. For him, Jesus Christ was not the scapegoat or the sin offering. But the Lord played a major role in the drama of reconciliation: 'For our sake he made him to be sin who knew no sin, so that in him we might become the righteousness of God' (II Cor. 5.21).

Again it proves that Paul's thought developed further, perhaps even while he was writing. To an increasing degree he put Jesus Christ in the centre. He is the one who forms the bridge between God and humankind. He can be that bridge because the community is the body of Christ.

Finally, the apostle produces a new thought. He makes a link between Christ and 'sin'. Here we must realize that once again the apocalyptist is speaking, who saw world history in the perspective of the struggle between good and evil, light and darkness, faithfulness to God and sin against God. In this text sin is a power hostile to God.[22] Paul does not write that Jesus becomes a 'sinner' as we are. This text does not speak of an exchange or of representation. For the apostle the drama went far deeper. It is not in the first place about the individual but about the whole cosmos. Christ is sacrificed to the powers hostile to God – 'made sin'. Thus human beings are freed from this power – 'a new creation' – and reconciliation between God and humankind and among human beings begins to become a reality.

II

The second letter to the community of Philippi

Growing opposition in Macedonia and Greece

We discussed the problem of the unity of the canonical letter of Paul to the community in Philippi earlier, so I shall give only a short summary of the discussion here. The apostle spent some time in prison in Ephesus. That did not prevent him from sending a cheerful and friendly letter to Philippi. Relations were particularly good. Words like happiness and joy largely define the atmosphere of the letter. Clearly there were no internal tensions in the community of Philippi, and the text is also silent about possible opponents of Paul.

This is true of the first two chapters of the letter to the Philippians. The third chapter also begins in the same spirit: 'Finally, brothers and sisters, rejoice in the Lord . . .' (Phil. 3.1). Evidently the apostle intended to end his letter quickly. But if we continue reading the canonical letter, we suddenly find ourselves in another world: 'To write the same things to you is not irksome to me and is safe for you. Look out for the dogs, look out for the evil-workers, look out for those who mutilate the flesh' (Phil. 3.1–2).

The warnings do not mince words. Paul speaks bluntly: dogs, evil-workers, those who mutilate the flesh. The idyll is drastically disturbed. Joy and happiness have given place to indignation and anger. What in heaven's name has happened? Of course, a person's mood can change. It is conceivable that Paul had to stop dictating for one reason or another. As a prisoner he was dependent on the whims and caprices of his gaolers. Perhaps the pause in dictation lasted longer than expected. When Paul could continue, his mood had changed. That could have happened. But very probably it did not. Paul was an emotional man, but he was not unstable. He knew what he wanted and had experienced a great deal. It took more than an enforced pause to put him off balance. The cause has to be sought in Philippi. Clearly the situation within the community there had radically changed. In my view the scholarly hypothesis that Paul sent not one but two letters to Philippi[1] gives a satisfactory explanation of the course of events. I discussed letter A (Phil. 1.11–3.1a; 4.2–7, 10–23) in a previous chapter; we now need to look at letter B, which was written later (Phil. 3.1b–4.1, 8–9).

The content of letter B confronts readers with a situation which is worlds apart from that in letter A. There is not a word about Paul's imprisonment. He was again a free man. By then he had left Ephesus and had crossed over from Troas to Macedonia (II Cor. 2.12). There is no doubt that on this occasion he visited Philippi for the second time. His remark in letter B also refers to this: 'I have *often* told you about them' (Phil. 3.18). The Acts of the Apostles pays strikingly little attention to this episode from the life of Paul: 'When he had gone through these parts (= Macedonia) and had given them much encouragement, he came to Greece. There he spent three months' (Acts 20.2–3). This is not the first time that the author of Acts surprises us by the brevity of his report. By now experience has taught us that he usually had his reasons for this. The image that he tried to sketch of the early Christian community needed to correspond as far as possible to his ideal: the life of the primitive community in Jerusalem (Acts 2.41–47; 4.32–35). Unity prevailed there and discord was alien; the community was governed by love and was not torn apart by theological conflicts. Was reality different from the ideal? That was certainly the case. Acts is not always silent about this (Acts 6.1), but time and again the author seems to be extremely restrained in mentioning disputes within the early Christian community.

The result is that there are sometimes major differences between the letters of Paul and the Acts of the Apostles. That again proves to be the case here. The apostle was not silent about them: 'For even when we came into Macedonia, our bodies had no rest but we were afflicted at every turn – fighting without and fear within' (II Cor. 7.5). Those who have become accustomed to read between the lines in Acts will understand why there is only a vague mention of Paul's stay in Greece. It is said to have lasted three months. Where was he all this time? Why doesn't the author of Acts tell us where he stayed? The answer is obvious: where else will Paul have stayed but in Corinth? He had already lived there for eighteen months. He knew a lot of people. The author of Acts prefers not to remind his readers of the serious conflicts which there had been between the apostle and the community in the past. Better the fine ideal than harsh reality.

In the familiar surroundings of the great Greek port Paul will have found the necessary calm to write a new letter to the community of Philippi. He had to do this. The situation was changing rapidly. During his previous journey through Macedonia and Greece Paul had regularly come into conflict with the Jews in cities like Thessalonica, Beroea and Corinth. He had visited their synagogues. Some people were won over, but others regarded him as a danger to the Jewish tradition (Acts 17–18). Developments continued. Paul was not the only itinerant preacher of the gospel of Jesus Christ. We have already met Apollos. From Alexandria he went via Ephesus also to Corinth (Acts 18.24). There were no modern means of communication, but that did not mean that it was impossible to make long journeys. In order to be able to send their legions quickly from one province to another, in the course of time the Romans had built an impressive network of roads throughout the empire. There was a good deal of trade, and there were many voyages around the Mediterranean for this purpose. Cargo ships also had room for passengers. Paul and his companions had often sailed in this way from Asia Minor to Greece and back again. Jewish pilgrims went to Jerusalem from near and far (Acts 2.1–13).[2] The Diaspora was large and widespread, not only all over the whole of the Roman empire but as far as ancient Persia. Jews were in a position to travel easily.

After his three-year stay in Ephesus Paul arrived in Macedonia in Greece to discover that he was still coming up against opposition within the early Christian community. That even seemed to be the case in his beloved Philippi. The apostle to the Gentiles had gained rivals, Jewish Christian preachers who did not put the emphases in the same place as he did. We have already come across them in II Corinthians. In the second letter which Paul sent to Philippi he also felt compelled to oppose their views with all his might.[3]

The content of letter B

The beginning of the letter sets the tone: 'Look out for the dogs, look out for the evil-workers, look out for those who mutilate the flesh' (Phil. 3.2). Paul warns the community and he does so in an extraordinarily sharp tone. The strange word 'mutilate' enables us to sketch a profile of his opponents. Paul's terminology is again a good example of the sarcasm that he was not afraid to use as a weapon on particular occasions. 'Mutilating' is a gibe at his opponents, who clearly attached great importance to the Jewish rite of circumcision. In his letter to the Galatians, written soon afterwards, in a similar way he would mock those who put so much emphasis on circumcision: 'I wish those who unsettle you would mutilate themselves' (Gal. 5.12). Such an outburst can hardly be called diplomatic – it is pretty coarse – but the apostle cannot be accused of being unclear and not daring to make a choice.

Paul left just as little room for misunderstanding in his second letter to the community of Philippi. In the first place he gave a surprising new definition of the concept of circumcision: 'For we are the true circumcision, who worship God in spirit, and glory in Christ Jesus, and put no confidence in the flesh' (Phil. 3.3). The argument recalls passages in II Corinthians in which in a similar way he relates passages from the Old

Testament tradition – in particular the one about the new covenant – to faith in Jesus Christ (II Cor. 3.6). Against this background we can imagine that Paul no longer meant 'circumcision' in a physical but in a spiritual sense.

That does not mean that he was now ashamed of his past: 'Though I myself have reason for confidence in the flesh also. If any other man thinks he has reason for confidence in the flesh, I have more: circumcised on the eighth day, of the people of Israel, of the tribe of Benjamin, a Hebrew born of Hebrews; as to the law a Pharisee, as to zeal a persecutor of the church, as to righteousness under the law blameless. *But whatever gain I had, I counted as loss for the sake of Christ.* Indeed I count everything as loss because of the surpassing worth of knowing Christ Jesus my Lord. For his sake I have suffered the loss of all things, and count them as refuse, in order that I may gain Christ and be found in him, not having a righteousness of my own, based on law, but that which is through faith in Christ, the righteousness from God that depends on faith' (Phil. 3.4–9).

Quite clearly Paul's thought is very much on the move, and the text quoted leaves us in no doubt about that. His opponents compelled him to be more specific than before. The Jewish Christians who emphasized the abiding significance of the commandments of the Torah for the Christian community forced Paul – who was also a Jewish Christian – to be negative about the value of the Torah, perhaps more negative than he would have wanted to be. However, unfortunately experience teaches us that in discussions the different standpoints soon tend to be expressed in black and white, though all those involved in the debate really know in their hearts that in most questions the issues are much less clear. Paul was certainly also aware of this. That will emerge among other things from his attitude in the letter to the Galatians. However, in this part the apostle gives the impression that he has left the Torah behind him as 'refuse'.

That Paul was thinking hard also emerges from the new content which he gives to the concept of 'righteousness'. In terms of tradition there is a close connection between 'righteousness' and the Torah. So the book of Psalms begins: 'Blessed is the man who walks not in the counsel of the wicked, nor stands in the way of sinners, nor sits in the seat of scoffers; but his delight is in the law of the Lord, and on his law he mediates day and night' (Ps. 1.1–2). The righteous man is the one who observes the commandments of the Torah: 'the Lord knows the way of the righteous' (Ps. 1.6). Paul also gives this tradition a new interpretation: 'my righteousness is not based on the law but on faith in Christ' (Phil. 3.9). In the last two letters of Paul that we possess – Galatians and Romans – this theme will be discussed at more length.

There is also a passage in the second letter to the community in Philippi which expresses the intensity of the bond that Paul felt with Christ: 'That I may know him and the power of his resurrection, and may share his sufferings, becoming like him in his death, that if possible I may attain the resurrection from the dead' (Phil. 3.10–11).[4] That is Paul's ideal, the goal of his life. Literally and figuratively, Christ Jesus has made him his own (Phil. 3.12). He has not yet reached the goal, but he is on the way, and will not be deterred by anything or anyone: 'forgetting what lies behind me and straining forward to what lies ahead, I press toward the goal for the prize of the upward call of God in Christ Jesus' (Phil 3.13–14).

As in II Corinthians, the perspective is that of the apocalyptist that Paul always was, shifted from the imminent future to heaven: 'But our commonwealth is in heaven, and from it we await a saviour, the Lord Jesus Christ, who will change our lowly body to be like his glorious body, by the power which enables him even to subject all things to himself' (Phil. 3.20–21).[5]

12

The letter to the Galatians

Paul in Galatia

The scene changes. The letters that we have discussed so far were addressed to three communities in Macedonia and Greece: Thessalonica, Corinth and Philippi. This geographical limitation is quite striking. But the way which Paul followed regularly took him through the vast territory of Asia Minor. During his first missionary journey, in the company of Barnabas he visited the cities of Iconium, Lystra and Derbe among others (Acts 13.50–14.28). Since some time before the beginning of our era this south-easterly part of Asia Minor had been incorporated into the Roman empire, these places belonged in the province of Galatia. This name still gives rise to misunderstandings. Who were the 'Galatians' to whom Paul was addressing his letter? He knew the people there, since he left no doubt that he had already been there (Gal. 1.8; 4.12–20). Was that during the first missionary journey? It is possible but not certain.

The Roman province was called Galatia because there was a region which already bore this name. The province comprised that region, but also areas to the south. Therefore the cities mentioned above must also be included within it. When Paul began his second missionary journey, according to Acts he first visited Derbe and Lystra again (Acts 16.1) and after that travelled 'through Phrygia and the region of Galatia'. Unfortunately the author does not tell us whether he was also active as a preacher of the gospel there. However, that does seem probable, since in the description of the beginning of Paul's third missionary journey the following passage occurs: 'After spending some time there (= Antioch) he departed and went from place to place through the region of Galatia and Phrygia, strengthening all the disciples' (Acts 18.23).

It remains difficult to say to precisely which Galatians Paul addressed his letter. The apostle himself did not make this clear. He wrote succinctly: 'to the communities of Galataia' (Gal. 1.1). In exegetical literature this question has regularly given rise to a discussion, but the discussion must in fact be regarded as fruitless. We can never be completely sure. Did Paul send a letter to the Galatians who were living in the province – like the inhabitants of Iconium, Lystra and Derbe? Or to the inhabitants of the region? The answer to these questions can have consequences for the dating of the letter. If he was writing to the inhabitants of the province the letter can be dated early and could even be Paul's earliest letter. If he was addressing the inhabitants of the region, that would mean a later date.

The exegete faces a dilemma. After mature consideration – and contrary to a view I expressed earlier[1] – I now defend the view that Paul could not have written this letter at an early stage of his activities. However, the question 'Province or region?' is not decisive in this debate. My choice of a late date rests on considerations which have to do with the content of the letter. A comparison with other letters of Paul shows that the topic which is discussed in Galatians is in fact closely connected with problems which he discussed in II Corinthians and in the second letter to the community in Philippi. Indeed I can imagine that he conceived the letter during his stay of three months in the city of Corinth.[2]

The occasion for writing the letter

Paul did not beat about the bush, but got straight to the point. In embryo the heading to the letter contains two themes which will prove central to what follows. Without any doubt they are the two subjects which were the specific points of dispute That is why the apostle wrote his letter to the Galatians: 'I, Paul, an *apostle – not from men nor through man, but through Jesus*

Christ and God the Father who raised him from the dead – and all the brethren who are with me. To the churches of Galatia: Grace to you and peace from God the Father and *our Lord Jesus Christ, who gave himself for our sins to deliver us from the present evil age*, according to the will of our God and Father; to whom be the glory for ever and ever. Amen' (Gal. 1.1–4).

The words in italics indicate the two themes. Here we need further clarification. The first theme can be summed up simply: Paul's disputed apostolate. The second theme needs more explanation. I would describe it like this: the meaning of the death of Jeus Christ for a community which is composed of Jews and Gentiles.[3] Paul felt it necessary to react to the question how Gentiles could share in the promises which God had made to the people of Israel. His opponents had a clear answer: this promise also applied to Gentile Christians, provided that they were prepared to observe the commandments of the Torah. Paul opposed this 'option' with all his might and all his apostolic authority. The order in which he presented the two themes was not in fact a coincidence, but was well-considered and thought through.[4]

Not only exegetes but also dogmatic theologians often venture to expound the letter to the Galatians. They do so in the steps of Luther and inspired by him. Luther thought that in the letter he had found the central theme of Paul's gospel: the justification of the godless through faith and grace alone.[5] In the sixteenth century Luther wrestled with the question how he could find a gracious God. His reading of Paul's letters – above all Galatians and Romans – led him to the liberating insight that he was justified by God not through doing good works (= 'the works of the law'), but through faith in Jesus Christ.[6] Obviously this reading of the texts is also worth considering. However, the exegete is confronted with the question what Paul meant by his words. Paul was no Luther. Between the apostle and the reformer there is not only a gap of many centuries; in addition they lived in totally different worlds. Paul was not a mediaeval monk. He was not tormented by feelings of guilt or fear of the devil.[7] He was not in search of a gracious God. Through scripture and tradition he already knew that God from his youth. Paul was an apocalyptist and therefore he longingly awaited the definitive intervention of God in the history of this world. All the evil powers, sin and death, would then be destroyed once and for all. The unexpected encounter with the crucified and risen Lord had opened Paul's eyes to the fact that a new period had dawned in the history of God and the world. He did not know how long this period would last. He hoped for the speedy coming of the Lord. In this situation he felt called to go to the Gentiles with the saving event. In the cross and resurrection the frontier which kept Jews and Gentiles apart had been done away with, the spell had been broken and the way to unity had been opened up. Paul took this way with great conviction. Gradually he discovered the problems. Above all the Torah threatened to become an insuperable barrier. He writes at length about that question in the letter to the Galatians.

Those who have read the previous chapters of this book will recognize that these themes are not being discussed for the first time. Paul clearly did not meet with growing opposition only in Macedonia and Greece. This also happened in the region of Galatia. Paul reacted fiercely. Instead of following the opening of the letter with a thanksgiving – as he usually did – he disregarded all obligations and got straight to the point. His fierce, polemical tone still speaks volumes: 'I am astonished that you are so quickly deserting him who called you in the grace of Christ and turning to a different gospel – not that there is another gospel, but there are some who trouble you and want to pervert the gospel of Christ. But even if we, or an angel from heaven, should preach to you a gospel contrary to that which we preached to you, let him be accursed. As we have said before, so now I say again, if anyone is preaching to you a gospel contrary to that which you received, let him be accursed' (Gal. 1.6–9). The clarity of these words leaves little to be desired. The apostle's self-confidence has unmistakably grown. He warned the Galatians that he would not be persuaded to change his mind even by an angel from heaven!

There has been much discussion in books about the New Testament on the profile of the opponents.[8] Of course it is impossible to discuss the question in detail in this book. In my view, the ideas of the people who caused disturbances in Galatia were not very different from those of Paul's opponents in Macedonia and Greece. They too belonged to the group of Jewish Christians who were actively calling for observance of the commandments of the Torah within the early-Christian communities in the Jewish Diaspora far beyond the frontiers of the land of Israel. This was not only a tense but also a dramatic and even tragic debate: the Jewish Christian Paul, as a young man a fervent zealot for the Torah, was increasingly coming into conflict with other Jewish Christians who could not accept his view of the Torah in relation to Gentile Christians. The conflict must have been an enormous burden on Paul. He was torn apart by inner conflicts. Deep in his heart he will have had little difficulty in recognizing that his opponents were right. From a Jewish perspective their insights were completely understandable and respectable in every way.[9] Why should Gentile Christians not put themselves under the saving influence of the Torah? However seductive that standpoint might have been even for Paul, he continued to oppose it with all his energy.

According to some exegetes the discussion in the communities of Galatia was extra complex because Paul had to fight on two fronts: on the one hand against Jewish Christians who emphasized the significance of the law and on the other hand against Gentile Christians who defended the view that Christian freedom was so radical that any commandment had lost its value. It cannot be denied that the letter to the Galatians is characterized by internal tensions – especially between Galatians 3–4 on the one hand and Galatians 5–6 on the other. In due course it will emerge that I think that there is another explanation for these tensions. Paul was not fighting on two fronts but was in conflict with himself. Here he revealed again that he was living in two worlds. Saul may at one point have become Paul, but Paul always continued to have something of Saul in him.

The content of the letter

Paul's letter to the communities in Galatia stands out from the other letters which have been discussed so far by virtue of its clear structure.[10] There were two main problems, and the apostle discussed them in succession: criticism of his apostolate (Gal. 1.11–2.10) and the relationship between Christ and the Torah (Gal. 2.11–5.1). The structure of the last two chapters is much looser. They contain not only conclusions which can be drawn from what has gone before, but also notions which bring these new elements to bear and put what was said earlier in another perspective. Any reader of the letter to the Galatians will note this: the letter is attractive but also very complex.

Paul had found not only the time but also the leisure to discuss the complicated role of the Torah in the early Christian community in a profound and structured way. Despite the self-control which he had unmistakably imposed upon himself, now and then he gave his emotions free rein. Here are a couple of examples. He bluntly rebukes the recipients of the letter: 'Foolish Galatians, who has bewitched you?' (Gal. 3.1). Some time later he reminds the same 'foolish' Galatians in a passionate argument of the sacrifices which they proved ready to make for him on his first visit (Gal. 4.12–20). Immediately after that he creates a surprising allegory on the Old Testament story of Hagar and Sarah (Gal. 4.21–31). In the concluding part of the letter he allows himself a coarseness which is already signalled earlier: 'I wish those who unsettle you would mutilate themselves' (Gal. 5.12).

The first theme – the criticism of Paul's apostleship – need not be discussed at length further here. It has already been considered abundantly in earlier chapters. Paul's apostolate was and remained controversial. The arguments were obvious: he had not belonged to the exclusive circle of the twelve disciples of Jesus; moreover his name continued to be associated with persecutions which had had painful consequences for at least part of the early Christian community in Jerusalem. In the long run people may have been inclined to forgive him this 'youthful sin', but they could never forget it completely. The consequence was that at the most inconvenient moments his apostolate was again put in question. His past was open to discussion and remained so, and that made him both controversial and vulnerable.

We know that Paul often had to defend his apostolate (II Cor. 10–13). He himself was passionately engaged in this, and over the years constructed a line of defence which was difficult to counter. In the letter to the Galatians he developed an argument which was meant to provide his apostolate permanently with the necessary legitimation: 'For I would have you know, brothers and sisters, that the gospel which was preached by me is not man's gospel. For I did not receive it from man, nor was I taught it, but it came through a revelation of Jesus Christ' (Gal. 1.11–12). After recalling his former way of life as a zealot for the Torah, he laid the following unassailable foundation for his apostolate: 'But when God who had set me apart before I was born and had called me through his grace was pleased to reveal his son to me, in order that I might preach him among the Gentiles, I did not confer with flesh and blood, nor did I go up to Jerusalem to those who were apostles before me, but I went away into Arabia; and again I returned to Damascus' (Gal. 1.15–17). On one point Paul would not yield: his apostolate was not created or instituted by men, but solely by God. With this conclusion he ended the discussion for good. He no longer hesitated. He himself would never doubt his authority again.

It was necessary for him to be able to feel more authoritative, because the second theme that he had to treat required of him not only a great deal of shrewdness and creativity but also such an aura of apostolic authority that the Galatians were ready to allow themselves to be convinced by him. Paul hoped that he could speak a word of reconciliation. We know that he was unsuccessful. That is tragic, but no one can blame him, least of all us. We look back and can note possibly wrong interpretations and digressions. Paul looked forward hopefully into an uncertain future. His solution seemed viable for the short period still left to the community. However, time went on. The

Christian community grew further. The number of Gentile Christians increased. In this situation Paul's solution did not seem to offer any solution for a tricky problem. He strove for unity, but without realizing it created a division which could not be overcome. He expected the speedy coming of the Lord, which would put an end to all disputes and differences of opinion. At that moment it was impossible for the apostle to suspect that the time would not be short (I Cor. 7.20) and that the world would go on to reach 2000.

The discussion of the significance of the Torah for Gentile Christians was not new. During the meeting of apostles in Jerusalem some years earlier the fundamental questions had already been discussed at length. Here is a quotation to recall that debate: 'Unless you are circumcised according to the custom of Moses, you cannot be saved' (Acts 15.1). In other words, are the commandments of the Torah also valid for Christians with a Gentile background? After mature consideration, the apostles in Jerusalem found a compromise solution. 'Therefore I (= James the brother of the Lord) judge that we should not trouble those of the Gentiles who turn to God, but should write to them to abstain from the pollutions of idols and from unchastity and from what is strangled and from blood' (Acts 15.20). Here the demand for Gentile Christians to observe the whole Torah – and thus also to be circumcised on their conversion – seems to have been dropped for good.

However, gradually that did not prove to be the case. The compromise had the effect of so many compromises: it satisfied no one. It did not go far enough for one group and went much too far for another. This latter feeling was prevalent above all in groups of Jewish Christians. They refused to accept the decision and continued to fight actively for their conviction that the validity of the Torah needed to be maintained undiminished. That applied to all members of the Christian community and thus also to Christians with a pagan background. They would accept no exceptions to the rule. They regarded Christian faith as a faith which was *par excellence Jewish, messianic*. In this they were zealous for the Torah with a zeal which will not have been foreign to Paul. These Jewish Christians forced him in a direction which he perhaps found it difficult to take. They compelled him to make statements which he would have preferred not to make. He had already clashed with representatives of this movement in Macedonia and Greece. Their influence had also extended to Asia Minor. In the meantime reports had reached him that they were causing disturbances in the communities of Galatia. Now that he had found peace in Corinth he took the far-reaching decision to expound his view as a matter of principle and on a scriptural basis.

What is the value of the commandments of the Torah? Are they valid always and everywhere and unassailable? Paul grew up in a Pharisaic milieu in the Diaspora. As a young adult he went to Jerusalem and there received training from Gamaliel, a distinguished and widely respected Pharisee (Acts 22.3). From him Paul had not learned rigidity and immovability, but wisdom, prudence, moderation and flexibility in the exposition of scripture and tradition. Perhaps in his early years he acquired more zeal and less tolerance, but in the course of time he thought back with more pleasure to Gamaliel's instruction. There were different tendencies in the Pharisaic movement – including the schools of Hillel and Shammai – which discussed the interpretation of the commandments with one another and had often arrived at different views. The adherents of Pharisaism had not withdrawn from society – like the Essenes of Qumran. They were married, earned enough to provide for their family and thus had both feet in everyday reality. They were 'conservative', but not rigid and adamant. They wanted to preserve tradition, but realized all too well that it was not always possible to apply the commandments strictly.

Paul grew up in the Diaspora. His short stay in Jerusalem was the exception to the rule that he spent his life largely *outside* the frontiers of Jewish territory. During his long missionary journeys he lived, for example, for eighteen months in Corinth and even for three years in Ephesus. He knew the Greek Hellenistic world from his own experience. Therefore he must have been aware that the commandment that Gentiles should be circumcised was a great obstacle for an early Christian community. It is conceivable that in this situation Paul slowly began to ask himself whether the commandment was really unassailable. The meeting of the apostles at Jerusalem drew a distinction between Jewish Christians on the one hand and on the other Christians who had come from paganism. For understandable reasons, Paul's opponents were not satisfied with this division of the community. They strove for unity within the early Christian community and put the Torah at the centre. Paul attacked this orthodoxy fiercely, and did so in a 'scriptural' way. He sought in scripture and tradition texts and motifs which could shed another light on the question.

The Bible is a rich and variegated book. That experience is not strange to modern readers, and scriptural experts living in the first century of our era were also aware of it. In the course of church history theologians have made efforts to prove the opposite. Despite appearances to the contrary, texts in the Bible are suppposed not to contradict one another. Since the previous century that presupposition has no longer applied in exegesis. Today the question of the 'centre' of both the Old and New Testaments is very much a matter for discussion.[11] In the present theological debate exegetes raise questions which often fill theologians interested in systematic theology with anxiety. If the Bible is variegated, how can the church ever form a close unity?[12]

Paul, the scriptural expert, was thoroughly aware of the tensions within scripture and tradition. Indeed he was not afraid to set biblical texts against one another. That was not new for him. In Jerusalem he had sat 'at the feet of Gamaliel'. One expert would produce a view and support it by adding: 'scripture says . . .' Another expert in scripture and tradition would oppose that view and with a reference to another text claim: '. . . but scripture also says . . .' Those who expound the Bible always face the question: which biblical text is to be preferred? Which commandment is so important that it can and may outdo the others? Paul will have had no difficulty in recognizing that circumcision is of the utmost importance for the Jewish tradition. He himself had been circumcised and did not think it necessary to make a secret of the fact (Phil. 3.6). That did not prevent him from considering the question whether the commandment requiring circumcision was really so important that it had to be tolerated as a deterrent to Gentiles who wanted to join the Christian community.

Paul knew his Bible. He was aware that God had made a covenant with the people of Israel, but he was also familiar with the story of the call of Abraham and the promise which was made to him: 'And I will make of you a great people, and I will bless you, and make your name great, so that you will be a blessing. I will bless those who bless you, and him who curses you I will curse, *and by you all the families of the earth shall bless themselves*' (Gen. 12.2–3). It is clearly no coincidence that Paul chose the words in italics as the starting point for his scriptural argument. He will have put his work as apostle to the Gentiles in that perspective.

This exposes the dilemma quite clearly. On the one hand there is the promise to Abraham which has a universal scope, and on the other there is the Torah with its concrete commandments, which lays down conditions and draws lines of demarcation. Which type of thinking is to be preferred? Paul's argument is fascinating and worth following closely: 'Brothers and sisters, to give an example form everyday life: no one annuls even a man's will, or adds to it once it has been ratified. Now the promises were made to Abraham and his offspring. It does not say, "And to offsprings," referring to many; but, referring to one, "And to your offspring," which is Christ. This is what I mean: *the law, which came four hundred and thirty years afterwards, does not annul a testament previously ratified by God, so as to make the promise void*' (Gal. 3.15–17). God's promise to Abraham – "in you shall all the generations on earth be blessed" – can be compared with a testament. It cannot be changed by anything or anyone other than the testator. Paul was convinced that God had not changed his 'testament'. Even the Torah is therefore subordinate to the promise to Abraham.

That Torah came no less than four hundred and thirty years later. The polemical intent of this statement is difficult to deny. Paul's opponents referred back to the Torah and the concluding of the covenant on Mount Sinai; he himself went even further back in time and arrived at Abraham, with whom God's efforts with the people of Israel and all the peoples on earth had really begun.

This option for the priority of the promise over the Torah makes Paul ask: 'Why then the law?' (Gal. 3.19). His answer is surprising and will have sounded like a curse to his Jewish-Christian opponents: 'the law came . . .' – the observation already shows little respect, but the sequel makes things even worse – 'because of transgressions' (Gal. 3.19). In the letter to the Romans which he would write some time later, Paul developed this paradoxical thought further. The law has a negative significance and effect. Without precepts and rules there would be no transgressions (Rom. 4.15; 5.13). As soon as a law is enacted, transgressions begin to become a reality (Rom. 7.7–25).

Paul relativized the significance of the Torah not only by a chronological argument – four hundred and thirty years later – but also by suggesting that the promise to Abraham came directly from God while the Torah of Moses did not: 'It was ordained by angels though an intermediary. Now an intermediary implies more than one; but God is one' (Gal. 3.20). The argument certainly wins no prizes for clarity and consistency, but we need not doubt Paul's intention. That is also clear from the question which he went on to put: 'Does the law then conflict with the promises of God' (Gal. 3.21). The confrontation between two scriptural motifs has now reached its climax. What would have happened had Paul answered this question in the affirmative? That is what Marcion did in the middle of the second century, and in so doing he thought that he was following in the apostle's footsteps. The church of Rome declared Marcion a heretic. He was the first in a long series. At the beginning of the twentieth century he gained the approval of no less than the influential German theologian Adolf von

Harnack.[13] The heretic had been forced to leave the church, but his ideas still haunted it. The problem was not solved, nor can it be solved in Paul's footsteps. All down the centuries the Christian tradition has wrestled with the significance of the Old Testament as a whole and the commandments of the Torah in particular.[14]

Paul did not take the step which according to Marcion he should have done. He did not argue for the abolition of the Torah. Of course he could not. His Jewish background made it impossible for him to take this course. Since then theology and the church have been confronted with an insoluble problem. The Torah is subsidiary to God's promise to Abraham, but not in conflict with it. Paul answered his own question as follows: 'by no means', in other words, the law is certainly not in conflict with the promises of God. Readers can now easily get lost in the maze of Paul's speculations. The arguments as it were fall over one another and it is not simple to take them at their true worth. In the first place the Torah has also entered the sphere of 'sin' – again the apocalyptist is speaking here (cf. II Cor. 5.21). After this negative evaluation of the Torah Paul continues his argument with two examples which are meant to make it clear how the Torah and the promise/faith are really related: (a) 'Now before faith came, we were *confined under the law*, kept under restraint until faith should be revealed. (b) So that the law was *our custodian until Christ came*, that we might be justified by faith. But now that faith has come, we are no longer under a custodian' (Gal. 3.23–25).[15]

Anyone who reflects on these words cannot escape the impression that the apostle gradually not only relativized the significance of the Torah but even limited it to a particular period in the history of Israel: from Sinai to Christ. In this period the Torah watched over the people of God, protected them and accompanied them on the way to the goal: the coming of Jesus Christ. From that moment the Torah has lost its significance. For Paul that is a liberating event. Boundaries disappear and the differences between people are radically removed: 'For in Christ Jesus you are all children of God, through faith. For as many of you as were baptized into Christ have put on Christ. There is nether Jew nor Greek, there is neither slave nor free, there is neither male nor female; for you are all one in Christ Jesus' (Gal. 3.26–28). And with this liberating thought Paul rounds off his argument, in which he had begun from the priority of the promise to Abraham: 'And if you are Christ's then you are Abraham's offspring, heirs according to promise' (Gal. 3.29).

Are things now clear? From what follows it is evident that Paul was not satisfied. He thought it desirable to elucidate his view with other words and images: 'I mean this, that the heir, as long as he is a child, is no better than a slave, though he is the owner of all the estate; but he is under guardians and trustees until the date set by the father. So with us; when we were children, we were slaves to the elemental spirits of the universe' (Gal. 4.1–3). In the previous part Paul argued from scripture; in these verses he is trying to clarify his perspective with an example which many will recognize. It is conceivable that the apostle opted for this extra explanation because he realized that he had to reckon with two groups of readers. He hoped to convince the Jewish Christians in the community that he was right with his scriptural arguments, while the comparison was meant above all for Gentile Christians, who perhaps had difficulty with his exegesis of scripture. That in this part he is addressing the Gentile Christians in particular is evident from the following passage: 'Formerly, when you did not know God, you were in bondage to beings that by nature are no gods, but now you have come to know God, or rather to be known by God, how can you turn back again to the weak and beggarly elemental spirits, whose slaves you want to be once more? You observe days, and months, and seasons, and years! I am afraid that I have laboured over you in vain' (Gal. 4.8–11).

Did Paul realize that he was treading a dangerous path with this combination of arguments? Consciously or unconsciously he made a connection between the statement 'the law was our custodian until the coming of Christ' (Gal. 3.24) and the thought that he expressed in the above quotation: we were not yet of age, slaves, subjects of the powers of the universe. For the apocalyptist Paul it was not difficult to give the Greek term translated here by 'powers of the universe' a meaningful place in his view of human beings and the world. The shadow side was that the Torah was more or less identified with those cosmic powers. It will be clear that, from a Jewish perspective, with this argument Paul had alienated himself from the Old Testament Jewish tradition.

Did Paul indeed bid a final farewell to the Torah?[16] The apostle went a long way in his efforts to remove all obstacles which made it difficult for Gentiles to follow the way to Christ. The promise to Abraham had priority over the Torah of Moses. The steps that Paul took led him along a way which in fact could end up with only one conclusion: the Torah had to be abolished. But the apostle did not draw this conclusion. Why not? Why did he hesitate? Or is it wrong to speak of hesitation? Once more we need to realize that while Saul indeed had become Paul, that Paul had also always remained Saul. It was impossible for him to think in terms of 'abolishing the Torah'.

In Christian theology Paul's letter to the Galatians has long played a central role in the discussion of the value of 'the law'. The apostle is said to have spoken about this in negative terms – 'Christ is the end of the law' (Rom. 10.4), and this is said to mean that in his view the Jewish view of the law must also be condemned.[17] I believe that this view is based on a stubborn and widespread misunderstanding. Paul's polemic in the previous chapters has not been that of a Christian against Judaism. He was writing some decades before that tragic schism became reality. In the concrete situation of the problems which were causing confusion in Galatia, he did not argue in principle but *contextually*.[18] Paul opposed Jewish Christians who thought that Gentile Christians had to be circumcised and needed to obey all the commandments of the Torah. He powerfully rejected this thought and therefore wrote with characteristic sarcasm: 'I wish those who unsettle you would mutilate themselves!' (Gal. 5.12).

Paul relativized the significance of circumcision – 'For in

Christ Jesus neither circumcision nor uncircumcision is of any avail, but faith working through love' (Gal. 5.6) – with the consequence that he felt compelled to relativize the significance of the whole Torah. However, he did not argue for abolition. As a consequence, unsuspecting readers of the letter will be surprised by a more positive attitude towards the Torah in the closing chapters: 'for the *whole law* is fulfilled in this one word: "You shall love your neighbour as yourself"' (Gal. 5.14). The whole law? Not a few select commandments but evidently all commandments. Including the commandment relating to circumcision? Paul seems to be contradicting himself, and strictly speaking he does. Some exegetes seek their salvation in a counsel of desperation: these words are said not to be Paul's but to have been added later.[19] In my view we can easily imagine how conflicts arose in the apostle's thought. Perhaps it is no exaggeration to suppose that sometimes he felt that they threatened to tear him apart. He passionately invited Gentile Christians to join the Christian community and at the same time it was existentially impossible for him to bid farewell to the Torah. He thought that he had found a solution to this tricky problem. The Torah might not be a hindrance to Gentile Christians if they wanted to become followers of Jesus Christ. In that case they need not be circumcised first. Christianity is not a Jewish sect. The universal promise to Abraham precedes the Torah. The old boundaries have disappeared. Anyone who has found the way to the Christian community lives by 'the fruit of the Spirit: love, joy, peace, patience, kindness, goodness, faithfulness, gentleness, self-control; against such things there is no law' (Gal. 5.22–23). Anyone who wants to know what a Christian way of life means will find trustworthy guidance in the Torah.

Paul's ideal was a Christian community which would form a unity despite the fact that it consisted of both Jewish Christians and Gentile Christians. He saw the promise to Abraham as the foundation of this unity. History showed that this ideal was difficult to realize. In his longing for unity Paul created a situation which led to division. Within one and the same community there lived Gentile Christians who were not circumcised and Jewish Christians who observed the Torah fully. These were two groups which constantly moved further from each other and finally ended up as different faith communities: a Gentile-Christian church and Jewish-Christian groups which as it were fell between two stools – they were out of the synagogue but did not feel at home in the Gentile-Christian church.

The Torah is central to the letter to the Galatians. Other theological themes are discussed exclusively in relation to that question. That is equally true of the significance of the crucified Christ. Paul does not offer us a completed christological study in this writing either. It can indeed be established that to an increasing degree he put Christ at the centre of his thought. In apocalyptic literature it is not unusual to divide history into periods. Paul also did that, but he did so in an original way: the creation – the promise to Abraham – the Torah of Moses – the coming of Jesus Christ – the *parousia* of the Lord God's definitive victory. He was aware of living in an interim period, between coming and *parousia*. In that interim the age-old promise to Abraham had taken on a new impetus in Christ, the mission among the Gentiles. Here we discover as it were between the lines Paul's motivation for going to the Gentiles and fulfilling his calling.

For Paul, the coming of Jesus Christ is the great turning point in history: 'But when the time had fully come, God sent forth his son, born of woman, born under the law, to redeem those who were under the law, so that we might receive adoption as sons' (Gal. 4.4–5). The image used here is not easy to interpret. Given the context, the contrast between being a slave and being a son (Gal. 4.1–3), it seems likely that Paul wrote these words with the image of a slave market in his head. However, the question which then arises is: if the son has redeemed those who were under the law, to whom did he pay the ransom? We can rule out the possibility that here Paul could have meant God. Perhaps it would be sensible not to ask too much of the image. With the help of a comparison which is to be explained from the context, Paul wanted to express the fact that the coming of Jesus Christ results in liberation and freedom. This thought is essential for the letter to the Galatians: 'for freedom Christ has set us free' (Gal. 5.1).

In the passage from Galatians 4 quoted above, liberation takes place through the *coming* of Christ. Earlier in the letter the apostle wrote some sentences in which a connection was made with the dying of Christ on the cross: 'Christ redeemed us from the curse of the law, having become a curse for us – for it is written, "cursed be every one who hangs on a tree" – that in Christ Jesus the blessing of Abraham might come upon the Gentiles, that we might receive the promise of the Spirit through faith' (Gal. 3.13–14). Throughout the argument the passage quoted performs a key function, but again it has to be said that the interpretation causes difficulties. Here too it is legitimate to ask to whom the ransom is paid. It seems very improbable that God would ask for this contribution. Despite the fact that the passage quoted plays an important role in the dogmatic discussion about vicarious suffering and reconciliation and atonement, the exegete again cannot avoid concluding that Paul was not formulating a generally valid 'doctrine' but arguing contextually.

The starting point for this is the thought, which was essential to Paul, that 'in Christ Jesus the *blessing* of Abraham would come upon the Gentiles' (Gal. 3.14). In Old Testament terms the 'blessing' stands over against the 'curse'. In the preceding pericope Paul had already drawn attention to that aspect (Gal. 3.6–12). In his theological reflection he now brought his own experiences to bear. Once as a persecutor of the Christian community he had seen the crucified Jesus, with a reference to scripture and tradition, as a 'curse'. This vision motivated him to be active as a 'zealot'. On the basis of the Torah it could be concluded that the crucified Jesus and his followers had been cursed by God. On the way to Damascus Paul – by now this had happened long ago – came to a conclusion as bewildering as it was surprising, namely that the one who had been crucified and cursed by God had risen from the dead.

Thus God changed 'curse' into 'blessing'. That was paradoxical, but Paul knew that it was true. The vision that he had made it possible for him to associate the Christ event intensively with his own fate. As readers we need to realize that in the first place his statement is very *personal*. When he writes that 'Christ became a curse for us', the words 'for us' refer to himself. He is called by God to proclaim the gospel of Christ in the world of the Gentiles so that 'the blessing of Abraham should come upon the Gentiles' (Gal. 3.14). It is understandable that later generations read more into these words, and this perhaps would have met with Paul's approval. When he wrote these texts, it was not his intention to make statements of eternal value.

How much Paul felt that he was bound up with Christ is unambiguously clear from the following text: 'For I through the law died to the law, that I might live to God. I have been crucified with Christ; *it is no longer I who live, but Christ lives in me*; and my mortal life is a life by faith in the Son of God, who loved me, and gave himself for me' (Gal. 2.19–20). Here too Paul is not speaking in general terms but very personally about his relationship to Jesus Christ. There seems no doubt that here again he recalled the vision on the way to Damascus. The persecutor became an apostle. His life changed radically. He became another person – a Christ person. He already lived as it were in the messianic kingdom. Paul also gave an indication of living in two worlds in this passage: 'Christ lives in me' and 'my mortal life'. The way to the new creation has been pioneered by Christ. Therefore Paul can write: 'in the Son of God, who loved me and gave himself for me' (Gal. 2.20).

To introduce his argument Paul reminded his readers in Galatia of a conflict which he had years earlier with no less a person than Peter (Gal. 2.11–14). There is nothing new under the sun. In Antioch both influential apostles already had a difference of opinion over the meaning of the Torah. According to Paul Peter did not dare to make a choice, and on this occasion he clearly discussed the matter with Peter: 'We ourselves, who are Jews by birth and not Gentile sinners, yet who know that a man is not justified by works of the law but through faith in Jesus Christ, even we have believed in Christ Jesus, in order to be justified by faith in Christ, and not by works of the law, because by works of the law shall no man be justified' (Gal. 2.15–16). To repeat myself: Paul was not polemical against Judaism, and his arguments were contextual. This passage is not about 'two types of faith':[20] Jewish, which is supposed to be based on justification through doing the works of the law, and Christian, which presupposes that justification is possible only through faith in Jesus Christ. That difference certainly applies to the years after the schism between Judaism and Christianity. However, in this dramatic scene we do not have the Jew Peter confronting the Christian Paul but two Jewish Christians, both of whom are wrestling with the meaning of the Torah for Gentile Christians. At the beginning of his letter Paul sharply observed that those who thought that conditions had to be laid down for Gentile Christians – in particular the command to be circumcised – were showing that they expected their salvation – justification – from 'the works of the law' and not from 'faith in Christ Jesus'. The conclusion was obvious: in that case what is the significance of Christ?

Paul wrote a long and complicated letter to the community in Galatia. Did his words have any effect? We do not know, but certainly soon afterwards the apostle would discuss a number of topics which are central to this letter in his letter to the community in Rome. Again it will appear there that his arguments were not arguments on matters of principle but contextual.

13

The letter to the community in Rome

A different kind of letter

There is little if any doubt among New Testament scholars about the authorship of Paul's last letter.[1] The notion that his writing addressed to the Christian community in Rome is the absolute climax of his whole work is centuries old. Those in search of his 'theology' are said to have here the key to his thought. In the previous chapters I have not started from this classical presupposition and have deliberately taken another course. At this stage I do not judge my well-considered choice of a chronological and biographical approach to have been wasted labour or time. The letter to the community of Rome is without doubt a fascinating and profound work. Indeed it is no exaggeration to describe it as the crown of the apostle's literary oeuvre that has come down to us, but it does not so transcend his other letters that they can only be understood in the light of this last work. The course that I have followed up to now discloses the significance and value of each individual letter. Paul was a creative man. His writings are always worth reading and studying. There is not a disappointing letter among them. I have no reason to revise that conclusion because his last letter is more systematic than its predecessors.

Paul's last letter has gained much authority and influence. It has played a central role at crucial moments in the history of the church and theology. The names of Augustine, Luther and Barth may again be mentioned here.[2] The great respect for the letter has also arisen as a result of its position in the New Testament canon. It is not the conclusion to the series of authentic letters by Paul but opens this series. Some exegetes infer from this that already at an early stage in church history the letter to the Romans was seen as the most important Pauline work.[3] I am inclined to doubt the validity of such an assertion. The place of a work in the New Testament canon says little about the value that people attached to it in early church history. Every reader of the New Testament can easily note that both the Gospels and the letters are in the first instance arranged by length. Matthew has twenty-eight chapters, Luke twenty-four and John twenty-one. Mark seems to be the exception to the rule. Despite its brief extent of sixteen chapters it comes second. This can easily be explained. Of the four Gospels, Matthew and Mark correspond most closely to each other. That was also noted in the first centuries of church history. It was therefore natural to make Mark follow immediately after Matthew. Both Gospels now belonged indissolubly together.

In the series of Paul's letters, in length Romans and I Corinthians compete for the crown. It was in fact inevitable that Romans should come first. Logic required I Corinthians to be followed by II Corinthians. However, the second letter to the community of Corinth is three chapters shorter than Paul's two longest letters. If Romans rather than I Corinthians opened the series, virtually all problems would be solved and the other letters to communities could be arranged in order of decreasing length (to make it quite clear, I have put in brackets the letters I do not regard as authentic): Romans sixteen chapters; I Corinthians sixteen; II Corinthians thirteen; Galatians six; (Ephesians six;) Philippians four; (Colossians four;) I Thessalonians five[4]; (II Thessalonians three;) after that follow, also in decreasing length, the letters addressed to persons: (I Timothy six chapters; II Timothy four; Titus three) and finally Philemon, the shortest of all, which consists of only one chapter.

The letters which I discussed in the previous chapters were addressed to communities which Paul had visited once or more and to people – Philemon and his household – whom he had met earlier. His writing to the community of Rome forms a

striking exception to this rule. Paul had travelled much through
Asia Minor, Macedonia and Greece, but he had not yet been to
Italy. That makes the exegesis of the letter difficult. In Corinth,
Philippi, Thessalonica and Galatia problems had arisen, conflicts which threatened the unity of the community. Messengers
brought disturbing news and asked Paul for advice. In his letter
to the community of Rome he was not reacting to questions
which were put to him, but himself took the initiative. This
observation raises the question why he thought it necessary to
send a letter to a community which he had not yet visited.

The community of Rome

The apostle to the Gentiles did not found the community in
Rome. It had already existed for some time before he announced
his coming. Its origins lie hidden in the mists of history. The
edict of the emperor Claudius,[5] discussed earlier, shows that at
the latest in the second half of the 40s of the first century unrest
developed in the Jewish community of Rome because of
the preaching of the gospel of Jesus Christ. On the orders of
Claudius the Jews – including Jewish Christians – were driven
out of the city. They went in many directions in search of new
abodes and livelihoods. During his second missionary journey
Paul met the Jewish couple Priscilla and Aquila in Corinth.
After being driven out of Rome they had provisionally made a
home in the Greek port. They were hospitable and gave lodging
to the apostle (Acts 18.2–3).

Later church tradition names Peter as the founder of the
community in Rome and as its first bishop.[6] A passage from
the Gospel of Matthew was seen as the credentials for his
authority and that of his successors.[7] Modern historians who
have to base their views on verifiable facts feel compelled to
note that there is no concrete evidence. The formation of
the early Christian legend has completely covered over the
historical course of events. Did Peter travel to Rome before
Paul? If that may have been the case, then it is at least strange
that the name of the first 'bishop' is not mentioned in the letter

to the community of Rome. The author of Acts relates that after his miraculous liberation from prison Peter went 'elsewhere' (Acts 12.17). Did he go to Rome then? That is not impossible, but the vagueness of the report inevitably raises new questions. Suppose that Peter really did go to Rome, why does the author not mention that explicitly? Does he deliberately keep silent about Peter's destination because he was so concerned with Paul that he attached more importance to the further stages of Paul's journey to Rome?

Those in search of an answer to these questions are surrounded by guesses and speculations. The data are too limited for it to be possible to make a reconstruction of the course of events which is to any degree plausible. It can be noted that the author of Acts gradually lost his interest in Peter's activities. After his departure 'elsewhere', indicated earlier, in due course the apostle returned to Jerusalem. He was present at the important meeting of apostles in the city (Acts 15.7–11). After that he disappears from the scene for good. Legends often say more than biblical stories, but these reports are seldom if ever reliable. The only responsible scholarly conclusion is that we do not know when the community in Rome was founded or by whom. The role of men like Paul and Peter in the dissemination of Christianity is not to be overestimated. Pioneer work was done by anonymous believers, like the followers of Stephen who were driven out and dispersed. Unknown men and women, pilgrims from the Diaspora, itinerant traders, soldiers and slaves laid the foundations for the communities which according to church traditions were founded by apostles.[8]

The edict of Claudius had far-reaching consequences for the composition of the Christian community in Rome. With the expulsion of the Jews, the Jewish Christians also disappeared from the city. Suddenly a community had come into being which counted exclusively Gentile Christians among its members. Was that a unique situation for this time? It does not seem rash to say that it was. The Jewish Diaspora was large and widespread. Jews lived in many cities in the Roman empire. On his long journeys Paul found that synagogues abroad were places where he could meet people who had been born into and brought up in the same Jewish faith as he had. There in those familiar surroundings he began his preaching of the gospel of Jesus Christ. There he found a hearing, but there were also fierce disputes. From the local synagogue Paul tried to interest non-Jews in his convictions. Without the Jewish Diaspora the rapid dissemination of the Christian faith would have been impossible.[9] Paul lived in the interim before the schism which in the 70s and 80s was to drive Jews and Christians far apart. He became a follower of Jesus Christ without denying his Jewishness. At this time the boundaries had not yet been drawn definitively. His terminology proves that. In his letters the 'Christian' Paul is not writing polemic against Judaism. Against what group within the variegated Judaism of his time would he have written this polemic? The Sadducees? The Zealots? The Essenes? Hellenistic Diaspora Judaism? Or the Pharisees? But that would raise the question which tendency within Pharisaism. Followers of Hillel, of Shammai, of Gamaliel, his former teacher? For us, living many centuries after the schism between Judaism and Christianity, it is impossible to imagine that there was a relatively short period in history – around fifty years – in which there was no controversy between Judaism and Christianity as such. But Paul lived in this time. He did not yet know the opposition between Jew and Christian, and we look for it in vain in his writings. In his perspective the world was divided into 'Jews' and 'Gentiles' – 'circumcised' and 'uncircumcised'. He did not opt for the one and oppose the other. Thanks to his vision on the way to Damascus he knew that he was called to bring the latter group – the Gentiles – into contact with the gospel of Jesus Christ. He did not dispute Judaism, but he hoped to be able to bring about unity between Jews and Gentiles (Gal. 3.28). That he finally failed to do this may be said to be the tragedy of his life.

In Rome, as a result of the edict of Claudius, of necessity and temporarily there was a situation which would be commonplace only after the schism between Judaism and Christianity in the second half of the first century: a Christian community which consisted exclusively of members from a Gentile background. The emperor Claudius was murdered in 54. His successor, Nero (54–68), presumably repealed the edict a short time after his accession. From that moment Jews and Jewish Christians returned to Rome. It is evident, for example, from the last chapter of Paul's letter that his friends Aquila and Priscilla were again living in the metropolis (Rom. 16.3). They had seen much of the world in a period of around five years: from Rome to Corinth, then to Ephesus and after that back to Rome.

Travel plans

The apostle does not leave his readers in Rome uncertain for long about the purpose of his writing. After the long heading (Rom. 1.1–7) he gets straight to the point: 'First, I thank my God through Christ Jesus for all of you, because your faith is proclaimed in all the world . . . I want you to know, brothers and sisters, that I have often intended to come to you (but thus far have been prevented) in order that I may reap some harvest among you as well as among the rest of the Gentiles. I am under obligation both to Greeks and to barbarians, both to the wise and to the foolish, so I am eager to preach the gospel to you also who are in Rome' (Rom. 1.8–15). Anyone who reads these verses closely cannot fail to note that they are remarkably ambiguous. The apostle begins by praising the Christians in Rome in unmistakable terms. Their faith is known far and wide. At the end of the passage quoted, however, he says that he cherishes the wish 'to preach the gospel to you also who are in Rome'. Do the words of praise at the beginning contain the conviction that he alone preached the gospel in the right way? If Paul might have expressed this thought in writing in a polemical situation (Gal. 1.6–12), in the letter to the community in Rome he does not allow himself to be led into making such bold assertions.

Towards the end of the letter the apostle produces a new

argument for his visit to Rome: 'This is the reason why I have so often been hindered from coming to you. But now, since I no longer have any room for work in these regions, and since I have longed for many years to come to you, I hope to see you in passing as I go to Spain, and to be sped on my journey there by you, once I have enjoyed your company for a little' (Rom. 15.22–24). In the end Rome does not prove to be Paul's final destination, but the starting point for new mission territories. His plans are such that one is inclined to feel that the adventurous apostle is beginning to excel himself: 'At present, however, I am going to Jerusalem with aid for the saints. For Macedonia and Achaea have been pleased to make some contribution for the poor among the saints in Jerusalem' (Rom. 15.25–26). This information allows us to date the letter with a probability bordering on certainty. Paul had earlier written about this collection in his second letter to the Corinthians (II Cor. 8–9). At that time he was travelling around Macedonia and then planned to go to Corinth. Having arrived there he stayed three months. His departure did not go according to plan. He wanted to travel by ship to Syria, but 'because a plot was made against him by the Jews he resolved to return through Macedonia' (Acts 20.3).

Paul had made good use of his last stay in Corinth. At all events he had had a number of intensive conversations with members of the community. A good deal had happened. The fierce conflicts had left few untouched. Charges had been made time and again and accusations had been exchanged. Thanks to the correspondence and Titus' attempts at mediation, things had quietened down. Paul could return to a community which was once more slowly becoming better disposed towards him. In this positive atmosphere he found time to correspond with the community in Philippi, to write a well-constructed letter to the Galatians and to complete an extensive letter addressed to the community in Rome.

Paul's plans were clear: first to deliver the proceeds of the collection to Jerusalem, and then to go via Rome to Spain, for 'I no longer have any room for work in these regions' (Rom.

15.22). Readers can hardly believe their eyes. Did the apostle really think that his activities in Macedonia and Greece could be regarded as complete? Was he so driven by an 'apocalyptic haste' that there was no longer any time for rest and reflection? He had visited cities like Thessalonica, Philippi and Corinth several times. He had not made any mention, for example, of Athens. How could he then say that there was no longer 'any room for work'? It seems to me that the text must be interpreted in a different way. In a previous chapter it became clear that Paul had come up against increasing opposition, especially in Macedonia and Greece. With much difficulty and a great deal of effort he had restored relations with the community in Corinth, but the peace was brittle and vulnerable. A satisfactory solution had yet to be found for a large number of differences. It is possible that the apostle therefore wanted to go on to new mission fields, far away in Spain, far away from his opponents in Macedonia and Greece, and also far away from Jerusalem.

Paul's mood when he was in Corinth and wrote the letter to the community of Rome is difficult to fathom precisely. Was he disappointed? Or even weary of it all?[10] It is not surprising that sometimes he felt overwhelmed. So much depended on him, and there was so much to do. Even an optimist would sometimes feel defeated. However, the apostle was not despondent. His last letter shows that he still had many plans. Or must we see his planned journey to Rome and Spain as a 'flight forward'? By the irony of history his plans were again thwarted. From Corinth he travelled to Jerusalem. The Acts of the Apostles contains an extensive account of the difficulties that he experienced there (Acts 21.15–23.22). Finally Paul ended up in prison in Caesarea. He remained there some time (Acts 23.23–26.32). Because he had appealed to the emperor he was finally brought as a prisoner to Rome (Acts 27–28). In this way he arrived in the capital of the Roman empire. Whether after that he was able to go on to visit Spain is completely unknown.

Contextual theology

Paul announced his coming at the beginning and at the end of his letter. He did so in a strikingly courteous way. It seems that he made an effort to present himself as well as possible. The Christians in Rome did not need to be anxious about him. In a short time they would meet a man who knew and respected the rules of courtesy and hospitality. Did Paul write his letter to the community in Rome only for this reason? Were that really the case, he could have contented himself with a short letter of at most a few chapters. However, the letter is considerably longer. Between the information about his travel plans at the beginning and at the end of his work the apostle gives an extended exposition of his theological views. What did he intend with this? Did he want not only to inform the Christians about his coming but also to bring them up to date with his 'theology'?

In the previous chapters we have come to know Paul as a man with an awareness of concrete reality. His letters inspired and irritated people because he did not argue in the abstract but contextually. His thought had a practical bent. That was his strength. He reacted to questions and sought solutions to problems which had arisen in the various communities. Nowhere in the letters which I have discussed so far did Paul make any attempt gratuitously to develop a theological system which he then thought that he had to impose on his readers as authoritative. This profile of the apostle is doubtless surprising. He was not the systematic thinker who has become both famed and notorious in the course of church history, admired by some and reviled by others because he was thought to have been rigid and to have had a one-track mind, allowing no room for other views. Rather, on closer inspection Paul seems to have been more of a chameleon, who was not carried along by unshakeable certainty but tried to find his way tentatively, seeking and discussing. It is the apostle's greatness that he ventured into areas which had previously been trodden by virtually no one. The questions and problems which led to situations of conflict are still sharply engraved on our memories: the *parousia* of the Lord; cross and resurrection; the significance of the Torah for Christians with a pagan background. Paul did pioneer work. He was not tied to a desk, but on journeys of discovery tried gradually to map out unknown territory.

At first sight the greater part of the letter to the community in Rome – chapters 1–11 inclusive – runs directly contrary to the apostle's way of working sketched out here. He no longer discusses or hesitates, but radiates certainty and assurance. Given the lack of concrete questions which needed to be answered, Paul will have seen his chance to present his theology, not least as an introduction of himself. Anyone who reads the letter with an open mind will not be surprised that in the course of the history of the church and the history of dogma it has often been interpreted as a summary of Paul's teaching.[11] Whether that is correct remains to be seen.

The question still remains: *why* did the apostle write such an extensive and profound letter to a community which he barely knew, if at all? Of course he shared his ambitious travel plans with the members of the community, but that was not the only reason why he wrote to Rome. He wanted more. However, there is a dispute over his precise aim(s). During his stay in Corinth Paul must have felt that he had arrived at a turning point in his life. He first needed to go to Jerusalem with the collection. After that he wanted to implement old plans and travel further west: first Rome, then Spain.

At some points in time people need to order their thoughts. It is easy to suppose that during his stay in Corinth Paul also felt this need. He had hectic years behind him, culminating tragically in imprisonment in Ephesus and the fierce conflict with the Corinthians. Time did not stand still, and developments continued apace. He could not complain about his success, but he also experienced the shadow sides of his successful activity. The tensions within the early Christian communities in Asia Minor, Macedonia and Greece increased. Where did Paul himself stand? There had hardly been time for reflection. He had not had the leisure for a well-considered stocktaking. In Corinth he finally found the opportunity to concentrate. After all the other questions had been deal with, he made a beginning of putting his views down on paper. Perhaps he did that initially with no other intention than to clear his mind. In my view we cannot possibly speak of a theological 'testament'.[12] As is evident from the letter to the community of Rome, the apostle did not yet plan to retire, to lead a quiet life and rest his weary head.

Paul, the man of two worlds, knows from his own experience that people can sometimes be 'drawn in two directions' (Phil. 1.23). He sought rest, but was not accustomed to sit still for long. At the same time the plan matured in his mind to fulfil an old wish: to travel to Rome. He did not know the community there and so he needed to announce his coming. Thus far the course of events is plausible. There remains the reason why he thought he had to add his personal views to the letter. Did he want to inform the members of the community in this way about his theological thought? That seems very likely. However, I hesitate to accept the suggestion. I do so because I find it psychologically difficult to explain how Paul could suddenly act so out of character. Until then his theology had been contextual. Questions and problems which had arisen in communities challenged him to reflect and react. Experience had taught him that situations often differ greatly and that standard answers usually could give no solace. I cannot therefore imagine that contrary to his custom the apostle would simply have presented the community in Rome with a long and complicated explanation of his theological views. Those who have come to know Paul's way of working will not be content with the traditional viewpoint – the letter to the community of Rome as a dogmatic compendium – and will look for other explanations.

The first question which then arises is: was Paul really completely ignorant of the situation of the Christian community in Rome? It is certainly true that in his letter he hardly reacts to concrete questions, if at all, but that does not mean that those whom he was addressing were a completely unknown quantity to him. The last chapter of his letter sheds another light on things. It contains a long row of names of men and women who lived in Rome and were members of the community there. The hint is easily taken: Paul knew many people in Rome. The next step is a short one. Thanks to these personal contacts he was well up with the local situation.

These considerations lead to the following conclusion. Paul's last letter is certainly unique, but that does not mean that it is fundamentally different from the rest of his letters. Despite appearances to the contrary, the apostle remained faithful to himself. The reports which he received from Rome led him to include in the letter which he sent as an introduction to the community in Rome the passage which he had written in the first instance to clear his own mind. Paul remained a practical man. The difference from his other letters is that he was less dependent on concrete questions and as a result his argument seems to have an abstract, theoretical character. But anyone who reads this letter carefully will discover that here too a *contextual* theologian is speaking.[13]

Strengths and weaknesses in the community in Rome

The special situation within the Christian community in Rome after the repeal of the edict of Claudius will have surprised and fascinated Paul. The return to the city of the Jewish Christians who had been driven out posed problems which had not arisen earlier. We can imagine that the apostle imagined himself in a world turned upside down. For around five years Gentile Christians had kept the community in Rome in existence. Now they saw that they had to create a proper place in their midst for their Jewish-Christian brothers and sisters. This might seem a simple task, but anyone who knows about complicated human relationships will understand that in such a situation tensions can sometimes run high. Who could lay claim to the oldest rights? Was it the Gentile Christians who had had the say for some years after the expulsion of the Jewish Christians? They had begun to determine the atmosphere and perhaps were afraid that the influx of a relatively large number of new members could seriously disturb the existing order. Or was it the Jewish Christians who had returned? In the period before the edict of Claudius they had been the leaders, and some might have boasted that they presided over the birth of the community.

It was not the first time that Paul was confronted with tensions between Jews and Gentiles within the Christian community. However, in Rome the roles were reversed. Leadership rested with the Gentile Christians. They encountered the returning Jewish Christians with some suspicion. Given Paul's own Jewish background it is understandable that this matter was very close to his heart. In my view that is also the true reason for his writing such a lengthy letter. The report on his travel plans might seem to be the occasion, but in reality it was just a useful pretext. The apostle was disturbed by the reports which reached him. The unity of the community was at stake. As before he tried to meet this danger with all his creativity.

Anyone who today tries to read an old and complicated writing like the letter to the community of Rome can no longer do so without skilled help in the form of a commentary or some other form of guide.[14] My advice may at first surprise and perplex readers, but on closer inspection it will prove to be worth considering. My recommendation would be to read the letter in reverse order, i.e. not begin with the first chapter but at the end, and then go backwards. The original readers would not of course have needed such advice. They would understand better than we do what the apostle had to say to them. As those directly affected they would have had no difficulty in as it were reading between the lines and understanding the unexpressed intentions. Centuries later, we pick up the letter and easily forget that Paul was not writing to us. We remain outsiders in a discussion which is alien to us. The apostle is not addressing us, and there is every reason to suppose that he would be amazed if he saw that we were still reading and studying his letter.

For those interested in theology, the last chapter of the letter has little to offer: a long series of names of – with one exception

– unknown men and women (Rom. 16.1–16). But for those with some understanding, this overwhelming number of names – more than in the apostle's other letters – can be a significant indication. The long letter full of complicated theological views ends surprisingly. Suddenly it is disclosed that Paul knew a lot of people in Rome. After this discovery we can read the preceding chapters with other eyes. The apostle is not theorizing. He did not write a timeless compendium of his teaching valid everywhere and for all times. Although he had not yet visited Rome, he knew the situation from hearsay. Through personal contacts he knew that the community risked being torn apart by internal tensions. While he was reflecting in Corinth on the situation he came to realize that the notes that he had drafted to clear his own mind could be extremely pertinent. That gave rise to the letter to the community of Rome: a marvellous combination of theoretical views, personal reflections and contextual theology.

The closing chapter is preceded by a section (Rom. 12–15) in which in relatively sober words Paul gave his view of the situation in the community in Rome. In keeping with the spirit of the whole letter he did so very cautiously, in a well-considered way and without sarcastic or ironical remarks. Evidently he did not want to provoke the parties needlessly. In the letter which he had sent some time previously from Corinth to communities in Galatia his approach had been less gentle. On this occasion he did not spare his readers and often gave his emotions free rein. Although there are agreements between the topics in the two letters, the letter to the community Rome is quite a different work from the letter to the Galatians. Paul was well aware of what he was doing. He had been to Galatia several times. He knew the situation there personally and not just from hearsay. In his writing he makes no secret of the fact that he had a special bond with members of the communities in Galatia and shared emotional memories (Gal. 4.12–20). The persons addressed to an important degree determine the colour of a letter. Therefore the community in Rome received a letter which is not dominated by emotions. Paul was trying to calm people down. He remained detached and hoped in this way to create the calm which was necessary for restoring unity.

The readers of this part of the letter will come across various themes which are familiar to them. The following passage could be regarded as a summary of the long chapters in I Corinthians 12–14 devoted to the question of unity: 'For as in the one body we have many members, and not all the members have the same function, so we, though many, are one body in Christ, and individually members one of another. Having gifts that differ according to the grace given to us, let us use them: if prophecy, in proportion to our faith; if service, in our serving; he who teaches, in his teaching; he who exhorts, in his exhortation; he who contributes, in liberality; he who gives aid, with zeal; he who does acts of mercy, with cheerfulness' (Rom. 12.4–8). This succinctness is surprising, and makes it clear that the unity of the community in Rome is threatened in a different way from that in Corinth.

As we know, Paul lived some decades before the schism between Judaism and Christianity became a reality. As a follower of Jesus Christ he did not break with the Jewish tradition. He was creative, but also 'conservative', in the sense that he conserved – preserved – what he thought valuable. He took it for granted that the Torah was part of this. Certainly some commandments posed problems in contacts with Gentile Christians, but that did not lead him to argue for a Christianity without the Torah. His letter to the community of Rome shows no sign of this. Thanks to his wide knowledge of scripture and tradition he knew that the word 'love' expressed the basic tenor of the Torah: 'You shall love your neighbour as yourself. I am the Lord' (Lev. 19.18). Paul did not first learn to spell the word 'love' when he encountered the risen Lord on the way to Damascus. Having grown up in the world of the Torah, from his youth he knew that 'love of neighbour' is seen as the summary of the commandments: 'Love does no wrong to a neighbour, therefore love is the fulfilling of the whole law' (Rom. 13.10; cf. Gal. 5.14; 6.2). It is not difficult to summarize the differences between Jesus and Paul,[15] but given what the

Synoptic Gospels say, at this point they were in fundamental agreement. When asked about the greatest commandment, Jesus replied: 'You shall love the Lord your God with all your heart and with all your soul and with all your mind. That is the first and great commandment. The second is like it: You shall love your neighbour as yourself. On these two commandments hang all the law and the prophets' (Matt. 22.37–40).[16]

In full accord with the Old Testament-Jewish tradition, in Paul's view the word 'love' now gave colour and content to the life of the Christian community. It is because Paul was so original that he seldom if ever repeated himself and always looked for images or notions which he could best apply to the situation of those whom he addressed. So instead of the lofty words of the 'hymn of praise to love' in I Corinthians 13, in his last letter he wrote a passage which is striking for the concrete instructions which it gives: 'Contribute to the needs of the saints, practise hospitality. Bless those who persecute you; bless and do not curse them. Rejoice with those who rejoice, weep with those who weep. *Live in harmony with one another*; do not be haughty, but associate with the lowly; never be conceited. Repay no one evil for evil, but take thought for what is noble in the sight of all. If possible, as far as it depends upon you, live peaceably with all' (Rom. 12.13–18).

The words in italics are of crucial importance for a proper understanding of the purpose of Paul's letter: 'Live in harmony with one another.' This is not a completely new thought for him (see e.g. Phil. 2.1–4). In his letter to the community of Rome, however, he was moving in an area into which he had hardly ventured hitherto. 'Live in harmony' takes on a wider meaning. It is no longer limited to the personal life of men and women in their mutual relations, but at the same time is applied to the attitude which has to be adopted towards the authorities: 'Let every person be subject to the governing authorities. For there is no authority except from God, and those that exist have been instituted by God. Therefore he who resists the authorities resists what God has appointed, and those who resist will incur judgment' (Rom. 13.1–2).

As I have remarked often, Paul was a contextual theologian. It is certainly no coincidence that he thought it relevant to speak of the authorities in his letter to the community of Rome in particular. On his way he had had more than one encounter with representatives of the Roman authorities. We even know the names of some of them: Sergius Paulus, proconsul on Cyprus, 'a man of intelligence' (Acts 13.7), and Gallio, the proconsul of Achaea, who refused to pronounce judgment in a matter which did not concern him (Acts 18.12–17). Nor would that be all. When Paul travelled to Jerusalem from Corinth shortly after writing his letter to the community in Rome, he soon got into difficulties. He was arrested and imprisoned in Caesarea (Acts 21.15–24.9). Extensive hearings followed, first before Felix, the Roman governor of Judaea, and then before Felix's successor, Porcius Festus (Acts 24.10–26.32). One cannot catch Paul out in revolutionary tendencies in any of these cases. He was 'zealous' but not a Zealot. He was not ashamed of being a Roman citizen. Sometimes this got him out of difficulties (Acts 16.35–40). In his defence in Caesarea he appealed to the emperor in Rome (Acts 25.6–12). Given the content of his letter to the community in Rome, there is no reason to doubt the historical reliability of these reports in Acts.

The members of the Christian community in Rome were literally and figuratively close to the supreme authority. They knew from their own experience what that could mean. Why did Paul write this part about attitudes towards the authorities? Were some members of the community planning to oppose this authority? That seems improbable, but it is not completely impossible. Political unrest was by no means an unknown phenomenon in Rome. Since the reign of the emperor Augustus, the much-famed *Pax Romana*[17] had been endangered more than once. In particular the accession of the unpredictable, capricious emperor Caligula (37–41) had posed a serious threat to the stability of the gigantic empire. Claudius restored order and extended the empire further. He was killed in 54 by poisoning. His successor Nero (54–68) was only sixteen years old and inexperienced when he was proclaimed emperor. The situation in the Roman metropolis was therefore anything but secure. Paul will have had good reason to warn the community not to let itself be caught up in a dangerous adventure. Moreover he was caught as it were between two fires. In that period unrest was also increasing in the land of the Jews. The Zealot movement was gaining adherents. An outburst of violence seemed almost inevitable. It is conceivable that some Jewish Christians who had come back had been infected by the revolutionary Zealot fire and that Paul had also heard that they were not concealing their ideas within the community. Paul advises calm and reflection: 'For the authorities are God's servant, for your good' (Rom. 13.4).[18]

Paul the apocalyptist was a man with a practical slant. He dreamed of change but he remained a realist. The content of his letters is stamped by this ambiguity. Those who are not favourably inclined towards the apostle could accuse him of imbalance and opportunism. According to some this is particularly the case in his notoriously disputed argument about obedience to the authorities in Romans 13. In the course of church history his advice has not been gratefully accepted by everyone.[19] For some he has proved to be a man with conservative views who was wary of revolutionary changes and without hesitation was submissive to the existing order. Others praise him and see him as a man who was an anti-revolutionary heart and soul, a man who had permanently endorsed the power of the authorities – from high to low, from kings to elders. Paul himself would have reacted to these descriptions with bewilderment. He wrote a letter to the community in Rome and thought it necessary to include a few words of warning. These words of his are also time-conditioned. He was not talking about a state authority which was to be valid for all centuries. To make the point once again: the apocalyptist Paul could not have guessed for a moment that his letters would continue to be read down the centuries.

Paul called for a 'harmonious' life. As we saw earlier, that was no luxury, as the community in Rome threatened to be torn apart by conflicts. In his letter the apostle spoke of a conflict between 'weak' and 'strong'. He thought that he himself could be said to be one of the 'strong'. Because in his last surviving letter the usual sarcastic and ironical phrases are almost completely absent, the following remarks sound more self-confident that what we are accustomed to hear from him: 'We who are strong enough ought to bear with the failings of the weak, and not to please ourselves; but let each of us please his neighbour for his good, to edify him' (Rom. 15.1–2). Paul was not a party to the conflict in Rome. He took the side of the 'strong' above all so as to be able to put in a good word for the 'weak'.

Who were these 'weak' in the community in Rome? There has been much discussion of this question in exegetical literature, but a consensus seems difficult to achieve.[20] The indications in the letter are far too vague for us to be able to sketch out a clear profile: 'As for the man who is weak in faith, welcome him, but not for disputes over opinions. One believes he may eat anything, while the weak man eats only vegetables. Let not him who eats despise him who abstains, and let not him who abstains pass judgment on him who eats; for God has welcomed him' (Rom. 14.1–3). It was not the first time that Paul had been confronted with this problem. In his correspondence with the community in Corinth he once expressed a remarkably qualified view about eating meat that had been offered to idols (I Cor. 8.1–13; 10.23–11.1). In this discussion, too, he asked for consideration to be given to the position of the 'weak' . He himself did not belong to that group. He evidently had no difficulty in eating meat offered to idols. His argument in the letter to the Corinthians was one which was bewilderingly and disarmingly clear: we do not believe in idols. In other words, meat offered to idols is ordinary meat. There is no intrinsic objection to eating it (I Cor. 8.1–13). The Gentile Christians should have followed his advice. For Jewish Christians the situation was more complicated. They had their food laws. In the conflict in Corinth Paul operated very cautiously (I Cor. 10.23–11.1). He also did so in the letter to the community of Rome. He said that he was 'strong', but he had sympathy for 'the weak in the faith'. He was sympathetic to their struggles. The apostle will have thought of the difficult position of the Jewish Christians within the community in Rome. At the end of the 40s they had been driven out of the city, and now they had returned to a community in which they could no longer feel really at home. The Gentile Christians were in the majority and showed little understanding of fellow-believers who wanted to obey the commandments of the Torah. Paul made an effort to reconcile the parties: 'One man esteems one day as better than another, while another man esteems all days alike. Let every one be convinced in his own mind. He who observes the day, observes it in honour of the Lord. He also who eats, eats in honour of the Lord, and he too gives thanks to God' (Rom. 14.5–6).

The pieces of the theological puzzle which is constituted by Paul's last letter are slowly coming together. The apostle's aims are becoming more or less visible. The reports which reached him about the special situation of the Christian community in Rome had made him think. He had experienced a great deal, but this situation was new to him. Jewish Christians saw themselves compelled to win a place in a Gentile-Christian community. The world seemed to have been turned upside down. Paul was sufficiently at home in the Old Testament-Jewish tradition to be amazed at this course of events. Long ago God made a covenant with the people of Israel. Gentiles were not completely excluded, but they could share in salvation only through Israel. After the Babylonian exile, above all in the Diaspora the phenomenon of 'godfearers' and 'proselytes' developed, Gentiles who felt attracted to the Jewish religion. The meaning of the word 'proselyte' is significant in this connection: 'one who has come'. In the community in Rome the roles had been reversed: now the returned Jewish Christians seem to be the proselytes, they had come. Suddenly they were 'the weak in faith'. Their faithfulness to the commandments of the Torah – food laws and sabbath – was regarded as irrelevant by 'the strong'.

Jews and Gentiles

In Paul's last extant letter, he theologized *par excellence* from a very *personal* context. He tried to keep a distance and controlled his emotion. That was an admirable achievement, since he was deeply involved in the discussion. He counted himself one of the 'strong', but also felt in solidarity with the 'weak'. He himself was a Jewish Christian. The Torah played an essential role in his life. However, he had also learned to differentiate its precepts. That had proved necessary, since otherwise his preaching would have little or no success in the Gentile world. For that reason he was opposed to Jewish Christians who gave such a central place to the commandments that Gentiles could become followers of Jesus Christ only through the Torah. Paul saw this as an unnecessary detour. As could be inferred from the letter to the communities in Galatia, he himself was ready to relativize the significance of the Torah (Gal. 3–4). Here the apostle was fighting on just one front: for the Gentile Christians and against Jewish Christians who caused serious difficulties for his missionary work among the Gentiles. The complicated situation within the community in Rome compelled him to fight on several fronts at the same time. He took the 'weak' under his wing and tried to make the 'strong' realize that they were wrong to think themselves superior to the others. However, in turn there were limits to Paul's solidarity with the 'weak'. He understood their reverence for the Torah, but at the same time impressed on them that the coming of Jesus Christ into this world had fundamentally changed existing conditions. So the significance of the Torah needed to be reformulated,[21] and Jews could not avoid recognizing that they had to share their age-old privileges with Gentiles who belonged among the followers of Jesus Christ.

Paul did not take sides in the tensions in Rome. That was wise and sensible, but it is also true that he had no alternative. More than ever he was pulled in two directions. Both groups could count on his sympathy. As was his custom, this time too he tried to approach the question in a 'pastoral' way. Of course great demands were put on his capacity to differentiate in his arguments. Anyone who has followed my advice and read the letter backwards will still have a vivid recollection of his exhortation to 'live in harmony with one another' (Rom. 12.16). These words form the guideline for interpreting those chapters which are usually regarded as the systematic part of the letter (Rom. 1–8 and 9–11). However, I doubt whether Paul would have agreed with such a description. Despite appearances to the contrary, it was not his intention to give an elegant, well-considered account of his theological insights. He was moved to the very depths by the question how Jews and Gentiles could live in harmony with one another. He wanted to help the community in Rome with an answer to this question. From his own experience the apostle knew that this problem could also be found elsewhere. He raised it with his usual missionary zeal. Therefore in the personal notes which he wrote in Corinth he had provisionally sought to discuss the whole question of the place of Israel and the significance of the Torah.

I would suggest that to understand Paul's theological insights readers should remember that the apostle to the Gentiles did not live in our time. He is not a contemporary. He does not know what we know. The ways of Judaism and Christianity have parted widely. Christian theology proved a rich source of anti-Jewish remarks. Paul very soon became one of the villains. He became the spokesman of the Christian sense of superiority to the Jewish tradition. He is said to have unmasked Judaism as legalism. This view has been foisted on the apostle, but he himself had no part of it. He wrote his letters some decades before the schism between Judaism and Christianity in the second half of the first century. He himself was a Jew. For us, who live so many centuries later, it is hard to understand, but he did not yet think in terms of oppositions like Jews versus Christians or church versus synagogue.[22] For him, the world was divided into Jews and Gentiles. As a result of the vision that he had had on the way to Damascus, now long in the past, he saw it as his task to proclaim the gospel of Jesus Christ in the world of the Gentiles. He probably discovered only gradually that in so doing he was producing a new opposition: Jewish Christians versus Gentile Christians. In this situation Paul reacted ambivalently. That is also true of the letter to the community of Rome. He had the fortunes of the Gentile Christians very much to heart, but he was and remained a *Jewish* Christian.[23]

After this short interlude, let me repeat the question I raised earlier: how can Jews and Gentiles in a Christian community – in the first place in the specific situation in Rome, but then elsewhere – live together in harmony? In his letter Paul tried first to make it clear that they needed to accept and respect one another in every way. Here the apostle came forward as the reconciler of oppositions. He did that carefully and subtly. When confronted with the arrogance of the Gentile Christians he emphasized the age-old priority of the Jews and thus also of the Jewish Christians. Certainly the roles were reversed in Rome, but that did not mean that the Gentile Christians might claim special rights. At the beginning of his letter we have words which are a programme for action: 'For I am not ashamed of the gospel. It is the power of God for salvation to every one who has faith, *to the Jew first* and also to the Greek' (Rom. 1.16). This theme runs right through the letter like a scarlet thread. That emerges, for example, in the closing chapters, when the apostle gives the following description of Jesus Christ: 'Welcome one another, therefore, as Christ has welcomed you, for the glory of God. For I tell you that *Christ became a servant to the circumcised* to show God's truthfulness, in order to confirm the promise given to the patriarchs, and in order that the Gentiles might glorify God for his mercy' (Rom. 15.6–9). The words in italics may perhaps sound strange to our ears. The way of Jews and Gentiles did not run parallel. Christ was in the first place 'minister of the uncircumcised'. Some decades later the evangelist Matthew would put a similar remark into the mouth of Jesus: 'I am sent only to the lost sheep of the house of Israel' (Matt. 15.24).

As a consequence of the special situation, the Jewish Christians may then be reckoned among 'the weak'; they can boast of an age-old venerable tradition. In principle the Jews have priority over the Gentiles. God has chosen the people of Israel above the Gentiles. Therefore the Jewish Christians need to be accepted and treated with respect. Paul works out this theme still further in chapters 9–11. Then it emerges once more how much importance he attached to this aspect. The introduction betrays the passion which came over the apostle as he was writing: 'I am speaking the truth in Christ, I am not lying; my conscience bears me witness in the Holy Spirit, that I have great sorrow and unceasing anguish in my heart. For I could wish that I myself were accursed and cut off from Christ for the sake of my brethren, my kinsmen by race. They are Israelites, and to them belong the sonship, the glory, the covenants, the giving of the law, the worship and the promises; to them belong the patriarchs, and of their race, according to the flesh, is the Christ. God who is over all be blessed for ever. Amen' (Rom. 9.1–5).

These words came straight from the heart. Paul did not theorize and write in abstract about 'the Israelites', as if for him they were only anonymous figures. He did not just regard them as a theological problem.[24] For him they were a living reality. Probably he even had particular individuals in mind as he wrote, men and women whom he had once known and who had meanwhile disappeared from his life. Paul had experienced a good deal. Fractures had become visible in his own biography. Suddenly the zealot for the Torah popped up as a convinced and active disciple of Jesus Christ. Many did not welcome this unexpected U-turn. In his letters he was silent about the consequences of the vision on the way to Damascus for his personal contacts. Perhaps members of his family and friends had been offended and turned their backs on him. In the dramatic argument quoted above he nevertheless declared himself ready to sacrifice everything to help his 'kinsmen by race'. Someone who makes remarks like that shows that he has not yet said a final farewell to the Jewish tradition.[25]

Paul shows that once more in what comes next in this part of his letter. All his life he had been on the frontiers: a Diaspora Jew, a zealot for the Torah, a follower of Jesus Christ, apostle to the Gentiles. Time and again he crossed the frontier which kept Jews and Gentiles apart. God had called him to preach the gospel of Christ all over the world (Gal. 1.16). Did he do that with joy? Did he realize that his successful support of the Jews could have negative consequences for the Gentiles? In Rome, as the result of a combination of circumstances, a situation had arisen in which the Gentile Christians were in the majority. It would soon prove that such developments would also take place in other communities. Perhaps the Jewish-Christian circle accused him of paying too much attention to the Gentiles. We can infer from Paul's letter that he had reflected on this question. He found a surprising solution: 'As I am an apostle to the Gentiles I magnify my ministry in order to make my fellow-Jews jealous, and thus save some of them. For if their rejection means the reconciliation of the world, what will their acceptance mean but life from the dead?' (Rom. 11.13–15). In Paul's view, Jews and Gentiles belong together. He did not think that his move into the Gentile world meant that he had turned his back on the Jews. On the contrary, even his preaching of the gospel to the Gentiles would ultimately benefit the Jews. Again it has to be said that anyone who cherished such thoughts cannot possibly be said to have bid a final farewell to his Jewish background. Despite all that had happened in the past, Paul continued to be concerned about the future of Israel. He will have been encouraged by the thought that even the task which God had given him could in a surprising way contribute to the salvation of Israel.

Paul wrote very passionately about this extremely complicated question. It will not surprise anyone that his Jewish background led him to begin from the presupposition that God had chosen the people of Israel. Moreover he was certain that God would keep his promise faithfully (Rom. 9.6–13).[26] The coming of Jesus Christ caused a break in the relationship between God and his chosen people which was as unexpected as it was tragic. Was that the end of the special role of the people of Israel? Did the break have to be regarded as irrevocable? Paul in fact gave two different answers to these questions. In the first place he called himself the living proof of God's faithfulness: 'The question now is, has God rejected his people? By no means! I myself am an Israelite, a descendant of Abraham, a member of the tribe of Benjamin' (Rom. 11.1). For Paul, the Jewish Christians are the proof that God has not rejected his people. But he was not satisfied with just this answer. Since the coming of Jesus Christ the people of God had been split in two: on the one hand a relative small group of Jewish Christians, and on the other the vast majority of the Jews who were either indifferent to the gospel or who vigorously opposed it. What would happen to them in the future? Paul also expressed his views on this problem: 'The next question is: have they stumbled so as to fall? By no means! But through their trespass salvation has come to the Gentiles, so as to make Israel jealous. Now if their trespass means riches for the world, and if their failure means riches for the Gentiles, how much more will their full inclusion mean?' (Rom. 11.11–12).

In a few sentences Paul formulated a quite fascinating but also speculative notion. Gentiles owe their deliverance and salvation in every respect to Israel. This perspective should also cause the Gentile Christians in Rome to treat more gently their fellow-believers who because of their obedience to the commandments of the Torah regarded them as 'weak' . Whichever way one turns, the Gentile-Christian community is not viable without the Jewish Christian tradition. Paul emphasizes this thought with a selection of images and comparisons (Rom. 1.11–24). That finally brought him to his second answer to the question of the future of Israel. Not only is Israel, in his own person and that of all the other Jewish Christians, still the elect people of God, but even that part of the people which has turned away from Jesus Christ is not lost for ever. That is Paul's conviction. The sentences which he devoted to this notion reveal that after all these years he had still remained an apocalyptist. Moreover no one can blame the apostle for in fact raising more questions than he seems to answer. Again he was in virgin territory. Apocalyptists write to encourage the 'elect'. They will not be lost. What did that perspective mean for the

future of Israel as the elect people of God? Trusting in God's
promise, Paul ventured a great leap: 'I want you to understand
this mystery: a hardening has come upon part of Israel, until the
full number of the Gentiles come in, and so all Israel wil be
saved' (Rom. 11.25–26).

Down the centuries, Paul's view of the abiding significance
of Israel as the chosen people of God has provoked many
reactions. His positive remarks about the abiding significance
of Israel in Romans 9–11 have often not earned him gratitude.
It is pointed out that in the first chapters of his letter the apostle
had spoken in more negative terms about the place of Israel. In
theological circles involved in Jewish-Christian dialogue, in
general these chapters from the letter to the community in
Rome are regarded as an important basis of such dialogue.
What would Paul have thought about his exegetes? We cannot
ask him any longer, so we can only guess. This time we need to
be cautious. Those who make the apostle too quickly and too
easily their spokesman are not aware that a wide gulf of almost
two thousand years separates us from him. He was an apocalyptist who lived in the expectation that the *parousia* of the
Lord would be taking place very soon. He hoped for a speedy
revelation of the 'mystery'. For us after so many centuries it has
become almost impossible still to interpret his words as a
prophecy. Too much has happened. Dark shadows lie over the
history of the Jewish people. Why did God wait so long to
unveil the 'mystery'? Judaism and Christianity have grown
further apart than Paul could have ever have thought possible.
Many questions remain unanswered. The text causes us confusion. At all events Romans 9–11 can teach us one thing: in his
hope that God would remain faithful to the people of Israel to
the end, the apostle to the Gentiles confessed his solidarity with
his own Jewish background in an impressive and moving way.

'The righteous shall live by faith'

Paul was a complicated thinker. He lived in different worlds.
No one can doubt his solidarity with the Jewish tradition. The

Gentile Christians in the community in Rome could suspect what awaited them when he paid his visit. With good reason, in the introduction to his letter the apostle wrote about his 'eagerness to bring the gospel to you, Romans' (Rom. 1.15). What was the *content* of that gospel? At all events it was a *Jewish* gospel. However, we do Paul an injustice if we leave it at that. To get a real grasp of the argument in the first part of his letter we must go back to the past, back to the vision with which it once all began. When Paul was reflecting in Corinth on the content of his writing to the community, his apocalyptic experience already lay twenty years behind him. From his letters written earlier we can infer that he could never wipe the event from his memory, nor did he want to. 'I have seen Jesus our Lord', he wrote with some pride to the Corinthians (I Cor. 9.1). His life changed radically. The zealot became a disciple. Sometimes he uses quite sharp words to describe this change: 'For his sake I suffered the loss of all things, and count them as refuse, in order that I may gain Christ and be found in him' (Phil. 3.8–9). To these words he added a further explanation in which there is the echo of a theme which wil be developed further in the letter to the community in Rome: 'not having a righteousness of my own, based on law, but that which is through faith in Christ' (Phil. 3.9).

The apocalyptic vision revealed that the crucified Jesus had been raised from the dead by God. In an unexpected way 'curse' was turned into 'blessing' (Gal. 3.13). For Paul this discovery meant that Jesus Christ – to put it more pointedly: the event of the cross and resurrection – was of central importance for the history of all humankind. That is the thought that he expressed at the beginning of the letter: 'For I am not ashamed of the gospel: it is the power of God for salvation to every one who has faith, to the Jew first and also to the Greek. For in it the righteousness of God is revealed through faith for faith; as it is written, "He who through faith is righteous shall live"' (Rom. 1.16–17).

The parties which caused these tensions within the community of Rome were given a bewildering message in the following pericopes (Rom. 1.18–3.20), which robbed them once and for all of all their supposed privileges: 'What then? Are we Jews any better off? No, not at all; for I have already charged that all, both Jews and Greeks, are under the power of sin' (Rom. 3.9). Paul emphasized that Jew and Gentile were in the same boat. Neither had any reason to feel superior to the other. In this drastic way he hoped to make the members of the community realize that they needed to follow his advice to live in harmony with one another: 'For God knows no respect of persons' (Rom. 2.11).

In this part of the letter Paul was not afraid to make sharp statements – not only to the Gentiles (Rom. 1.18–32) but also to the Jews (Rom. 2.1–3.8). Without beating about the bush he censures their reprehensible behaviour: 'But if you call yourself a Jew and rely upon the law and boast of your relation to God, and know his will and approve what is excellent, because you are instructed in the law, and if you are sure that you are a guide to the blind, a light to those who are in darkness, a corrector of the foolish, a teacher of children, having in the law the embodiment of knowledge and truth – you then who teach others, will you not teach yourself? While you preach against stealing, do you steal? You who say that one must not commit adultery, do you commit adultery? You who abhor idols, do you rob temples? You who boast in the law, do you dishonour God by breaking the law?' (Rom. 2.17–23). If earlier I said that Paul was more cautious and subtle in his letter to the community of Rome, sadly an exception has to be made for this passage. The apostle fiercely enters the battle, and makes sharp accusations. Whom did he have in view? Perhaps the readers in Rome could answer this question, but we no longer can. Again, all we can do is guess. Did his criticism apply to the behaviour of some Jewish Christians in Rome? Or was he thinking, while he was in Corinth, still full of bitterness, back to the conflicts with his Jewish-Christian opponents that had made life so sour for him in Asia Minor and Greece? Or was he speaking over the heads of Christians in Rome to the Jews in Jerusalem and everywhere else who refused to accept Jesus Christ as their saviour? Whichever possibility one chooses – my preference is for the second, see below – there is no doubt that in this passage Paul's polemic is ungracious. Evidently he allowed himself to be carried away in the fire of his argument to speak out bluntly. In later centuries these words encouraged alienation between Jews and Christians rather than preventing it.

In the letter to the communities in Galatia Paul had already created the opposition between 'the works of the law' and 'faith in Jesus Christ'. In that same work he made a connection between law and sin (Gal. 3.22). Meanwhile he had clearly developed his thought further on this point. It is out of the question that the works of the law could save sinful human beings: 'For no human being wil be justified in his sight by works of the law, since through the law comes knowledge of sin' (Rom. 3.20). It is difficult to interpret Paul's criticism precisely. Again it is not clear against whom he is writing this polemic. In Christian circles it is customary to suppose that in his letter he was above all addressing the synagogue.[27] I think that highly improbable. It is wrong to assume that in the time of Paul Jews in the synagogues believed that they would be justified by God through doing works of the law. In the first place, Judaism in the first century of our era was extraordinarily variegated, and the Pharisaic movement, too, consisted of numerous schools and tendencies.[28] Secondly, Jewish belief in the Eternal One down the centuries has been much richer and more variegated than has often been supposed in Christian circles, and still is. Indeed a term like 'legalism' in no way does justice to Jewish piety in the first century of our era.[29] Paul must have known that. He must be blamed for having caused this misunderstanding by unclear terminology. He played the words 'law' and 'faith' off against each other, whereas in the Old Testament-Jewish tradition they relate to each other.[30]

These considerations confront the exegete with a new question: if Paul was not discussing with the synagogue, against whom was he being so fierce? The apostle was in the port of Corinth. The unpleasant skirmishes with his Jewish opponents were still fresh in his memory. They forcibly emphasized the abiding validity of the Torah. Paul did not disagree with this. However, their zeal went so far that it seemed that observing the commandments of the Torah – doing the works of the law – was more important than faith in Jesus Christ. Paul opposed these conclusions, as he had already done in his letter to the communities in Galatia. In the discussion with his Jewish-Christian opponents he is led to make very negative statements about the Torah. Thus he states soberly that strictly speaking the commandments should confront people only with their impotence and sinfulness: 'through the law comes knowledge of sin' (Rom. 3.20).

Thus Paul reached the absolute nadir in his views about the possible privileges of Gentiles or Jews. Everyone stands before God with empty hands. The apostle was not the first to make this frightening discovery. Centuries earlier, one of the psalmists had begged God to be gracious to him in a mixture of hope and despair: 'Out of the depths I cry to you, O Lord! Lord, hear my voice! Let your ears be attentive to the voice of my supplications! If you, Lord, should mark iniquities, Lord, who could stand? But there is forgiveness with you' (Ps. 130.1–3). At the end of this moving psalm doubt and tribulation have given way to the certainty of faith: 'O Israel, hope in the Lord! For with the Lord there is steadfast love, and with him is plenteous redemption. And he will redeem Israel from all his iniquities' (Ps. 130.7–8). Some decades after Paul's letter, the evangelist Matthew would make a connection between the name of Jesus and the end of the psalm: 'she shall bear a son and you shall give him the name Jesus, for he shall redeem his people from their sins' (Matt. 1.22).

Scripture and tradition had taught Paul that the relation between God and human beings was vulnerable. His own experiences reinforced this thought. He knew that the cause had not to be sought with God, but on the human side. God remains faithful to the covenant that he made with Israel. His love is infinitely great. This conviction is also expressed in the psalms: 'The Lord is merciful and gracious, slow to anger and

abounding in steadfast love. He will not always chide, nor will
he keep his anger for ever. He does not deal with us according
to our sins, nor requite us according to our iniquities' (Ps.
103.8–10). Paul was a creative thinker. He interpreted old and
traditional notions of faith and brought them up to date. Time
did not stand still. In early Jewish apocalyptic the question of
God's love and faithfulness was again raised in a pressing way.
Evil powers seemed to have the upper hand. Where was God?
Horror-struck, people went so far as to wonder whether God
was still powerful enough to win the battle in world history
against evil and on behalf of his elect. Apocalyptists were both
realists and dreamers. They lived in the present with their gaze
directed towards the future. The world lay in darkness, but they
did not despair. Despite everything, they were convinced that
God would eventually win.

Paul was an apocalyptist. The letter to the community in
Rome leaves no doubt about that. It is striking that in this
particular letter he referred back so markedly to apocalyptic
insights. Over the years he had made long journeys. On the way
he met many people and came into contact with all kinds of
different religious notions. He was also open to other ideas
because of his variegated background. That is evident above all
from his correspondence with the community in Corinth. So as
to be able to speak the language of those whom he was addressing, he even seemed prepared to distance himself from apocalyptic thought (II Cor. 5.1–10). There is no question of that in
his last letter. The world lies in darkness, but full of optimism
Paul looks to the near future: 'I am convinced that the sufferings
of this present time are not worth comparing with the glory that
is to be revealed to us. For the creation waits with eager longing
for the revealing of the sons of God; for the creation was subjected to futility, not of its own will but by the will of him who
subjected it in hope, because the creation itself will be set free
from its bondage to decay and obtain the glorious liberty of the
children of God. We know that the whole creation has been
groaning in travail together until now' (Rom. 8.18–22).

That is apocalyptic language. Paul felt that the end of this world was approaching with rapid strides. The decisive battle between God and evil would not be long in coming. The realism of the apocalyptists had led them to redefine the term 'sin'. Human beings committed sins. They were sinners because they opposed the will of God and did not obey his commandments. It had always been thus, but the apocalyptic experience had taught that 'sin' was also a power which held people in its grip and degraded them to become slaves of its anti-godly purposes.[31] Paul also thought like this, and perhaps we may even conclude that such ideas influenced him strongly. Already in the letter to the Galatians he made a connection between law and sin (Gal. 3.22). In his writing to the community in Rome the theme of 'sin' played a prominent role. Gentiles sinned, but so did Jews (Rom. 1.18–3.20). For the root of the evil we must go far back into the past: 'Therefore as sin came into the world through one man and death through sin, and so death spread to all men because all men sinned . . .' (Rom. 5.12). In chapter 7 Paul himself got his head down and went deeply into the material. He was a lively author. Dedicated readers of his letters need not be bored for a moment. But the passage which I shall go on to quote wins the prize. It is the most personal passage that he has left to us. Without any reserve he gives readers an opportunity to look into the depths of his soul: 'I lead a sinful life, sold as I am under sin. I do not understand my own actions. I do not do what I want, but I do the very thing that I abhor. Wretched man that I am! Who will deliver me from this body of death?' (Rom. 7.14–24).

With this emotional cry from the heart Paul has caused many headaches for his interpreters down the centuries.[32] Was he really speaking about himself here? Many people in the past and present could not and cannot imagine this, and think that he was referring to the spiritual distress of 'the man who lives outside Christ'. I do not share that view. On the basis of Paul's apocalyptic view of human beings and the world I think it quite understandable that he should have made such an emotional outburst. It seems to me quite clear from the beginning that this is a text of a very personal character: 'But *I, I* lead a sinful life, sold as *I* am under sin' (Rom. 7.14). One says that about one-self and not about others.

The choice of this interpretation of the text immediately raises a new question. What is the relationship between chapters 6 and 7 of the letter to the community in Rome? In chapter 6 Paul wrote: 'How can we who died to sin still live in it? Do you not know that all of us who have been baptized into Christ Jesus were baptized into his death? We were buried therefore with him by baptism into death, so that as Christ was raised from the dead by the glory of the Father, we too might walk in newness of life. For if we have been united with him in a death like his, we shall certainly be united with him in a resurrection like his. We know that our old self was crucified with him so that the sinful body might be destroyed, and we might no longer be enslaved to sin. For he who has died is freed from sin' (Rom. 6.2–7). Much could be said about this fasci-nating text, but a lengthier discussion is impossible here.[33] Paul was a many-sided man. He first wrote explicitly about the meaning of baptism in the letter to the Galatians: 'For as many of you as were baptized into Christ have put on Christ' (Gal. 3.27). After that, clearly the theme did not let him go. The image that he uses in the passage quoted above is certainly sur-prising. There is no unanimity in scholarly literature about its historical origins.[34] Paul wrote the letter in Corinth. As we know, at this time the Greek port was a real melting pot of religions. It is not impossible that the apostle derived the image from rituals which were customary at the initiation of new members into the mystery religions.

Those who are baptized begin on a new life. The old has been put off and one 'puts on Christ'. The candidate is immersed and then rises as if from the dead to the new spiritual existence. Was Paul talking to himself? Was he hopelessly entangled in his own arguments? Those who think that they may expect a systematic argument from the apostle will have to recognize that the remarks above are very disjointed. How could some-one who has first claimed to be 'free from sin' then confess in a passionate argument that he was still in the power of sin? Paul's letter to the community in Rome is not a theological treatise, a summary of his 'doctrine'. The apostle was a contextual thinker. He was aware of living in two worlds. In the letter to the Galatians, written earlier, he had expressed himself briefly as follows: 'I have been crucified with Christ; it is no longer I who live, but Christ who lives in me; and the life I now live in the flesh I live by faith in the Son of God who loved me and gave himself for me' (Gal. 2.19–20). As a believer he knew that he was a liberated person. At the same time, as an apocalyptist he was sufficient of a realist never to trivialize the power of sin – not even for his own life.

In the apocalyptic view of the relationship between God and human beings the forgiveness of sins plays less of a role than the battle against the power of sin.[35] In this sense, too, Paul was unmistakably an exponent of early Jewish apocalyptic: the word forgiveness does not come to the forefront in his letters. The vision that he had on the way to Damascus certainly changed the content of his thought, but not the framework within which it developed further. He expressed the significance of Jesus Christ in apocalyptic terms: 'But now the righteousness of God has been manifested apart from law, although the law and the prophets bear witness to it, the righteousness of God through faith in Jesus Christ for all who believe. For there is no distinction; since all have sinned and fall short of the glory of God, they are justified by his grace as a gift, through the redemption which is in Christ Jesus' (Rom. 3.21–24). It will escape no one who has read the text carefully that Paul again ran the risk of getting tangled up in his own ideas. Evidently there is 'law' and 'law'. Therefore he could make what at first sight is the enigmatic statement that the 'law and prophets' (= scripture) already bore witness that God's righteousness had been revealed outside the law (= the works of the law).

The term 'the righteousness of God' is of crucial significance for the first part of the letter and demands our attention. A tremendous number of scholarly books and articles have been written on this subject.[36] Why did Paul choose the term? He remained faithful to the end to his apocalyptic view of human beings and the world. In the eschatological drama which was being played out, God would have a final reckoning with the evil powers and with the godless. In the apocalyptic view of the future, the judgment of the living and the dead was central (Dan. 12.1–3). At the end of time God would pronounce judgment and evil would be punished.

Who can escape the wrath of God? A relatively simple answer to this question is still given in the prophetic literature: 'For behold the day comes, burning like an oven, when all the arrogant and all evildoers will be stubble; the day that comes shall burn them up, says the Lord God, so that it will leave them neither root nor branch. But for you who fear my name the sun of righteousness shall rise, with healing in its wings. You shall go forth leaping like calves from the stall' (Mal. 4.1–3). The tendency is clear: the righteous – those who observe the commandments of the Torah – will be acquitted by God. Therefore the prophet Habakkuk could also say that 'the righteous shall live by his faith' (= his faithfulness to God/the Torah) (Hab. 2.4). The apocalyptic literature generally speaks of the salvation of the 'elect' (Mark 13.22). Paul was not satisfied with these interpretations. His sense of standing before God with completely empty hands was so great that he thought that he had to raise the intimidating question: 'who will save me from this body of death?' (Rom. 7.24). Is God's anger so great that no one will be acquitted in his judgment?

The unexpected vision on the way to Damascus opened his eyes to a new reality, the revelation of God's righteousness. Paul realized that the judgment need no longer be terrifying. Whether he made this discovery immediately is difficult to say. Given the content of his letters, it seems to me that he only gradually became increasingly aware of it. The term 'the righteousness of God' can easily lead to misunderstanding. Precisely what 'righteousness' is this? To interpret it properly it is important for us to remember the apocalyptic framework of the judgment of God. In that judgment all stand before God, and in Paul's conviction they stand with empty hands. Those who want to be acquitted in the judgment – 'justified' – have not themselves but exclusively God to thank. That is God's grace. 'The righteousness of God' is therefore the acquittal which God bestows on men and women. They receive 'God's righteousness' and are 'justified' by him.

This train of thought was not completely new. The word was not unknown in the Old Testament-Jewish tradition. What was special was that Paul associated this 'righteousness of God' directly with Jeus Christ. As I have said, the consequences of this insight presumably dawned on him only gradually. The basis was laid by the vision on the way to Damascus. At that moment the apostle arrived at the discovery that the crucified Jesus had been raised by God from the dead. Since then he had felt that he was living in two worlds. He felt reborn, a new person, taken up in the Spirit into the messianic world which had already become a reality in faith by the raising of Christ by God (Rom. 8.1–17). However, he was sufficient of a realist to sense that at the same time 'the whole creation has been groaning in travail together until now' (Rom. 8.22). The tension was great: the new had already come, but the old had not yet disappeared. Paul knew that he was a sinner (Rom. 7.14–25), and he was aware that in the death and resurrection of the crucified Jesus the judgment definitively lay behind him and that having been acquitted he might gratefully enjoy 'the righteousness of God'.

In Paul's reflection on this event the old words of the prophet, 'The righteous shall live by faith', took on new meaning for him (Rom. 1.17; Gal. 3.11). Whatever the prophet meant, there was no possibility of misunderstanding: the believer owed his life to his faithfulness to God and the Torah (Hab.2.4). In the Qumran writings the biblical text is in fact paraphrased in this spirit: 'Interpreted, this concerns all those who observe the Law in the House of Judah, whom God will deliver from the House of Judgment because of their suffering and because of their faith in the Teacher of Righteousness.'[37] Paul took another course. The righteous shall not live by *his* faith but by faith. The terminology is probably deliberately ambiguous. In the letter to the

Galatians Paul wrote the words 'before the coming of faith' (Gal. 3.23). Two explanations seem possible: before the coming of the faith *of Christ* or before the coming of Christ who gave us faith. Similar thoughts will have run through Paul's head when he interpreted the prophetic text: the righteous shall live by the faith of or by faith *in* Jesus Christ. It is certain that in this framework Paul can never have meant that 'faith' was a human quality. Against this background we can understand how he could give his own desperate question 'Who will redeem me from this body of death?' the liberating answer: 'Thanks be to God through Jesus Christ our Lord!' (Rom. 7.25). The following conclusion was more or less obvious: 'There is therefore now no condemnation for those who are in Christ Jesus' (Rom. 8.1).

In the death and resurrection of Jesus Christ God revealed his righteousness. For Paul, the implications of this event were all-embracing. I wrote earlier that he was a creative man. But in this specific case words and images fell short and he could not express the consequences in all their breadth. Sinners are acquitted: 'for Christ died for the godless at the appointed time when we ourselves were completely helpless' (Rom. 5.6). His death has benefited us – the godless. For Paul, Jesus' death and resurrection belonged indissolubly together: 'Jesus, who was put to death for our trespasses and raised for our justification' (Rom. 4.25). The enmity between God and human beings has been done away with: 'Justified by faith we have peace with God through our Lord Jesus Christ. Through him we have obtained access to this grace in which we stand, and we rejoice in our hope of sharing the glory of God' (Rom. 5.1–2).

Anyone who has become convinced that God's righteousness has been revealed in Jesus Christ will give Jesus a central place in his thought. Paul also did that in his letter to the community in Rome. His creativity put him in a position to express his conviction in a variety of images and ideas. Here are some of them. He described the new humanity briefly and powerfully as being 'in Christ' (Rom. 8.1). Anyone who is 'in Christ' is not subject to the judgment but acquitted. Through Christ we live in peace with God, and the alienation which kept God and human beings apart is fundamentally abolished: 'Whom God put forward *as a means of expiation by his blood,* to be received in faith. This was to show God's righteousness, because in his divine forbearance he had passed over former sins' (Rom. 3.25). The words in italics attract our attention. They are not easy to translate. In the Greek there is a word which could be rendered 'mercy seat' (Heb. 9.5). In his letters Paul only very exceptionally made use of language and ideas from the cult. In the pericope devoted to 'reconciliation' in II Corinthians his choice fell on words and concepts which had nothing to do with sacrifices and temples but were derived from legal language (II Cor. 5.17–21). In the sentences quoted above, the apostle made an exception to the rule. Why he did so it is difficult to say. Most exegetes think that he did not devise these words himself. This is not his 'language'. But it fascinated him, and he resolved to use it in his letter.[38] For someone with a Jewish background, the meaning was not difficult to interpret. The words 'blood' and 'mercy seat' refer to the ritual of the Day of Atonement (Lev. 16). To avoid misunderstanding I should point out that Jesus is not being compared with the scapegoat which was sent out into the wilderness laden with the sins of the people, which did not die but was released (Lev. 16.22). Rather, another ritual took place on the Day of Atonement. The blood of sacrificial animals was sprinkled on the mercy seat: 'so he cleanses the altar from the uncleannesses of the Israelites and hallows it' (Lev. 16.19). The cleansing of the altar created the possibility of removing the alienation between God and human beings. This was a symbol for atonement and reconciliation: sins could be removed from society and people were again in a state in which they could be reconciled to God and their neighbours.

14

A retrospect

Paul was a Jew. He saw the light of day In the Diaspora. His parents introduced him to the ideals of the Pharisees. He grew up in Tarsus in Asia Minor, a Greek Hellenistic city which in culture and religion even rivalled Athens. From his birth he was 'a man of two worlds'. He shared that fate with many Jewish men and women past and present. When he had reached adulthood he went to Jerusalem. In that centuries-old city he was initiated into scripture and tradition as a pupil of the wise and moderate Gamaliel. Paul did not tread in the footsteps of his eminent teacher. In his early years he found it difficult to adopt a moderate standpoint. He became a zealot for the Torah. His target was members of the early-Christian community who observed the commandments less strictly than he thought permissible. In his zeal he knew no forgiveness.

Paul expected the speedy destruction of this 'sinful' world. In his thought he was influenced by apocalyptic ideas about the future of human beings and the world. On the way to Damascus he received 'a revelation', an apocalyptic vision that changed his life radically. The zealot became a convinced follower of Jesus Christ. Paul has given us little information about the content of the vision. He did not write an apocalypse like the last book of the Bible. The summary reports in his letters suggest that in a visionary way he came to discover that Jesus, who had suffered the 'accursed' death of crucifixion, had been raised by God from the dead.

The persecutor became the preacher of the gospel. His 'teaching' developed gradually. Even in the last letter of his to have been preserved he has not left us a succinct summary of his 'dogmatics'. Here Paul was not denying his spiritual origins. Through his upbringing and teaching in a Pharisaic milieu, from his youth he had been trained to think, act and argue in a concrete and practical way. Pharisees treated the law with the utmost seriousness. However, they did not live like monks, but had both feet firmly in society. In that concrete situation they sought the meaning of particular commandments of the Torah.

Paul was also very interested in the practical consequences of belief as a follower of Jesus Christ. He particularly took to heart the ups and downs of the young Christian communities. He was plied with questions. In most cases these were questions which had not arisen earlier. The apostle reacted with answers which consisted of a remarkable mixture of certainties and qualified views. Paul was an emotional man. Often he knew the people to whom he was writing. He had lived for no less than eighteen months in Corinth. He made an effort to heal breaches and to remove misunderstandings. The letter to the communities in Galatia is a fine example of his way of working. His mind was razor sharp. He would have no compromises. This seemed to set the tone and mark out the boundaries clearly. He sarcastically called his readers 'stupid Galatians' (Gal. 3.1). However, in the course of time he became gentler. With the force of scriptural arguments he tried once again to give the inhabitants of Galatia, who had been greatly confused by his opponents, firm ground under their feet. At a given moment he even became very personal. In emotional words he reminded them of the help that he had received from them on his first visit (Gal. 4.12–20). Towards the end of the letter his anger emerged once more. With great sarcasm, he remarked scornfully, 'I wish those who unsettle you would mutilate themselves' (Gal. 5.12). It is understandable that such outbursts hardly play a significant role in the later dogmatic discussion. Emotions are extremely difficult to systematize. But they are indispensable for a good insight into intentions and motives.

From the biographical information in Paul's letter to the Galatians it seems that as a result of his vision on the way to Damascus he came to realize that he had the task of preaching the gospel of Jesus Christ in the Gentile world (Gal. 1.16). He was not the first person to feel called to do that. Others had already gone before him, sometimes driven by necessity, as was the case with the followers of Stephen who, not least because of the zealotry of the young Saul/Paul, had been driven from Jerusalem and began to build a new life above all in Antioch. There are legends from which it can be inferred that, for example, the apostle Thomas was engaged In widespread activities as a preacher of the gospel. He is said to have travelled eastwards from Antioch: to Syria, ancient Mesopotamia, India – as if he wanted to rival Alexander the Great in his desire for travel. But Thomas wrote no letters which have been preserved by posterity and he did not have the good fortune to have his missionary journeys described in a writing which attained canonical status. Paul did, and some letters – he will certainly have written more than the seven which have been preserved – were regarded as authoritative. They were included in the canon of the New Testament almost without discussion. Thanks to his own letters and thanks to Acts it is possible to gain a picture of the thought of a Pharisee who became a follower of Jesus Christ.

Apparently Paul planned his journeys. A popular view is that he went to work strategically in founding Christian communities in Asia Minor, Macedonia and Greece. However, honesty compels us to put question-marks against this view. It has proved repeatedly in the previous chapters that his plans were thwarted in all kinds of ways. He was driven out or arrested. He regularly found himself compelled to make hasty departures. Was that coincidence? An unfortunate combination of circumstances? Did Satan prevent him from taking the way that he had planned? Or did the Spirit of God compel him to choose a different route? Paul was aware that his life was guided in a special way, but that meant that he was never certain whether he could carry out his plans.

After his Damascus experience, the zealot who thought that he had to draw the line between Jews and Gentiles as sharply as possible worked for some decades with the utmost conviction as the apostle to the Gentiles. Apocalyptists realized that the coming conflict between God and the evil powers would have consequences for Jews and Gentiles. No one would be able to escape the rapidly approaching cosmic catastrophe. Would exclusively Jews be saved? Scripture and tradition are not clear about this. Certainly the people of Israel is assigned a special role, but there is also the promise to Abraham, which has a universal scope (Gen. 12.3). Despite himself, the reluctant prophet Jonah had a great success in pagan and hostile Nineveh. It could be said that Paul trod in the footsteps of this prophet. Unlike Jonah, he went very willingly with his liberating message to the Gentiles. Jonah had to go eastwards, to the city of Nineveh, the centre of power at that time. The apostle to the Gentiles went ever further westwards. By then the centre of power had shifted from east to west. The book of Acts ends with the report that after many tribulations Paul arrived in the Roman metropolis.

What was the content of the gospel that Paul proclaimed in Asia Minor, Macedonia and Greece? His letters do not make it easy for us to sketch out a clear and precise picture. They reveal that the apostle was active over a wide area, but that he was not yet in a position to write a coherent theology. We have to assume that he never attempted to do so. He did not come from a world in which 'dogmatics' were written. Paul reacted to reports which reached him. He answered questions, sought solutions to problems, and tried to restore relationships which had gone wrong.

The apocalyptist who had become a disciple of Jesus Christ brought a message which was heard with perplexity and amazement by Gentiles. His monotheistic view of God will have aroused the least opposition. Many people had great difficulties with his apocalyptic view of present and future. However, that did not stop Paul telling his ideas to the world. The time was short. The destruction of the world was coming ever closer. Who would be able to escape the wrath of God? Paul thought that he had found an answer to this question. Thanks to his Damascus experience his gaze had been directed permanently to Jesus Christ: the crucified man who had been raised from the dead by Jesus. In his letter to the community in Thessalonica he formulated his hopeful faith: the parousia of Christ will save us from the wrath of God (I Thess. 1.10).

Paul was an apocalyptist and believed in the resurrection of the dead. As a Diaspora Jew he must have been aware that he would encounter much misunderstanding in the Gentile world. But he remained true to his convictions. The vision on the way to Damascus confirmed his belief: God raises the dead. However, that must also have surprised him and made him wonder. Apocalyptists usually expected a collective resurrection from the dead. All men and women would be raised, and not 'just' an individual. For Paul, the resurrection of Jesus was not in fact an incident in history but a beginning. He is the firstfruits (I Cor. 15.20). He has gone before us. We shall follow.

During the time of the life and death of Jesus Paul was still living in Tarsus. He never met Jesus in the flesh and did not belong to the circle of his disciples. He saw him for the first time in the vision. From that time Paul ardently hoped for the speedy coming, the parousia of the Lord. He expressed his strong bond with Jesus Christ in many different ways in his letters. Sometimes his impatience was so great that he could hardly wait. He wanted to die in order to be able to be with the Lord as quickly as possible (Phil. 1.23). In apparent contradiction to this, Paul also knew the assurance and certainty that the bond with Christ was so intense that he need no longer look forward tensely to the future. The parousia of the Lord had already been realized. Christ lived in him (Gal. 2.20). After the vision on the way on the way to Damascus Paul moved in two worlds. His apocalyptic view of human beings and the world led him to the conclusion that the old 'sinful' world had not yet disappeared, but the resurrection of the crucified Jesus by God disclosed that the messianic kingdom had already dawned. It proves from his letters that Paul repeatedly experienced this 'ambiguity' in his own life. His existence was overshadowed by sins (Rom. 7.14–25), and at the same time he ventured to call himself 'messianic' man, a Christ man.

Paul lived on the frontier of different worlds. His theological insights were not unshakeable, but developed gradually. His thought was contextual. His many-sidedness and creativity put him in a position to live in his readers' world of ideas. He tried to speak their language. Sometimes the result of this effort was that the apocalyptist made use of terms and images which one might expect more from a Gnostic. Paul ventured to take this course. The gospel of Jesus Christ was variegated. It had come into being in an apocalyptic context, but that did not mean that it had nothing to say to people with another world-view. Paul can direct his gaze towards the future, but also upwards, to heaven. That is what he did when in his correspondence with the community in Corinth he wrote of his longing 'to depart from this body' in order to be able to enter 'our heavenly dwelling' (II Cor. 5.1–10). The thought of the salvation of the whole person seems to have given way to the idea that the human spirit/soul is liberated from the earthly body.

Filled with zeal for the Torah, after his Damascus experience Paul became apostle to the Gentiles. The man on the frontier ran into a situation in which 'worlds' clashed. What significance did the commandments of the Torah have for Gentiles? Some Jewish Christians defended a clear standpoint. They refused to make a distinction. The authority of the whole Torah needed to be recognized in the Christian community, too – by both Jews and Gentiles. Paul opposed this view. He did not do so in principle but rather contextually. His years of living outside Jewish territory in the Diaspora confronted him with the difficulties which were the consequence of an 'orthodox' standpoint. Some commandments of the Torah – especially those relating to circumcision, the sabbath and cleanness – were a hindrance to Gentiles who wanted to join the Christian community. The apostle faced a difficult dilemma.

Paul's missionary activities bore fruit. The Christian community proved viable in the Gentile world. Success forced him to look more closely at Christian identity. Paul gradually saw himself compelled to choose between two evils. He regarded it as his task to save Gentiles. When it became clear that some commandments of the Torah were a hindrance, there seemed to him to be no alternative but to relativize the significance of the whole Torah. Doubtless Paul was taking a very daring step. History has taught us that his decision was not without its dangers. Also as a result of his view, Judaism and Christian have grown far apart. Paul certainly did not intend that. He still lived some decades before the schism between Judaism and Christianity. He was constantly aware of his Jewishness. By preaching the gospel of Jesus Christ he hoped to unite Jews and Gentiles (Gal. 3.28). The tragedy of his life is that the opposite happened.

How Jewish did Paul finally remain? At a given moment did he bid a final farewell to the Jewish tradition? The complexity of his thought emerges when an answer is sought to this question. Some autobiographical passages in his letters (II Cor. 11.22; Gal. 1.13–14; Phil. 3.5–8) indicate that he was proud of his Jewishness. But there is no denying the fact that at the same time he was to some degree distanced from it. He was not ashamed of his past, but on one occasion he sarcastically described it as 'refuse'. It was now a different age. The coming of Jesus Christ into this world opened his eyes and at the same time put a blindfold on the Jewish tradition (II Cor. 3.12–18). But Paul never denied that Jewish tradition, and he never argued for the abolition of the Torah. Rather, he did the opposite (Rom. 13.8–10; Gal. 5.13). The Gentile community would not be viable without the 'sap of the olive' (Rom. 11.17).

Paul remained a man of two worlds. He had 'two souls' which sometimes came into conflict. Saul had become Paul. The Diaspora Jew who had turned out to be a zealot became a disciple of Jesus Christ. His life changed decisively, but Saul did not disappear completely into the background, and the insights which he had acquired as a Pharisaic scribe were not suddenly wiped completely out of his memory. Paul's many-sidedness makes it almost impossible for us to pronounce a final judgment on him. Moreover, our knowledge is ultimately too limited for us to be able to do so with a quiet conscience.

In the vision on the way to Damascus Paul encountered the

crucified Jesus who had been raised by God from the dead. Cross and resurrection – this event was central to his thought. The apostle could only speak positively about the cross because he had discovered that the one who had been crucified had been raised by God from the dead. He did not regard the cross as a sacrifice but as a curse (Gal. 3.13). On the way to Damascus the paradox of faith was disclosed to him: the accursed man on the cross had been raised by God from the dead. That was the prelude to the new, messianic reality. Paul did not have the images and the words to express how he thought that he could interpret the meaning of Jesus Christ: salvation, redemption, renewal, freedom, peace, righteousness, love, reconciliation, inspiration, religious conviction, a way to go and an example to follow. Those who try to sum up this great variety of notions run the risk of failing to do justice to the richness of the apostle's thought.

Paul provoked opposition. He made friends, but also enemies. After his death the discussion went on. His attitude on a great many questions raised questions. Sometimes he had been too explicit and in other cases his thoughts were too vague and incomplete. The first corrections and supplements can already be found in the New Testament. In some letters Paul had left no doubt that he thought that the world would soon come to an end. Around the end of the first century such unconcealed apocalyptic expectations were increasingly felt to be problematical. The parousia of the Lord seemed further off than Paul had supposed. In that period of early church history an unknown author wrote another letter to the community in Thessalonica. He made it appear as if it was a letter by the apostle, but relativized the apocalyptic view which had been unambiguously expressed in the authentic letter of Paul to that community. Probably the unknown author hoped that his work would replace the original letter. He only partly succeeded. Now we have one voice set against the other in the New Testament.

Some people call Paul the founder of Christianity. Without wanting to belittle his significance for the spread of the

Christian faith, in my view he was not. Paul was a charismatic and not a born organizer. In his letters he is primarily concerned with the *unity* of the community. Relatively little about structures is to be found in his writings. In all probability that was already seen in the early church as a great lack. People always need structures to live within. That was especially the case when the *parousia* of the Lord did not take place and it proved necessary to organize the community as a firm and hierarchically ordered institution. Above all for that reason kindred spirits of the apostle wrote the Pastoral Epistles.

Paul was a contextual theologian. He reacted to questions and theorized little, if at all. His letters have the character of documents conditioned by time and place. That makes them fascinating, but at the same limits their value and importance. That was evidently regarded as a great difficulty even by the early Christian community. New, topical letters were written and attributed to Paul. Thus alongside the works mentioned above, the writings which have been included in the canon of the New Testament as the letter to the Colossians and the letter to the Ephesians also came to be produced. Developments in the community of Colossae after Paul's death made an authoritative reaction necessary. A creative disciple of the apostle – perhaps Timothy – composed a letter in which new errors were challenged as sharply as possible with the help of elements from the thought of his teacher. Later the letter to the community of Colossae served as an inspiring example for an unknown author who thought that he had to set down in writing his thoughts about christology and community in the letter to the Ephesians.

Even after that Paul has continued to fascinate and inspire. The many-sidedenss of his theological insights make it possible to sketch different portraits of him. His contextual letters confront us with the question of the meaning of his thought for our time. He did not write for people living almost two thousand years later. We must therefore recognize that much of what he wrote in his letter can no longer have any meaning for us. The Roman empire no longer exists. Greek-Hellenistic thought has become a thing of the past. The ways of Judaism and Christianity have grown far apart. The apocalyptic view of human beings and the world inspires few people. Today we think differently about inter-personal relations, about marriage and family, about the place of women in society, from Paul, who was a child of his time. Anyone who reads Paul's letters today repeatedly has the feeling of hearing a voice from a totally different world. Strangely enough, though, this voice continues to fascinate. We hear a passionate man speaking who knows that he has a vocation. He is aware of living in a divided and sinful world. It made him pessimistic, but he remained an optimist. The vision on the way to Damascus fundamentally determined his work and thought. He strove for unity between Jews and Gentiles – unity between people with different backgrounds. He had seen the 'risen' Jesus. After that he believed that life, not death, has the last word, that sin will not triumph, but the love and grace of God, that enmity and hatred will not continue to set the tone, but peace and reconciliation will win through. Anyone who cherishes such ideals can only say that this will happen soon. We should not blame Paul for making a mistake here. Despite this, the perspective of his life and thought remains worth considering.

Notes

Introduction

1. For a note about bibliography see the conclusion to this introduction. Titles listed in that bibliography are cited in short form.
2. 'Paul would develop into a religious genius with a rich imagination, certainly confused, but in a position to give a mythological and archetypal significance to the death of a Jewish hero, Jesus of Nazareth', A. N. Wilson, *Paul. The Mind of the Apostle*, London 1997.
3. R. Niemann (ed.), *Paulus – Rabbi, Apostel oder Ketzer?*, Stuttgart 1994.
4. See e.g. L. Grollenberg, *Paul*, London and Philadelphia 1978.
5. There is a short survey of the reception of Paul and research into Paul in J. Gnilka, *Paulus von Tarsus. Zeuge und Apostel*, Freiburg 1996, 9–17.
6. See K. H. Rengstorf (ed.), *Das Paulusbild in der neueren deutschen Forschung*, Darmstadt 1969.
7. See also J. Becker, *Paulus. Der Apostel der Völker*, Tübingen 1989, III: 'In order not to let the almost overwhelming literature on Paul result in endless notes which tend more to put readers off and which can be fully appreciated by only a few readers, after long consideration I have omitted the scholarly apparatus completely. As I trust any specialist colleague to detect where I have learned from others and particularly from him or her, or have a different opinion, I have not noted this fact specially.'

The 'historical' Paul

1. C. J. den Heyer. *Jesus Matters. 150 Years of Research*, London and Valley Forge 1996.
2. That means that in what follows I shall pay no attention to authors who think that they can base their publications on other sources.
3. R. Schnackenburg, *Jesus in the Gospels. A Biblical Christology*,

Louisville 1995.

4. G. R. Beasley-Murray, *Jesus and the Kingdom of God*, Grand Rapids 1986.

5. The great standard work in this area is still the collection made by H. Ristow and K. Matthiae (eds.), *Der historische Jesus und der kerygmatische Christus. Beiträge zum Christusverständnis in Forschung und Verkündigung*, Berlin 1961.

6. Cf. also H. Detering, *Paulusbriefe ohne Paulus? Die Paulusbriefe in der holländische Radikal Kritik*, Frankfurt am Main 1992.

7. For a critical discussion of the criterion of canonicity see N. Appel, *Kanon und Kirche. Die Kanonkrise im heutigen Protestantismus als kontroverstheologisches Problem*, Paderborn 1964, 215–27.

8. There are surveys of the changing evaluation of the letter to the Hebrews over the course of the centuries in A. Vanhoye (ed.), 'Hebräerbrief', *Theologische Realenzyklopädie* 14, Berlin and New York 1985, 292–6; E. Grässer, *An der Hebräer I: Hebr. 1–8*, Evangelisch-Katholischer Kommentar zum Neuen Testament XVII/1, Zurich and Neukirchen-Vluyn 1990, 15–38.

9. For a discussion of the various views see H. Feld, *Der Hebräerbrief*, Darmstadt 1985.

10. See also J. Reiling, *Hebreeën. Een praktische bijbelverklaring*, Tekst en Toelichting, Kampen 1994, 9–11.

11. H. Hübner, 'Paulus I', *Theologische Realenzyklopädie* 26, Berlin and New York 1996, 133–53.

12. J. Roloff, 'Pastoralbriefe', *Theologische Realenzyklopädie* 26, Berlin and New York 1996, 50–68.

13. W. Trilling, *Der Zweite Brief an die Thessalonischer*, Evangelisch-Katholischer Kommentar XIV, Zurich and Neukirchen-Vluyn 1980, 21–32.

14. For the problem of the delay of the *parousia* see E. Grässer, *Die Naherwartung Jesu*, Stuttgart 1973.

15. A. Lindemann, 'Zum Abfassungszweck des Zweiten Thessalonicherbriefes', *ZNW* 68, 1977, 35–47.

16. For the text-critical problem of Eph. 1.1 – the words 'in Ephesus' are missing from important manuscripts – see the commentaries.

17. See F. Mussner, 'Epheserbrief', *Theologische Realenzyklopädie* 9, Berlin and New York 1982, 743–53.

18. Thus e.g. E. Schweizer, *Der Brief an die Kolosser*, Evangelisch-Katholischer Kommentar XII, Zurich and Neukirchen-Vluyn 1980, 20–7.

19. In a later chapter I shall ask whether it is correct to speak of the 'conversion' of Paul.

20. C. Burchard, *Der dreizehnte Zeuge*, Göttingen 1970.

21. Cf. R. Pesch, *Die Apostelgeschichte I, Apg 1–12,* Evangelisch-Katholischer Kommentar V/1, Zurich and Neukirchen-Vluyn 1986, 24–7.

22. F. Bovon, *Das Evangelium nach Lukas, I, Lk 1, 1–9, 50,* Evangelisch-Katholischer Kommentar III/1, Zurich and Neukirchen-Vluyn 1989, 22–4.

23. In detail on the sources of Acts see G. Schneider, *Die Apostelgeschichte I: Einleitung. Kommentar zu Kap.1, 1–8, 40,* Herders Theologischer Kommentar zum Neuen Testament V, Freiburg 1980, 82–103.

2. The life of Paul. Biographical information

1. L. Storoni Mazzonali, *The Idea of the City in Roman Thought. From Walled City to Spiritual Commonwealth,* London 1970.

2. J. E. Stambaugh ad D. L. Balch, *The New Testament in Its Social Environment,* Philadelphia 1986, give a good introduction to this cultural world.

3. Cf. D. Hildebrandt, *Saulus/Paulus. Ein Doppelleben,* Munich and Vienna 1989.

4. K. L. Noethlichs, *Das Judentum und der römische Staat. Minderheitpolitik im antiken Rom,* Darmstadt 1996.

5. Cf. S. McKnight, *A Light among the Gentiles. Jewish Missionary Activity in the Second Temple Period,* Minneapolis 1991; M. Goodman, *Mission and Conversion. Proselytizing in the Religious History of the Roman Period,* Oxford 1994; L. H. Feldman, *Jew and Gentile in the Ancient World,* Princeton 1993, 288–382, comes to the opposite conclusion.

6. I. Levinskaya, *The Book of Acts in its Diaspora Setting,* The Book of Acts in its First Century Setting, Vol. 5, Grand Rapids 1996.

7. H.-F. Weiss, 'Judentum in Alexandrien', *Theologische Realenzyklopädie* 2, Berlin and New York 1978, 262–4.

8. See R. van den Broek, 'Hermes en zijn gemeente te Alexandrië', in G. Quispel (ed.), *De Hermetische Gnosis in de loop der eeuwen. Beschouwingen over de invloed van een Egyptische religie op de cultuur van het Westen,* Baarn 1992, 9–26.

9. G. Hölbl, *Geschichte des Ptolemäerreiches. Politik, Ideologie und religiöse Kultur von Alexander dem Grossen bis zum römischen Eroberung,* Darmstadt 1994.

10. For an account of Alexandrian wisdom theology see G. Schimanowski, *Weisheit und Messias. Die jüdischen Voraussetzungen der urchristlichen Präexistenzchristologie,* Tübingen 1985, 13–106; E. Schüssler Fiorenza, *Miriam's Child, Sophia's Prophet,*

New York and London 1997, 157–96.

11. See the excursus 'Paul's Roman Citizenship' in G. Lüdemann, *Early Christianity according to the Traditions in Acts. A Commentary*, London 1989, 240f.; see J. Gnilka, *Paulus von Tarsus. Zeuge und Apostel*, Freiburg 1996, 25–7.

12. G. Schneider, *Die Apostelgechichte, 2. Kommentar zu Kap 9,1–28,31*, Herders Theologischer Kommentar zum Neuen Testament V, Freiburg 1982, 29 n.57.

13. J. N. Bremmer, *Götter, Mythen und Heiligtümer im antiken Griechenland*, Darmstadt 1996.

14. C. Colpe, 'Die älteste judenchristliche Gemeinde', in J. Becker et al., *Die Anfänge des Christentums. Alte Welt und neue Hoffnung*, Stuttgart 1987, 59–72 (especially 71–2).

15. For a very extensive discussion of this problem see R. E. Brown, *The Death of the Messiah. From Gethsemane to the Grave. A Commentary on the Passion Narratives in the Four Gospels*, New York 1994, 1350–78.

16. H. Conzelmann, *History of Primitive Christianity*, London 1971, 45–7.

17. E. P. Sanders, *Judaism. Practice and Belief. 63BCE–66CE*, London and Philadelphia 1992, 421–4.

18. E. P. Sanders, *Jesus and Judaism*, London 1985, 270–93.

19. P. J. Tomson, '*Als dit uit de Hemel is . . .' Jesus en de schrijvers van het Nieuwe Testament in hun verhouding tot het Jodendom*, Hilversum 1997.

20. K. Hoheisel, *Das antike Judentum in christlicher Sicht. Ein Beitrag zur neueren Forschungsgeschichte*, Wiesbaden 1978.

21. C. Münz, *Der Welt ein Gedächtnis geben. Geschichtstheologisches Denken im Judentum nach Auschwitz*, Gütersloh 1995.

22. H.-F. Weiss,. 'Pharisäer I', *Theologische Realenzyklopädie 26*, Berlin and New York 1996, 473–81.

23. P. Schäfer, *Geschichte der Juden in der Antike. Die Juden Palästinas von Alexander dem Grossen bis zur arabischen Eroberung*, Stuttgart and Neukirchen-Vluyn 1982, 89–90.

24. For the relationship between the Pharisees and the Essenes see J. Maier and K. Schubert, *Die Qumran-Essener. Texte der Schriftrollen und Lebensbild der Gemeinde*, Munich and Basel 1982, 36–41.

25. Cf. S. K. Stowers, *Letter Writing in Greco-Roman Antiquity*, Philadelphia 1986; R. Dean Anderson Jr, *Ancient Rhetorical Theory and Paul*, Kampen 1996.

26. For an extended discussion of the topic cf. M. Hengel, *The Zealots*, Edinburgh 1989.

27. 'That the whole life of the Jewish people, from hour to hour of its

working days as well as on the solemn moments of sabbath and feast-
day, was dominated by the Law is evident from talmudic tradition,
Josephus and the New Testament, especially the writings of Paul,'
S. Safrai, 'Religion in Everyday Life', in S. Safrai and M. Stern (eds),
The Jewish People in the First Century II, CRINT I, Assen and
Amsterdam 1976, 793–84: 793.

28. B. Bar-Kochva, *Judas Maccabaeus. The Jewish Struggle against the
Seleucids*, Cambridge 1989.

29. In additon to Hengel's classic book *The Zealots* (n.26), cf. M.
Menken, 'Die Zeloten', *Vox Theologica* 45, 1975, 30–47; H. Schwier,
*Tempel und Tempelzerstörung. Untersuchungen zu den theo-
logischen und ideologischen Faktoren im ersten jüdisch-römischen
Krieg (66–74 n.Chr)*, Göttingen 1989.

30. R. Goldenberg, 'Hillel/Hillelschule', *Theologische Realenzyklopädie*
15, Berlin and New York 1986, 326–30.

31. K. Haacker, 'War Paulus Hillelit?', *Das Institutum Judaicum
Tübingen 1971–1972*, Tübingen 1972, 106–20.

32. See K. H. Schelkle, *Paulus. Leben–Briefe–Theologie*, Darmstadt
1981, 71–4.

33. G. Theissen, *Psychological Aspects of Pauline Theology*, Edinburgh
and Philadelphia 1987.

34. There is much literature on the chronology of Paul's life: A. Suhl,
Paulus und seine Briefe. Ein Beitrag zur paulinischen Chronologie,
Gütersloh 1975; R. Jewett, *Dating Paul's Life*, London and
Philadelphia 1997; G. Lüdemann. *Paul. Apostle to the Gentiles. I.
Studies on Chronology*, Philadelphia and London 1984.

3. From persecutor to preacher

1. This is the term in Acts for the followers of Christ, cf. E. Repo, *Der
'Weg' als Selbstbezeichnung der Urchristentums*, Helsinki 1964.

2. There is much information in E. P. Sanders, *Judaism. Practice and
Belief. 63BC–66CE*, London and Philadelphia 1992.

3. R. Riesner, *Jesus als Lehrer. Eine Untersuchung zum Ursprung der
Evangelien-Übelieferung*, Tübingen 1984.

4. E. Trocmé, *The Childhood of Christianity*, London 1997, 13–28.

5. K. Löning, 'Der Stephanuskreis und seine Mission', in J. Becker et al,
Die Anfänge des Christentums. Alte Welt und neue Hoffnung,
Stuttgart 1987, 80–101.

6. See the very extensive study (around 1000 pages!) by R. Eisenman,
*James the Brother of Jesus. Recovering the True History of Early
Christianity*, London 1997; cf. also Pierre-Antoine Bernheim, *James,
Brother of Jesus*, London 1997.

7. Cf. H. Kraft, *Die Entstehung des Christentums*, Darmstadt 1981, 226–40.

8. J. C. H. Lebram, 'Apokalyptiek als keerpunt in het joodse denken', *Nederlands Theologisch Tijdschrift* 30, 1976, 271–81.

9. N. Cohn, *The Pursuit of the Millennium*, London 1993.

10. A good introduction to this complex thought-world can be found in J. Schreiner, *Alttestamentlich-jüdische Apokalyptik. Eine Einführung*, Munich 1969; see also C. Rowland, *The Open Heaven*, London and New York 1982; U. H. J. Körttner, *Weltangst und Weltende. Eine theologische Interpretation der Apokalyptik*, Göttingen 1988.

11. H. Gese, 'Anfang und Ende der Apokalyptik, dargestellt am Sacharjabuch', in *Vom Sinai zum Zion. Alttestamentliche Beiträge zur biblischen Theologie*, Munich 1974, 202–30.

12. See J. Lebra, 'Daniel/Danielbuch', *Theologische Realenzyklopädie* 8, Berlin and New York 1981, 325–49.

13. See M. Poorthuis, *Het gelaat van de Messias. Messiaanse Talmoedlezingen van Emmanuel Levinas*, Hilversum 1992.

14. See E. E. Urbach, *The Sages. Their Concepts and Beliefs*, Jerusalem 1979, 669–90.

15. J. Schüpphus, *Die Psalmen Salmos. Ein Zeugnis Jerusalemer Theologie und Frömmigkeit in der Mitte des vorchristlichen Jahrhunderts*, Leiden 1977; G. S. Oegema, *De messiaanse verwachtingen en bewegingen gedurende de hellenistich-romeinsche tijd*, Baarn 1991, 94–7.

16. There is much literature on this question, see V. Hampel, *Menschensohn und historischer Jesus. Ein Ratselwort als Schlüssel zum messianischen Selbstverständnis Jesu*, Neukirchen-Vluyn 1990.

17. W. Harnisch, *Verhängnis und Verheissung der Geschichte. Untersuchungen zum Zeit- und Geschichtsverständnis im 4. Buch Esra und in der syr. Baruchapokalyse*, Göttingen 1969.

18. P. Volz, *Die Eschatologie der jüdischen Gemeinde im neutestamentlichen Zeitalter. Nach den Quellen der rabbinischen, apokalyptischen und apokryphen Literatur*, Hildesheim 1966 (= Tübingen 1934).

19. For what follows see B. Heininger, *Paulus als Visionär. Eine religionsgeschichtliche Studie*, Freiburg 1996.

20. The discussion was prompted by A. Schweitzer, *The Mysticism of Paul the Apostle*, London 1931.

21. 'Apocalyptic is not a peripheral curiosity for Paul but the central climate and focus of his thought', J. C. Beker, *Paul the Apostle. The Triumph of God in Life and Thought*, Edinburgh 1980, 144.

22. But in Jewish literature on Paul there is a tendency to speak of 'con-

version'. He is said to have turned away radically from Judaism: 'Whether or not Paul also tried to missionize Jews, the change is most easily described as a decision to change commitments from one religious community to another. In Paul's case, the change was from Pharisaism, in which Paul received his education, to a particular kind of gentile community of God-fearers, living without the law, and the change was powered by Paul's absorption into the spirit,' A. F. Segal, *Paul the Convert. The Apostolate and Apostasy of Saul the Pharisee*, New York and London 1990, 117.

23. II Cor. 11.16–12.13 is rightly characterized in scholarly literature as the 'fool's speech', thus e.g. M. Ebner, *Leidenslisten und Apostelbrief. Untersuchungen zu Form, Motivik und Funktion der Peristasenkataloge bei Paulus*, Würzburg 1991, 96.

4. *Between Damascus and Antioch*

1. That it is nevertheless possible to write a book of around 500 pages on this period is shown by M. Hengel and A. M. Schwemer, *Paul Between Damascus and Antioch. The Unknown Years*, London 1997.

2. Cf. R. Bultmann, *Theology of the New Testament* I, London 1952, 238f.; C. K. Barrett, *A Commentary on the Second Epistle to the Corinthians*, London 1973; R. Bultmann, *Der zweite Brief an die Korinther*, Göttingen 1976.

3. Cf. J. Becker, *Paulus, Der Apostel der Völker*, Tübingen 1989, 119–31.

4. H. Weder, *Das Kreuz Jesu bei Paulus. Ein Versuch, über den Geschichtsbezug des christlichen Glaubens nachzudenken*, Göttingen 1981, 225.

5. There is an extended discussion in R. Pesch, *Das Markusevangelium, 2.Teil, Kommentar zu Kap.8, 27–16,20*, Herders Theologischer Kommentar zum Neuen Testament,. Freiburg 1977, 1–27; R. Pesch, 'Das Evangelium in Jerusalem: Mk 14, 12–26 als älteste Überlieferungsgut', in P. Stuhlmacher (ed.), *Das Evangelium und Evangelien. Vorträge vom Tübinger Symposium 1982*, 114–55.

6. E. Güttgemanns, *Der leidende Apostel und sein Herr. Studien zur paulinischen Christologie*, Göttingen 1966, 126–35.

7. For more extensive comments on this see P. J. Tomson, '*Als dit uit de Hemel is . . .': Jesus en die schrijvers van het Nieuwe Testament in hun verhouding tot het Jodendom*, Hilversum 1997, 143–85.

8. K. H. Schelkle, *Paulus. Leben–Briefe–Theologie*, Darmstadt 1981, 236–43.

9. There is a flood of literature on this problem and very great

differences of opinion: Albert Schweitzer with his apocalyptic Jesus; Rudolf Bultmann, who rejected the apocalyptic Jesus but did speak of the eschatological Jesus; Ernst Käsemann, who offended his teacher Bultmann by coming to the conclusion that apocalyptic was the mother of Christian theology; on this see e.g. K. Koch, *The Rediscovery of Apocalyptic*, London 1972; W. Schmithals, *Die Apokalyptik. Einführung und Deutung*, Göttingen 1973, 114–30.

10. See J. Neusner, W. S. Green and E. Frerichs (eds), *Judaisms and their Messiahs at the Turn of the Christian Era*, New York 1987.

11. See E. P. Sanders, *The Historical Figure of Jesus*, London 1993, 240–3.

12. For a Jewish view see N. P. Levinson, *De Messias*, Baarn 1996.

13. For the following see in detail C. J. den Heyer, *De messiaanse weg I. Messianse verwachtingen in het O.T. en in de vroeg-joodse traditie*, Kampen 1983.

14. P. J. Tomson, *Paul and the Jewish Law. Halakha in the Letters of the Apostle to the Gentiles*, CRINT III/3, Assen and Minneapolis 1990, 51–3.

5. It began in Antioch

1. H. Conzelmann, *A History of Primitive Christianity*, London 1971, 138–9.

2. Gerd Theissen, *The First Followers of Jesus*, London 1978; G. Bouwman, *De weg van het Woord, het woord van de Weg. De wording van de jonge kerk*, Baarn 1985, 73–84.

3. There is a description of the history of the city in J. E. Stambaugh and D. L. Balch, *The New Testament in its Social Environment*, Philadelphia 1986, 145–9.

4. G. Lüdemann, *Early Christianity according to the Tradition of the Acts of the Apostles. A Commentary*, London and Philadelphia 1989, 137–9, thinks that these reports may be thought to be historically reliable and form evidence of the close contacts between 'the Antiochene community and the Jerusalem mother community . . . Both churches worked together from the beginning. The ecumene was no late fruit.'

5. W. Schneemelcher, *Das Urchristentum*, Stuttgart 1981, 123–333.

6. Cf. K. Löning, 'Der Stephanuskreis und seine Mission', in J. Becker et al., *Die Anfänge des Christentums. Alte Welt und neue Hoffnung*, Stuttgart 1987, 80–101; E. Trocmé, *The Childhood of Christianity*, London 1997, 29–38; P. J. Tomson, *Paul and the Jewish Law. Halakha in the Letters of the Apostle to the Gentiles*, CRINT III/3, Assen and Minneapolis 1990, 222–58.

7. The study by O. Cullmann, *Peter. Disciple-Apostle-Martyr*, London 1962, may be regarded as a classic; cf. C. P. Thiede, *Simon Peter. From Galilee to Rome*, Exeter 1986.
8. There is an extensive discussion in U. Luz, *Das Evangelium nach Matthäus*, 2: *Mt 8–17*, Evangelisch-Katholischer Kommentar zum Neuen Testament I/2, Zurich and Neukirchen-Vluyn 1990, 450–83 (= exegesis of Matt. 16.13–20 and excursus on Peter in the Gospel of Matthew).
9. With G. Lüdemann, *Early Christianity* (n.4), 171f., I think that Acts 15 and Gal. 2 describe the same visit of Paul to Jerusalem.
10. W. Pratscher, *Der Herrenbruder Jakobus und die Jakobustradition*, Göttingen 1987; E. Ruckstuhl, 'Jakobus', *Theologische Realenzyklopädie* 16, Berlin and New York 1987, 485–88.
11. For a discussion of the question whether or not Matthew was a Jewish Christian or after all a Gentile Christian see U. Luz, *Das Evangelium nach Matthäus* (n.9), 62–5.
12. For an extensive discussion of 'the last word of the exalted Jesus to the disciples' see J. Gnilka, *Das Matthäusevangelium, II.: Kommentar zu Kap. 14.1–28.20 und Einleitungsfragen*, Herders Theologische Kommentar zum Neuen Testament, Freiburg 1988, 501–12.
13. G. Eichholz, *Die Theologie des Paulus in Umriss*, Neukirchen-Vluyn 1972, 17–20.

6. The first letter to the Thessalonians

1. There is some discussion about the unity of the letter, but the arguments have not caused me to have any doubts. See also T. Holtz, *Der erste Brief an die Thessalonicher*, Evangelisch-Katholischer Kommentar zum Neuen Testament I/2, Zurich and Neukirchen-Vluyn 1986, 23–31.
2. See T. Baarda, ' "Maar de toorn is over hen gekomen" (I Thess. 2.16c)', in T. Baarda, H. Jansen, S. J. Noorda and J. S. Vos, *Paulus en de andere joden. Exegetische bijdragen en discussie*, Delft 1984, 15–74.
3. O. H. Steck, 'Israel und das gewaltsame Geschick der Propheten', in *Untersuchungen zur Überlieferung der deuteronomistischen Geschichtstheologie im Alten Testament, Spätjudentum und Urchristentum*, Neukirchen-Vluyn 1967.
4. W. Harnisch, *Eschatologische Existenz. Ein exegetischer Beitrag zur Sachanliegen von 1 Thessalonicher 4, 13–5, 11*, Göttingen 1973.

7. Correspondence with the community in Corinth (I)

1. Cf. R. Jewett, *A Chronology of Paul's Life*, Philadelphia and London 1979; G. Lüdemann. *Paul the Apostle to the Gentiles I: Studies in Chronology*, Philadelphia and London 1989; N.Hyldahl, *Die paulinische Chronologie*, Leiden 1986.

2. J. E. Stambaugh and D. L. Balch, *The New Testament in its Social Environment*, Philadelphia 1986, 162; G. Lüdemann, *Early Christianity according to the Tradition of the Acts of the Apostles. A Commentary*, London and Philadelphia 1989, 201–3; K. L. Noethlichs, *Das Judentum und der römischen Staat. Minderheitpolitik im antiken Rom*, Darmstadt 1996, 160.

3. There are differences of opinion over the precise date. Some, like Lüdemann, think that Claudius took the decision to expel the Jews from Rome soon after his accession as emperor. In my view a later period is more likely, cf. R. Riesner, *Die Frühzeit des Paulus*, Tübingen 1991, 164–9.

4. 'It cannot be claimed that with the arrival of Paul the gospel reached Rome. When Paul arrives, brothers come to meet him as far as the Forum Appii and Tres Tabernae (28.15). Christianity is not disseminated by the official heralds like Paul but by the soldiers, traders and slaves,' G. Bouwman, *De weg van het Woord, het woord van de weg. Der wording van de jonge kerk*, Baarn 1985, 13.

5. For what follows see B. Koet, 'Why did Paul shave his hair (Acts 16,16)? Nazirite and Temple in the Book of Acts', in M.Poorthuis and C. Safrai (eds), *The Centrality of Jerusalem. Historical Perspectives*, Kampen 1996, 128–42.

6. Paul is still often seen in this light in modern Jewish literature about him; cf. *Paul the Convert. The Apostolate and Apostasy of Saul the Pharisee*, New Haven and London 1990; H. Maccoby, *Paul and Hellenism*, London and Philadelphia 1991.

7. C. W. Griggs, *Early Egyptian Christianity. From Its Origins to 451CE*, Leiden 1991, 16–17.

8. W. A. Meeks, *The First Urban Christians. The Social World of the Apostle Paul*, New Haven and London 1983.

9. See the description of the city in Stambaugh and Balch, *The New Testament in its Social Environment* (n.2), 157–60.

10. R. Garrison, *The Graeco-Roman Context of Early Christian Literature*, Sheffield 1997, 27–40.

11. Stambaugh and Balch, *The New Testament in its Social Environment*, (n.2), 135–6.

12. R. J. McKelvey, *The New Temple. The Church in the New Testament*, Oxford 1969, 93–8.

13. L. J. Lietart Peerbolte, *The Antecedents of Antichrist. A Traditio-Historical Study of the Earliest Christian Views of Eschatological Opponents*, Leiden 1886, 258–96.

14. There is a difference of opinion over how many letters. Some exegetes arrive at eight; for a detailed and extended account see W. Schenk, 'Korintherbriefe', *Theologische Realenzyklopädie* 19, Berlin and New York 1990, 620–40.

15. 'The letters to the Corinthians have attracted much less attention in the church than that to the Romans. Here no great "doctrines" like "justification by faith" or "'predestination'" are discussed. The content moves on the level of daily life,' A. F. J. Klijn, *De wordingsgeschiedenis van het Nieue Testament*, Nijkerk 1987, 84.

16. There is an extensive treatment of the discussion in W. Schrage, *Der erste Brief an die Korinther, I, 1 Kor 1, 1–6,6*, Evangelisch-Katholischer Kommentar VII/1, Zurich and Neukirchen-Vluyn 1991, 51–6.

17. 'The Reformers were indisputably right when they appealed to Paul for their understanding of evangelical theology as a theology of the cross': that is the beginning of the chapter on 'The Saving Significance of the Death of Jesus in Paul', in E. Käsemann, *Perspectives on Paul*, London and Philadelphia 1971, 32–59. There is an extensive discussion of the objections to this view, but the last sentence makes it quite clear that Käsemann subscribes to the tradition: 'Since Paul, all theological controversy has radiated ultimately from one central point and can hence only be decoded at this point: *crux sola nostra theologia.*'

18. See H. Weder, *Das Kreuz Jesu bei Paulus. Ein Versuch, über den Geschichtsbezug des christlichen Glaubens nachzudenken*, Göttingen 1981, 227–33.

19. Cf. J. C. Beker, *Paul the Apostle. The Triumph of God in Life and Thought*, Philadelphia and Edinburgh 1980, 204–8.

20. J. Zmijewski, *Paulus – Knecht und Apostel Christi. Amt und Amtsträger in paulinischer Sicht*, Stuttgart 1986.

21. Cf. G. Friedrich, *Die Verkündigung des Todes Jesu im Neuen Testament*, Neukirchen-Vluyn 1985, 82–6; G. Barth, *Der Tod Jesu im Verständnis des Neuen Testaments*, Neukirchen-Vlyun 1992, 71–5.

22. Beker, *Paul the Apostle. The Triumph of God in Life and Thought* (n.19), 208–11, devotes a section to this problem: 'The Dogmatic Debate: Anselm and the "Classical" View of the Atonement'. This is typical of his remarks: 'The history of Christian thought shows the danger of separating or conflating the death and resurrection of Christ . . .' In other words, the dogmatic debate separates where Paul correlates.'

23. For marriage and divorce, see in detail P. J. Tomson, *Paul and the Jewish Law. Halakha in the Letters of the Apostle to the Gentiles*, CRINT III/3, Assen and Minneapolis 1990, 97–124.

24. 'Paul's higher evaluation of celibacy does not imply any devaluation of marriage or sexuality, far less of the woman. The reservations about marriage expressed in I Cor. 7 (cf. esp. vv.27b, 29b–35) are partly conditioned by the expectation of an imminent end,' H. Merklein, ' "Es is gut für den Menschen, eine Frau nicht anzufassen." Paulus und die Sexualität nach 1 Ko7', in G. Dautzenberg, H. Merklein and K. Müller (eds), *Die Frau im Urchristentum*, Freiburg 1986, 225–253: 252.

25. Tomson, *Paul and the Jewish Law* (n. 23), 189–220.

26. R. Garrison, *The Graeco-Roman Context of Early Christian Literature*, Sheffield 1996, 95–104 ('Paul's Use of the Athlete Metaphor in I Corinthians 9').

27. There are splendid examples of patristic exegesis in J. Daniélou, *Sacramentum Futuri. Études sur les origines de la typologie chrétienne*, Paris 1950.

28. See G. Stemberger, 'Jabne und der Kanon', and H. P. Rüger, 'Das Werden des christlichen Alten Testaments', *Jahrbuch für Biblische Theologie, 3: Zum Problem des biblischen Kanons*, Neukirchen-Vluyn 1988, 163–74 and 175–90.

29. 'However, for Paul the link between the "body of Christ or the Kyrios" which he surrendered "for us" on the cross with the community as "body of Christ" is made by the Lord's Supper. Here the text of I Cor. 10.16–17 is of central significance,' J. Hainz, 'Vom "Volk Gottes" zum "Leib Christi". Biblisch-theologische Perspektiven paulinischer Theologie', *Jahrbuch für Biblische Theologie, 7: Volk Gottes, Gemeinde und Gesellschaft*, Neukirchen-Vluyn 1992, 154–64: 153.

30. M. Barth, *Das Mahl des Herrn. Gemeinschaft mit Israel, mit Christus und unter den Gästen*, Neukirchen-Vlyun 1987, 52–183.

31. H. Patsch, *Abendmahl und historischer Jesus*, Stuttgart 1972; H. Feld, *Verständnis des Abendmahls*, Darmstadt 1976.

32. C. J. den Heyer, *De maaltijd van de Heer. Exegetisch en bijbeltheologische studie over Pascha en Avondmaal*, Kampen 1990.

33. There is a real divergence of opinion over the background of the image in the history of religion: is it Old Testament Jewish, Greek Hellenistic, Gnostic? See e.g. J. J. Meuzelaar, *Der Leib des Messias. Eine exegetische Studie über den Gedanken vom Leib Christi in den Paulusbriefen*, Assen 1961.

34. See H. Conzelmann, *First Corinthians*, Hermeneia, Philadelphia 1975, ad loc.

35. B. L. Mack, *Logos und Sophia. Untersuchungen zur Weisheits-theologie im hellenistische Judentum*, Göttingen 1973.

36. Conzelmann, *First Corinthians* (n.34), says of vv. 33b–36: 'This coherent section disrupts the context: it interrupts the theme of prophecy and disturbs the flow of the account. In content it contradicts 11.2ff., where the appearance of women in the community is presupposed.' Cf. E. Schüssler Fiorenza, *In Memory of Her. A Feminist Theological Reconstruction of Christian Origins*, New York and London 1983, 230–3; B. Witherington, *Women in the Earliest Churches*, Cambridge 1988, 90–104.

37. For more information on this pre-Pauline confessional formula see C. J. den Heyer, *De Messiaanse weg III. De christologie van het Nieuwe Testament*, Kampen 1991, 49–61.

38. See the (sub)title of the study by J. C. Beker, *Paul the Apostle. The Triumph of God in Life and Thought*, Edinburgh 1980.

8. *The first letter to the community in Philippi*

1. There is an extended discussion of the problems in J. Gnilka, *Der Philipperbrief*, Herders Theologischer Kommentar zum Neuen Testament X/3, Freiburg 1968, 5–18. In this commentary Gnilka discusses first letter A (1.1–31.a; 4.2–7,10–23) and then letter B (3.ab–4; 1.8–9).

2. For a recent survey of the state of the discussion see H. Balz, 'Philipperbrief', *Theologische Realenzyklopädie* 26, Berlin and New York 1996, 504–13.

3. J. E. Stambaugh and D. L. Balch, *The New Testament in its Social Environment*, Philadelphia 1986, 155–7.

4. Thus e.g. G. H. TerSchegget, *Het lied van de Mensenzoon. Studie over de Christuspsalm in Filippenzen 2:6–11*, Baarn 1975; O. Hofius, *Der Christushymnus Philipper 2.6–11. Untersuchungen zu Gestalt und Aussage eines urchristlichen Psalms*, Tübingen 1976.

5. P. Vielhauer, *Geschichte der urchristlichen Literatur. Einleitung in das Neue Testament, die Apokryphen und die Apostolischen Väter*, Berlin 1975, 41, rightly speaks of the 'flood of literature'.

6. A. Grillmeier, *Christ in Christian Tradition*, Vol.1, Oxford 1975, 20–3.

7. K. T. Kleinknecht, *Der leidende Gerechtfertigte. Die alttesta-mentlich-jüdische Tradition vom 'leidenden Gerechte' und ihre Rezeption bei Paulus*, Tübingen 1984, 189–90.

8. L. Ruppert, *Jesus als der leidende Gerechte? Der Weg Jesu im Lichte einen alt- und zwischentestamentlichen Motivs*, Stuttgart 1972.

9. H. Haag, *Der Gottesknecht bei Deuterojesaja*, Darmstadt 1985; J. C.

Bastiaens, *Interpretaties van Jesaja 53. Een intertextueel onderzoek naar de lijdende Knecht in Jes.51 (MT/LXX) en in Lk 22:14–38, Hand.3:12–26, Hand 4:23–31 en Hand 8: 26–40*, Tilburg 1993.

10. B. Lang, *Frau Weisheit. Deutung einer biblischen Gestalt*, Düsseldorf 1975; G.Schimanowski, *Weisheit und Messias. Die jüdische Voraussetzungen der urchristlichen Präexistenzchristologie*, Tübingen 1985.

11. G. Kittel, *Der Name über alle Namen II. Biblische Theologie/NT*, Göttingen 1990, 9–19.

12. For the reception of the Christ hymn by Paul cf. Kleinknecht, *Der leidende Gerechtfertigte* (n.7), 311–24.

9. Letter to Philemon

1. Thus e.g. P. Stuhlmacher, *Der Brief an Philemon*, Evangelisch-Katholischer Kommentar XVIII, Zurich and Neukirchen-Vluyn 1981, 20–4.

2. J. E. Stambaugh and D. L. Balch, *The New Testament in its Social Envrionment*, Philadelphia 1986, 40.

3. W. H. Ollrog, *Paulus und seine Mitarbeiter*, Neukirchen-Vluyn 1979, 101–6.

4. H. Balz, 'Philemonbrief', *Theologische Realenzyklopädie 26*, Berlin and New York 1996, 490, gives a short survey of the history of the exegesis of the letter.

10. Correspondence with the community in Corinth (II)

1. W. Schenck, 'Korintherbriefe', *Theologische Realenzyklopädie 19*, Berlin and New York 1990, 628–32.

2. Cf. R. Bultmann, *Der zweite Brief an die Korinther*, Kritisch-Exegetischer Kommentar, Göttingen 1976.

3. J. T. Nielsen, *2 Korintiërs. Een praktische bijbelverklaring*, Tekst en Toelichting, Kampen 1995, 119, comes to the opposite conclusion.

4. See D. Georgi, *Die Gegner des Paulus in 2.Korintherbrief. Studien zur religiösen Propaganda in der Spätantike*, Neukirchen-Vluyn 1964, 7–29.

5. J. Zmijewski, *Der Stil der paulinischen 'Narrenrede'. Analyse der Sprachgestaltung in 2 Kor 11,1–12,10 als Beitrag zur Methodik der Stiluntersuchungen neutestamenliche Texte*, Cologne 1978.

6. J. J. Gunther, *St Paul's Opponents and Their Background. A Study of Apocalyptic and Jewish Sectarian Teachings*, Leiden 1973.

7. L. L. Belleville, *Reflections of Glory: Paul's Polemical Use of the Moses-Doxa Tradition in 2 Corinthians 2.1–18*, Sheffield 1991.

8. See M. de Jong, *Paulus, struikelblok of toetssteen. Een studie van 2 Korinthiërs2.12–4:6 als bijdrage in het gesprek met Israël*, Kampen 1989.

9. S. Ben-Chorin, *Paulus. Der Völkerapostel in jüdischer Sicht*, Munich 1970; P. Lapide and P. Stuhlmacher, *Paulus – Rabbi und Apostel. Ein jüdisch-christlicher Dialog*, Stuttgart and Munich 1981; H. Maccoby, *The Mythmaker – Paul and the Invention of Christianity*, London 1986.

10. J. S. Vos, '"De letter doodt, maar de geest maakt levend." Het beeld van het jodendom bij Paulus en zijn uitleggers', in T. Baarda, H. Jansen, S. J. Noorda and J. S. Vos, *Paulus en de andere joden. Exegetische bigdragen en discussie*, Delft 1984, 146–70.

11. S. J. Hafemann, 'The Glory and Veil of Moses in 2 Cor. 3.7–14. An Example of Paul's Contextual Exegesis of the OT – A Proposal', *Horizons of Biblical Theology* 14, 1992, 31–49.

12. J. P. Versteeg, *Christus en de geest. Een exegetisch onderzoek naar de verhouding van de opgestane Christus en de Geest van God volgens de brieven van Paulus*, Kampen 1971.

13. For a detailed discussion see E. Gütgemanns, *Der leidende Apostel und sein Herr. Studien zur paulinischen Christologie*, Göttingen 1966, 94–126.

14. Thus already A. Schweitzer, *The Mysticism of Paul the Apostle*, London 1931; here the reader should be aware that for Schweitzer the terms 'mysticism' and 'apocalyptic' are connected.

15. See e,g. J. Staal, *Het wetenschappelijk onderzoek van de mystiek*, Utrecht and Antwerp 1978, and the extensive contributions on 'Mystik', *Theologische Realenzyklopädie* 23, Berlin and New York 1994, 553–89.

16. 'This pericope contains one of the most attractive and profound passages in Paul', J. T. Nielsen, *2 Korintiërs* (n.3), 66f.

17. G. Quispel, 'Paulus en Hermes Trismegistus', in G. Quispel (ed.), *De Hermetische Gnosis in de loop der eeuwen. Beschouwingen over de invloed van een Egyptische religie op de cultuur van het westen*, Baarn 1992, 243–56.

18. See K. Rudolph (ed.), *Gnosis*, Edinburgh 1984.

19. 'It is in his scheme of salvation, however, with its basic theme of the descent of the divine saviour to a fallen world, that the deepest affinities of Pauline with Gnostic thought can be located,' H. Maccoby, *Paul and Hellenism*, London and Philadelphia 1991, 52–3.

20. Cf. C. Breyenbach, *Versöhnung. Eine Studie zur paulinischen Soteriologie*, Neukirchen-Vluyn 1989.

21. G. Friedrich, *Die Verkündigung des Todes Jesu im Neuen Testament*, Neukirchen-Vluyn 1982, 95–105.

22. P. Sacchi, 'Die Macht der Sünde in der Apokalyptik', *Jahrbuch für Biblische Theologie 9: Sünder und Gericht*, Neukirchen-Vluyn 1994, 111–24.

11. *The second letter to the community of Philippi*

1. There is an extended discussion of the problems in J. Gnilka, *Der Philipperbrief*, Herders Theologischer Kommentar zum Neuen Testament X/3, Freiburg 1968, 5–11.
2. S. Safrai, *Die Wallfahrt im Zeitalter des Zweiten Tempels*, Neukirchen-Vluyn 1981.
3. See the excursus 'Die philippischen Irrlehre', in Gnilka, *Der Philipperbrief* (n.1), 211–18.
4. For a very detailed disussion (350 pages!) see V. Koperski, *The Knowledge of Christ Jesus my Lord. The High Christology of Philippians 3.7–11*, Kampen 1996.
5. D. J. Doughty, 'Philippians 3.20–21', *New Testament Studies* 41, 1995, 21.

12. *The letter to the Galatians*

1. See C. J. den Heyer, *Galaten. Een praktische bijbelverklaring*, Tekst en Toelichting, Kampen 1987, 7–14. For a defence of an early date see R. Zuurmond, *God noch gebod. Bibels-theologische notities over de brief van Paul aan de Galaten*, Baarn 1990.
2. Honesty compels me to recognize that here I am taking an exceptional position. Cf. H. Hübner, 'Galaterbrief', *Theologische Realenzyklopädie* 12, Berlin and New York 1984, 11: 'Ephesus is almost universally accepted as the place of composition.'
3. K. Stendahl, *Paul among Jews and Gentiles,* Philadelphia and London 1977.
4. J. Eckert, *Die urchristliche Verkündigung im Streit zwischen Paulus und seinen Gegnern nach dem Galaterbrief*, Regensburg 1971.
5. Cf. F. Mussner, *Der Galaterbrief,* Herders theologischer Kommentar zum Neuen Testmaent IX, Freiburg 1974, 71.
6. See e.g. E. Kinder and K. Haendler (eds), *Gesetz und Evangelium. Beiträge zur gegenwartigen theologischen Diskussion*, Darmstadt 1986.
7. H. A. Oberman, *Luther. Mensch zwischen Gott und Teufel*, Berlin 1982.
8. See the long section on attempts at solutions to the problem of the spiritual background to the opponents and their views in Mussner,

Galaterbrief (n.5), 11–29.

9. 'Theirs was an entirely reasonable position', E. P. Sanders, *Paul, the Law and the Jewish People*, Philadelphia and London 1985, 18.

10. See J. Smit, *Opbouw en gedachtengang van de brief aan de Galater*, Nijmegen 1986.

11. M. Oeming, 'Unitas Scripturae? Eine Problemskizze', *Jahrbuch für Biblische Theologie* 1: *Einheit und Vielfal biblischer Theologie*, Neukirchen-Vluyn 1986, 48–70; J. Reumann, *Variety and Unity in New Testament Thought*, Oxford 1991.

12. 'The historian must answer in the negative the question whether the New Testament canon is the basis of the unity of the church, because of the variability of the preaching in the New Testament,' thus E. Käsemann, 'Begründet der neutestamenliche Kanon die Einheit der Kirche?', in id. (ed.), *Das Neue Testament als Kanon. Dokumentation und kritische Analyse zur gegenwärtigen Diskussion*, Göttingen 1970, 124–33: 124.

13. A. von Harnack, *Marcion. Das Evangelium vom fremden Gott. Eine Monographie zur Geschichte der Grundlegung der katholischen Kirche*, Leipzig 1924/Darmstadt 1985.

14. H. D. Preuss, *Das Alte Testament in christlicher Predigt*, Stuttgart 1984.

15. In the Revised Version the Greek word *paidagogos* is rendered tutor, the slave whose task it was to accompany children of well-to-do Roman families from home to their teacher and back again.

16. An evocative quotation: 'In a fuller sense Paul is an antinomian. Now that the fullness of time has come, all commandments are finished for good,' thus Zuurmond, *God noch gebod* (n.1), 9.

17. For a classical view see N. H. Ridderbos, *Paulus. Ontwerp van zijn theologie*, Kampen 1966, 139–71.

18. Recently New Testament scholars have paid more attention to this aspect: H. Räisänen, *Paul and the Law,* Tübingen 1987; F. Thielman, *Paul and the Law. A Contextual Approach,* Downers Grove, Ill 1994. For a 'conservative' critical reaction see T. E. Spanje, *Inconsistentie bij P{aulus? Een confrontatie met het werk van Räisänen,* Kampen 1996.

19. Thus e.g. Smit, *Opbouw en gedachtengang van de brief aan de Galater* (n.10), 93–124.

20. The term is taken from Martin Buber, *Two Types of Faith*, London 1952.

13. The letter to the community in Rome

1. For a discussion of the authenticity of ch.16 see the commentaries. E. Käsemann, *Commentary on Romans*, Grand Rapids and London ²1982, describes the final chapter as 'Appendix: A Letter of Recommendation', 409. Apart from the last verses he attributes the chapter to Paul.
2. I did that earlier, see above, pp. 4–5.
3. Thus e.g. U. Wilckens, *Der Brief an die Römer. 1: Röm 1–5*, Evangelisch-Katholischer Kommentar zum Neuen Testament IV/1, Zurich and Neukirchen-Vluyn 1978, 49: 'A central role has been given to the letter to the Romans in the reception of the letters of Paul in the formation of the New Testament canon. That is evident from its position at the end or the beginning of the canonical letter part.'
4. An 'irregularity' presumably caused by the fact that there was a desire to put the two letters to the Thessalonians one after the other.
5. See above, p. 120.
6. Cf. B. Schimmelpfenning, *Das Papstum, Grundzüge seiner Geschichte von der Antike bis zum Renaissance*, Darmstadt 1984, 2–7.
7. I wrote about Matt. 16.18–19 earlier, on p. 94.
8. G. Bouwman, *De weg van het Woord, het woord van de Weg. De wording van de jonge kerk,* Baarn 1985, 13.
9. Cf. I. Levinskaya, *The Book of Acts in Its Diaspora Setting*, Grand Rapids 1996.
10. Thus T. C. de Kruijf, *De brief van Paulus aan de Romeinen*, Boxtel 1986, 297.
11. The famous characterization of the letter by Melanchthon as *compendium doctrinae* in his 1532 Commentary on Romans is typical; cf. *Melanchthons Werke in Auswahl*, Gütersloh 1952, 7.
12. See Wilckens, *Der Brief an die Römer* (n.3), 47f.
13. The hermeneutical key to Romans is primarily situational', J. C. Beker, *Paul the Apostle. The Triumph of God in Life and Thought,* Edinburgh 1980, 74.
14. The number of commentaries on the letter to the Romans is legion. I have already mentioned those by Käsemann, Wilckens and de Kruijf. For an excellent English commentary see J. Ziesler, *Paul's Letter to the Romans*, London and Philadelphia 1989.
15. Cf. E. Jüngel, *Paulus und Jesus. Eine Untersuchung zur Präzisierung der Frage nach dem Ursprung der Christologie,* Tübingen 1972.
16. R. Banks, *Jesus and the Law in the Synoptic Tradition*, Cambridge 1975, 164–73.
17. Cf. K. Wengst, *Pax Romana*, London 1987.

18. For more information about the historical circumstances see E. Bammel, 'Romans 13', in E. Bammel and C. F. D. Moule, *Jesus and the Politics of His Day*, Cambridge 1984, 365–83.
19. See e.g. J. H. Yoder, *The Politics of Jesus*, Grand Rapids 1972.
20. There is an extensive survey in the excursus on the 'strong' and the 'weak' in Rome, in U. Wilckens, *Der Brief an die Römer. 3. Röm 12–16*, Evangelisch-Katholischer Kommentar zum Neuen Testament IV/1, Zurich and Neukirchen-Vluyn 1978, 109–15.
21. Cf. F. Thielman, *Paul and the Law: A Contextual Approach*, Downers Grove 1994.
22. 'According to a prevalent reading he (= Paul) was the champion of the break between Christianity and Judaism. According to another reading that is quite wrong'; for the dilemma see P. J. Tomson, *'Als dit uit de Hemel is . . .' Jesus en de schrijvers van het Nieuwe Testament in hun verhouding tot het jodendom*, Hilversum 1997, 143–85: 185.
23. 'In this situation is it not astonishing how Jewish Paul still was but how little he wanted to be anything other than Jewish . . . Jesus Christ has not torn him as far away from Christianity as possible but attached him to Judaism as closely as possible. *The theology of Romans seems to us quite clearly to be a Jewish-Christian theology.'* F.-W. Marquardt, *Die Juden im Römerbrief*, Theologische Studien 107, Zurich 1971, 36f.
24. This happens often in theological literature, see the characterization of chs 9–11 as 'The Righteousness of God and the Problem of Israel', Käsemann, *Commentary on Romans* (n.1), 253.
25. I do not agree with the following statement either: 'We can only conclude that for Paul himself his conversion also meant a break and a departure from Judaism as it actually was. *From that moment he no longer wanted to be a Jew'* (my italics), T. Korteweg, 'Paulus: jood of christen? Enkele beschouwingen naar aanleiding van het woordje "nu"', J. T. Baker and D. C. Mulder (eds), *Eén bron, twee stromen. Overwegingen over het eigen van het christelijk geloof ten overstaan van het jodendom*, Zoetermeer 1994, 82.
26. See G. Sass, *Leben aus Verheissungen. Traditionsgeschichtliche und biblisch-theologische Untersuchungen zur Rede von Gottes Verheissungen im Frühjudentum und beim Apostel Paulus*, Göttingen 1995 (243–490 relate to Romans).
27. 'Here Paul develops the gospel of the righteousness of God with the saving power for both Jews and Gentile in dialogue with the *synagogue*,' Wilckens, *Der Brief an die Römer* 1 (n.3), 41–2
28. E. P. Sanders, *Judaism, Practice and Belief. 63 BC–66 CE*, London and Philadelphia 1992.
29. See K. Hoheisel, *Das antike Judentum in christlicher Sicht. Ein*

Beitrag zur neueren Forschungsgechichte, Wiesbaden 1978.

30. Cf. E. E. Urbach, *The Sages. Their Concepts and Beliefs*, Jerusalem 1979, 286–314.

31. P. Sacchi, 'Die Macht der Sünde in der Apokalyptik', *Jahrbuch für biblischer Theologie 9: Sünde und Gericht*, Neukirchen-Vluyn 1994, 111–24

32. There is an extensive survey of the discussion in H. N. Ridderbos, *Aan de Romeinen*, Kampen 1959, 162–71; for a more recent discussion see U. Wilckens, *Der Brief an die Römer. 2: Röm 6–11*, Evangelisch-Katholischer Kommentar zum Neuen Testament IV/1, Zurich and Neukirchen-Vluyn 1978, 97–117.

33. Cf. N. Gäumann, *Taufe und Ethik. Studien zu Römer 6*, Munich 1967.

34. See the long excursus on the background to Romans 6 in Wilckens, *Der Brief an die Römer 2* (n.32), 42–62.

35. Cf. L. J. Lietart Peerbolte, 'Vergeving in de Openbaring van Johannes', in C. Houtman et al. (eds), *Ruimte vor vergeving*, Kampen 1998, 57–70.

36. Here is a short selection: P. Stuhlmacher, *Gerechtigkeit Gottes bei Paulus*, Göttingen 1965; K. Kertelge, *'Rechtfertigung' bei Paulus. Studien zur Struktur und zum Bedeutungsgehalt des paulinischen Rechtfertigungsbegriffs*, Münster 1967.

37. 1 Qp Hab VIII. 1–2: translation by G. Vermes, *The Complete Dead Sea Scrolls in English*, London 1997, 482.

38. For more information, in addition to the commentaries see P. Stuhlmacher, 'Zur neueren Exegese von Röm 3.24–26', in *Versöhnung, Gesetz und Gerechtigkeit. Aufsätze zur biblischen Theologie*, Göttingen 1981, 117–35; C. J. den Heyer, *Jesus and the Doctrine of the Atonement*, London 1998, 34–65.

Index of Biblical References